THE MARSEILLES MAFIA

The Marseilles Mafia

The Truth Behind the World of Drug Trafficking

PIERRE GALANTE

and

LOUIS SAPIN

W. H. ALLEN · London
A Howard & Wyndham Company
1979

Printed and bound in Great Britain by
Butler & Tanner Ltd, Frome and London
for the publishers W. H. Allen & Co. Ltd,
44 Hill Street, London W1X 8LB

ISBN 0 491 02325 1

Acknowledgment

We are most grateful to John Cusack and Michael Antonelli of the DEA (Drug Enforcement Administration); to François Le Mouel and Lucien Aimé-Blanc of OCRTS (Office Central de Répression du Trafic des Stupéfiants); and to their wonderful staffs for a patient, loyal and total assistance.

Contents

Introduction

Even as recently as the early 1960s, no social group was more closed or clannish than that of the drug traffickers. It consisted largely of Corsicans and Marseilles racketeers who formed an underworld within the underworld. Despite persistent legends, they were not part of a structured, authoritarian hierarchy operating under the aegis of all-powerful bosses, enjoying police or political protection and merciless towards traitors. They formed short-lived, random associations which were themselves dependent on the trade's key factors: suppliers, chemists and clients.

Before the war trafficking had been organised, after a fashion, by Venture Carbone and François Spirito, who during the thirties ruled Marseilles. At first the scale was modest. They had used their white slavery posts on the Mediterranean for their supplies, and their contacts with American gangsters for the disposal of the end product: heroin. Heroin had replaced cocaine in the favours of the drug users. It had become the 'smart' commodity, the only one that could justify the very considerable investment and risks involved, even though these were offset by considerable gains.

The war put an end – or almost – to this clandestine traffic and scattered the leading men behind it. Trafficking revived once the war was over. It was still run by the Corsicans and Marseilles men; but they were now joined by various exiled Turkish or Lebanese suppliers. As before the war, the sailors on passenger and cargo boats secured the transport of the merchandise: raw morphine across the Mediterranean and heroin across the Atlantic. Almost all the drugs exported went through Le Havre, where Jean Joseph Andreani, a former Resistance fighter and the doyen of the 'quiet men', had settled. He was boss of the local underworld, the owner of a hotel, a taxi company and various night-clubs; he also supervised local prostitution. He acted as shipper for his Marseilles producers.

'We were operating quite openly,' he was to confide to Inspector Mugnier later. 'We were making high-quality goods for a well-heeled clientèle, Cartier stuff. We didn't put a foot wrong.'

During the fifties, the main bulk of the traffic was concentrated in the hands of four or five teams; they diversified their methods of routing, making use of the diplomatic bag for the larger consignments. In the Lebanon, the trafficker Samy Khoury had secured a near-monopoly of the smuggling of raw morphine. These rings relied on the assistance of experienced technicians who had been driven out of France at the Liberation by the threat of judicial action and who returned gradually after having forged transatlantic connections with Canadian or American *mafiosi*.

Heroin addiction was already a chronic disease, particularly in the United States. But it was still a benign problem that a small number of police officers, backed up by customs officials, had managed to keep within so-called reasonable limits. Governments did not consider it worth-while to spend large sums on the dismantling of these networks. Drug traffic was a poor fourth to gaming, prostitution and gangsterism in the pickings it afforded the American 'Crime Syndicate', heir to the gangs of the twenties and thirties.

In the sixties, with an increase in demand from the American market, the situation worsened. Italo-American buyers were competing with exiled Cubans and Puerto Ricans, who were profiting from the restraint exercised by certain families of *Cosa Nostra*. The number of addicts continued to rise. The problem spread throughout the United States, affecting all social classes. In the wake of marijuana and LSD, heroin swept through the university campuses. Several factors were behind the sudden expansion of the problem: first there was the Vietnam war; then growing reservations about the 'American way of life'; and, corollaries of both of these factors, sexual liberation and the rebellion of the young. For a whole generation of adolescents, drugs became the symbol of flight from the adult world. The epidemic soon affected other countries, spread primarily by the 'hippies'. It reached a point when civilisation itself seemed to hang in the balance.

This development was a godsend for the Marseilles traffickers. Over the years, the manufacture of heroin had become concentrated in various clandestine laboratories in Provence. Their chemists had acquired an international reputation. To meet increased demand, the laboratories multiplied, and the networks of the 'quiet men' were no longer sufficient to dispatch what they produced. The closed world of the traffickers opened its doors to let in new recruits of various origins. The more dynamic among them built up new networks. The fabulous profits they made, and the relative leniency of the penal code with regard to traffickers, attracted a whole crowd of go-getting thieves, crooks, gangsters and layabouts to the expanding trade, all demanding their bite of the cherry.

From 1965 onwards, the various networks which the traffic had produced were gradually expanded to cover the whole of the American continent, not to mention the Far East and central Asia. Cargo and passenger boats had already been utilised to transport the plastic sachets, each containing five hundred grams of white powder; now cars, trucks and trains began to be used as well, as did yachts and aeroplanes, both private and commercial. The couriers dreamt up multifarious schemes to outwit such checks as the overworked customs men could muster. Official reaction was slow. At first governments remained unaware of the increased traffic and of the danger it represented for society, despite the reports of the various officials, trying to fight it with pathetically inadequate resources. No one wanted to believe that the rot could be setting in so rapidly and so mercilessly, although statistics registered several hundred of thousands of addicts in the United States alone. When the United States Government announced that eighty per cent of the heroin introduced illegally into the States came from the Marseilles laboratories, France's protest actions were made in all good faith.

Washington reacted first. In April 1968, the American Government set up a federal agency to contain the rising tide: the Federal Bureau of Narcotics and Dangerous Drugs, under the authority of the Attorney General of the Department of Justice. The BNDD brought together the agents of the former Bureau of Narcotics (which had been part of the Treasury) and the officials of the Dangerous Drugs Department of the Ministry of Agriculture. Its European unit moved from Rome to Paris with somewhat increased manpower. But months and indeed years went by before France – the main party involved – and the other countries concerned joined in the fight whole-heartedly. The fact that it justified a summit conference between the Presidents of the United States and France was a pointer to the seriousness of the situation. Final victory did not come until 1973, after eight years of struggle. The Marseilles traffickers, their suppliers, their chemists, their American clients and their accomplices were eliminated from the illicit drug market. It was a short-lived victory because, four years later, the shadow that heroin casts over the future of the younger generation in various countries still persists, and the means deployed over eight years to contain the influx of Asian 'brown sugar' have proved ineffectual.

From 1968 until 1973, then, the world was shaken by a cultural earthquake; the havoc it wreaked was reminiscent of that caused by another phenomenon, the trafficking produced by the prohibition of alcohol in the United States between the wars, which poisoned the whole social life of America and whose effects can still be felt today.

Numerous books have been written about the damage done by drugs and the dangers they represent. Some have exposed those responsible for drug trafficking – more or less openly – without being able to adduce the conclusive evidence so difficult to obtain in this field. Others again have bolstered up the numerous legends which obscure a reality that is elusive enough without embroidery. Certain criminal circles have succeeded in holding their own against the combined offensives of the police of twenty odd countries over eight years, despite the very considerable repressive measures which have at last been made available to the authorities. A closer knowledge of these circles was crucial for a better understanding of the trafficking phenomenon and for an assessment of its true extent. This is the task that has absorbed the authors of *The Marseilles Mafia* for four years.

There is no need to emphasise the difficulty of the undertaking. For a description of key moments of contemporary history, we can turn to those who were their witnesses or heroes. We have recourse to official records, to the biographies of the protagonists, to specialist studies and commentaries. Some famous gangsters have boasted of their exploits freely, even smugly. But it is no use asking a drug trafficker to give a detailed account of how he succeeded in introducing into a country a kilo of heroin which brought with it the degradation and death of tens of thousands of innocent victims. It is equally useless to expect to find written evidence of this kind of activity.

'Drug trafficking is like a plate of spaghetti,' Thomas Puccio, the Attorney of the Eastern District of New York, said to us. 'The networks intertwine.' In order to find our way through this tangle, we had first to discover what the detectives concerned with the fight against drug trafficking had learned during the last few years. In France and in the United States as well as in other countries, detectives agreed to submit to cross-examination, to describe their investigations and in particular to describe their 'clients' so as to throw more light on the various facets of their personalities. We then studied the various cases in the files, with the relevant correspondence and conclusions. Over a period of about a year in Paris, and for several months in New York and Washington, we lived as officials of the French Office for the Prevention of Drug Traffic (the 'stups') or of the Drug Enforcement Administration (the 'narcs') which had succeeded the BNDD in July 1973. In the office made available to us, huge stacks of records rapidly piled up; we went through them systematically sheet by sheet.

When we had done this, our collaborators patiently agreed to further, more detailed questioning on points which our earlier investigations had failed to clarify. At this stage in the operation we were able to pick out the names of witnesses and of close friends of those figures who interested us but who were not as elusive as they were.

At innumerable meetings, we were able to put together a large number of statements about the private life of the traffickers, in most cases having promised to safeguard the anonymity of our sources. It was a fascinating but exhausting process, because each new confidence suggested new sources of information to be investigated.

The fifty kilos of documentation we amassed over two years included official records and studies, reports of fact-finding commissions of the American Senate and Congress, United Nations, reports on trafficking, files on the previous history of the main traffickers, various works on the Mafia and the 'Crime Syndicate', newspaper articles, trial reports and transcripts. We frequented court record offices, the Library of Congress, the museum of the Prefecture of Police in Paris, and of the 'Evêché' in Marseilles. Each new discovery led to new questions which our hapless victims continued to answer with good grace if with decreasing enthusiasm. 'We've been had once,' they said. 'We won't be had again.'

Of course, we also made use of journalist colleagues, who had followed most of the drug scandals. Finally the point was reached when all that was left for us was to go our separate ways and visit the Argentine, Brazil, Fort-de-France or elsewhere, to set the various events in their real contexts.

Once in possession of these imposing documentary tools, we had to sort them, classify them, work out case records and put them all on file before starting to write this book. When we did at last make a start, more than two-and-a-half years had gone by since we had first had the idea of writing an 'inside story' of drug trafficking. We wanted our account to be vivid but entirely authentic, with each incident, each fact, each word corresponding to a definite reference in our documentation, whether statement, official report, confession, transcript or record of hearings. As the typed pages piled up – we soon reached the thousandth – the pattern of the organisation began to emerge, with all its ramifications. Events which had seemed incomprehensible, information we had put aside because we had thought it improbable, found their places within the puzzle with an inevitability which confirmed their authenticity. It then became easier for us to prune our text, to cut out episodes superfluous to the unfolding of this incredible enterprise, devoted to the smuggling of a single substance: heroin. The quantities of heroin transported had to be measured in tonnes, the sums commanded in thousands of millions of francs.

We have refrained from making moral, social or political judgements in our account of drug trafficking and its consequences. Others have done this before us. We can only hope that our work will make a contribution to the history of our time.

1

Monsieur Drogue

For several years – until his downfall – Auguste Ricord was to be the star and indeed the symbol of the heroin traffic. Before describing his meteoric rise to fame, it may be as well to go back to his beginnings on the pavements of Marseilles, towards the end of the nineteen-twenties.

At that time the city offered brilliant prospects to its young layabouts. Some, sons of fishermen or peasants, had grown up in Corsica or in Provence, others in Marseilles itself, in the narrow allées of the Belle-de-Mai or Panier districts. A few months' apprenticeship after elementary school served to dissuade them from attempting to earn an honest living. Some – cabin boys or sailors on the steamship lines of the Near or Far East – became involved in the small-scale traffic of opium, or raw morphine.

They hung around idly in small groups on the pavements of the Canebière or the Vieux Port. They observed those of their elders who had made good sitting at café terraces, dressed in made-to-measure suits and silk shirts. These tycoons seemed to have nothing to do but amble from table to counter, from the Glacier to the Gerbe d'Or, from chez Félix to the Café Riche; when they were not actually delving into their pockets for thick wads of banknotes to pay for drinks, their life seemed to be an endless round of back-slapping.

For experienced gangsters, it was a time of plenty. Business had never been better. French girls enjoyed an excellent reputation in the brothels of Caracas, Buenos Aires, Beirut and Alexandria.

At the Bal des Camélias or various other dance halls in the suburbs, budding gangsters were climbing the first rung of the ladder. Here they 'picked up' guileless country girls who had come to find work in the city, beginners in search of adventure or more wideawake girls taking their first steps towards street-walking. All they had to do, with a cunning mixture of charm and intimidation, was to take the girls to the pavements or brothels of the coast, in preparation for longer journeys to Sidi Bel Abbés or Maracaibo, journeys which were rarely two-way.

Procuring was the golden stairway – providing you could climb beyond it. The brashest layabouts, having served their apprenticeship on it, proceeded upwards. Flaunting the same dazzling outfits as their elders, they strapped on the indispensable revolver and joined the underlings, bodyguards and assorted heavies surrounding the bosses of the hour.

In 1928 Auguste Ricord, aged seventeen, had reached this stage. He hovered around Carbone and Spirito, and even caught the attention of Simon Sabiani, their friend and protector, who had just been elected a Deputy and was also Deputy Mayor of Marseilles. Young Ricord lacked physical charm but not career potential. He was small, with a cunning weasel's face and a wiry body. He was an amateur boxer. A police report of the time described him as 'a petty crook, and quite unscrupulous. Sole interests: food, girls and money. No sense of humour, decency or dignity.'

His police record confirms his rise during the following decade. He received his first conviction in 1927, before his seventeenth birthday, for theft and extortion; and subsequently others for violence, carrying firearms and receiving.

In 1935 Ricord left Marseille, where the heat was on, and went to Paris accompanied by his henchwoman and half-sister Maria Traversi. She was also his fall-girl and accomplice and the wife of a minor official at the Assistance Publique, Baptistin Bonsignour.

Further convictions enable us to follow the trail of young Auguste, who already had a couple of prostitutes walking the streets for him. Receiving, acts of violence, assault and battery, carrying a weapon without a licence, smuggling absinthe and offences against the railway police marked his career between 1935 and 1940. He was living in rue Hauteville, but in August 1939 general mobilisation drove him underground. Until the arrival of the Germans, he continued to devote himself to his usual activities, to which he now added burglary, where his slight build and small stature served him well.

Towards the end of June 1940 the Germans occupied Paris. Ricord, in hiding in an apartment on the rue Mansart, just off Pigalle, received a visit which was to change the course of his life: a visit from a burglar, the scourge of the strong-boxes, Alfredo Palmieri, whom he had met with Spirito and who was supposedly serving a sentence in La Santé.

'The Germans released me. We did a deal. I need your help for a very simple job.'

This very simple job was the robbing of a printing works in Melun whose safe contained virgin French passports. They were urgently required by the Abwehr and Gestapo to enable them to mingle with the crowds of refugees who were still wandering the roads of France.

The team was promptly organised. It consisted of the boss, Palmieri, a small unsmiling Italian; Jean d'Agostino alias Jean Sisco, with a jaw like Fernandel's; Spirito the playboy of the Canebière and Ricord and his two bosom friends, Cesar, long-nosed and dark-eyed, currently a restaurant owner, and Joseph Oberto, known as 'Zé-la-Ganache', whose square jaw was stuffed with gold fillings.

The 'Corsican gang' soon made its mark in Paris. They worked for *Abteilung IV* of the *Befehlshaber der Sipo* on the Boulevard Flandrin, which was concerned with subversive activities and was part of the establishment at 31 Avenue Foch. Previously they had been employed by *Abteilung VI*, which dealt with political intelligence. They had taken part in an operation against a house eighty kilometres from Paris, occupied by members of the Resistance. During the siege Palmieri and two of his men were wounded. In their free time, the gang's members also began to learn the technique of 'bogus policemen' which was soon to enjoy a certain vogue.

If they were not in possession of police identification cards, the Corsicans – who incidentally were mostly Italian – could produce bilingual certificates with the words 'The German authorities are requested to assist the bearer of this card. In case of arrest, contact the appropriate department.'

Shortly before the war, in the restaurant Dupont Latin, Auguste Ricord had made the acquaintance of a young student of the applied arts and former pupil at the Lycée Fénelon, who was just emerging from an unhappy marriage with a musician from the Concerts Colonne. We shall call her Jeanne B. Shortly after the armistice they were living together in a flat on the rue Eugène Carrière. Auguste told her that he was a representative for the Pommery et Grau champagne company; she believed him, for a time.

'Subsequently I learned that this was just a cover. Auguste gambled heavily, which meant we had to live modestly. After having kept me for some time in a life style well above his means, he forced me on to the streets for a few months.' At the beginning of the Occupation, the crooks who worked for the occupying powers were not yet in the big time.

In January 1942, Palmieri managed to have seven licensed brothels in the Pas de Calais requisitioned by the Germans. He made one over to Ricord, in Saint Omer, for seventy-five thousand francs. Thus Jeanne rose to the rank of Madam. During that summer, the couple returned to Paris, hung around Melody's and the Grand Duc, went to Monte Carlo, lost all the money they had and were back in Pigalle again by the end of the year.

Meanwhile Palmieri had opened a purchasing agency on behalf of the Germans in the rue du Colisée. Tired of living in his hotel on the rue Blanche, he settled in the Avenue Victor Hugo, then in the Avenue Henri Martin in the sixteenth *arrondissement*. He had a Jewish mistress, Jacqueline, who also acted as his secretary. With his accomplices, he divided his time between his activities for *Abteilung IV* and various trafficking pursuits, notably in gold. The gangs' victims were mainly Jews. Arrests and searches gave Ricord the opportunity of driving around in a black Citroen.

Prosperity had come at last. The Ricords set up house at 50 Avenue Wagram with Maria Bonsignour, two Indo-Chinese servants and another young woman, Cookie, who shared Auguste's favours with Jeanne. A young man of about twenty was serving his apprenticeship alongside his elders: Louis Bonsignour, Maria's son.

The 'gang' could not continue with its extortions without arousing the attention of the French police. On 2 August 1943 four men in two cars stopped outside a cheesemonger's in the Dreux region. 'German police,' they announced in the sing-song accents of the Midi. They accused their victims of hiding defaulters from the obligatory labour forces; they searched the premises, confiscated two hundred and fifty litres of petrol, sixty litres of oil and finally agreed to draw a veil over the affair against a payment of four hundred thousand francs. A lorry driver in German uniform loaded up the booty. The Dreux police made investigations. One of the cars belonged to Ricord. The police went to 50 Avenue Wagram. They were greeted by Maria Bonsignour; Ricord was caught in mid-toilette. 'He was stripped to the waist with a gold chain around his neck. In the same room there were also two young women in a state of almost total undress Ricord produced an identity card issued by the Germans and the arresting officer pocketed it. "Ah, I see you're keeping that card," he said. "You'll see where that will get you." We took him off with the two young women to the police station in rue Bassano.'

Two hours later, the Germans ordered Ricord's release.

This was just one of the many jobs' in which the gang was involved and of which mention is made in the records of the Paris police. In 1944 the proceeds the gang netted enabled Ricord to buy the Heure Bleue, a night-club in Pigalle. This and two other establishments, the Chapiteau and the Ange Rouge, were authorised to remain open during curfew hours. The Heure Bleue was frequented by German officers and smart collaborationist Paris society.

But the months passed and the Allies landed in Normandy. Ricord sensed that a prosperous period of his life was drawing to a close. He would have to leave France as soon as possible. From a German officer in the Hotel Lutetia, Palmieri had obtained a safe conduct for himself and his gang to get to Milan.

On 15 August, as Leclerc's armoured cars were preparing to drive into Paris, three cars proceeded up the German columns along the road to Strasbourg. Their occupants were Ricord, Palmieri and several other survivors of the now dispersed gang. Some gang members had already reached the Spanish frontier. Louis Bonsignour was to reach Milan a little later together with two known criminals, Abel Danos and Raymond Naudy. After the war Danos was condemned to death and guillotined and Naudy was shot down at his arrest in Menton.

The members of the convoy had no material worries: 'Palmieri had at least fifteen million francs in foreign currency; Ricord had three million pesetas, gold coins and diamonds. After an overnight stop in Munich, the party went over the Brenner Pass. Thanks to the safe conduct, they crossed into Italy without difficulty, then split up. Palmieri went to join his friend Jacqueline and her two children in Varese, near Lake Como. Ricord settled in a family pension in Milan, and together with several former associates, launched into the black market in foodstuffs.

During autumn 1946 Lucien Dargelès, the owner of a bistro in Asnières, met a music hall artist called Domi Spada in the Faubourg St Martin. Dargelès expressed an interest in 'life on the road' and an admiration for its strolling players with their untrammelled, adventurous existence.

'Why don't we put an act together?' suggested Domi. 'I've had several offers of engagements in Italy, Switzerland and Belgium. We'd only need a couple of months' rehearsal.'

Lucien Dargelès was tempted. The partners-to-be signed a contract. All they now needed was a passport. Spada undertook to sort out this formality, so Lucien gave him his demobilization papers, certificate of good character and residence permit and the necessary four photographs. He never saw either Domi Spada or his papers again and finally informed the local police of his misfortune.

Meanwhile the passport was issued. From Spada it passed into the hands of Jean Lunardi, a survivor of the 'Corsican gang'. Following discrete and well-tried routes, the passport reached Spain where Ricord had travelled from Milan and had been waiting for it for several slow-moving weeks. He was now in possession of officially issued identity papers.

It was thus that on 8 December 1947 the *Argentina Star*, sailing from Spain, entered Buenos Aires harbour with a small, unremarkable passenger mingling with the crowd of European immigrants whose lives had been disrupted by the war. He was called 'Lucien Dargeles'.

A few months went by. Ricord – now known as Cori – had resumed his pimping activities in his new country. There was no shortage of Marseilles *confrères* in the local underworld: they had been running the prostitution business ever since the heyday of the white slave traffic. Ricord lived in the Calle Tucuman. From Prince Galitzin, son of the one-time Tsar's ambassador to Berne, he had bought a night-club, the Mayfair, in the Calle Lavalle, which he renamed Le Fétiche. In September 1948 a French music hall artist appeared with a certain amount of success there: he was the obliging Domi Spada.

Though still pursuing his career as procurer, Ricord was now opening a series of restaurants, one called the Texas, and also more clubs: the Erwin, chez Danielle. Maria Traversi had come to join him with Baptistin Bonsignour and her daughter Helène. Louis Bonsignour also arrived to join the family party.

Despite the protection of certain corrupt officials, Ricord did have some problems with the law. In 1951 he was arrested for corrupt practices and unlawful association, then released. He now thought it preferable to leave Argentina 'until things blew over'.

He returned there in 1956.

At the beginning of March 1957 Ricord was imprisoned for

drug trafficking, and white slavery in Argentina. This is the first mention of drugs in his career. And these were just small beginnings. But by now the sailors from the *Provence* and the *Bertagne* – by which most of the escapees crossed the Atlantic – were delivering small quantities of heroin, supplied mainly by Marius Ansaldi, a gangster known as 'le matelot'.

France applied for an extradition order for Ricord. But on 7 May, once again, he was released. At the beginning of June he was in Uruguay. In July he sank from sight but bobbed up the following year in Caracas, where he was running a club called Le Domino. He made frequent visits to Rio de Janeiro and was still involved in white slavery. He was glimpsed in Paraguay and Mexico with Louis Bonsignour. He now had a numbered account in a Swiss bank in Lausanne.

Maria had stayed in Buenos Aires where she ran the restaurant El Sol and received the escapees who continued to pour in. After a stay in her home at 1150 Tupac Amaru, in the Vicente Lopez district, they would use the restaurant (which was shortly to change its name to become the Auberge Provençale) as an accommodation address. Gradually they were incorporated into the Ricord Organisation.

2

The Bad Lads of Buenos Aires

Francisco Naval, a native of Marseilles and the manager of the French ex-servicemen's club in Buenos Aires, had gone to some trouble over the eleventh of November commemoration. Carnival novelties with the French national colours are hard to find in the Republic of Argentina, but he got together all he could find by way of red, white and blue lanterns, paper-chains and bunting in his office at 1435 Santiago del Estero. His wife Aloisa and sister-in-law Anita had spent the two days before the celebrations running up streamers and pennants on the family sewing-machine.

Colonel Duclos, a former Resistance fighter and president of the association, came up the entry corridor into the main hall, hung with flags commemorating the heroism of the French soldiers in both World Wars. He congratulated Naval on his efforts. He cast a glance over the gaming room where three or four tables were set aside for bridge players, over the billiard room, now a temporary refreshment room, and over the restaurant, its white cloths decked out with red, white and blue flowers.

His expression darkened when he saw the new barman, François, behind the bar; he was chatting to Marguerite, Francisco Naval's daughter, as she handed him the bottles to arrange on the shelves. The colonel drew the manager aside: 'I really don't like that boy; I hope these *collabos* and layabouts will have the decency not to show their faces on a day like this.'

Naval shrugged resignedly. The bad lads – as the French colony called them – were already well established masters of the place when he had taken over the running of the club. They had come over in the immediate post-war years. Quite a number of them had had brushes with the Argentinian police. But their money enabled the association to balance its books; and for squalid financial reasons the regulations allowed visitors free access to the bar and restaurant, the other rooms being theoretically reserved for members and well-wishers.

'It's difficult for me to refuse them entry as long as they behave reasonably,' ventured the manager. 'I know that a number of members have, unfortunately, stopped coming. François does the bar for nothing. We can't afford to pay a barman. But he always behaves properly and he's a perfect gentleman with Marguerite.'

François was a tall, solid, athletic-looking man. He had a broad face, wavy grey hair, thick lips and a cold, determined expression. If the colonel and Naval had known his past record, they would have had even more cause for concern.

François Chiappe, known as 'Rubber lips', had been one of the heroes of the mini-war which bloodied the pavements of Pigalle after the Liberation, and set the Corsicans against the North Africans who were making a bid for the streets of Montmartre. One evening in June 1955, as he was sipping an apéritif at a café terrace in rue Fontaine together with two footballer friends, a North African had leapt out of a car, clutching a sub-machine gun, and peppered the front of the bar. Chiappe was picked up, slightly wounded.

At the beginning of 1964, Chiappe was 'protecting' the proprietress of the bar Jour et Nuit in Montmartre for her man, Ange Valentini, who was in prison. The young woman had been importuned by one of her former lovers, a man from Guadeloupe, Valentin Laure, and his Algerian friend Barca Hamid. On 24 February, accompanied by three of his gang, Chiappe entered a bar-restaurant in rue de la Grande Truanderie and shot the two men down.

François now had no choice but exile. It was Barthélémy Guerini who made this possible, sending him to Buenos Aires on board the *Provence*, which had already dispatched other criminals on the run; they too had been met at their port of destination by Auguste Ricord. Known as 'Mémé', Guerini was one of five brothers who came from Corsica to Marseilles in the early thirties and were second only to Carbone and Spirito. After the war, with Carbone dead and Spirito in exile, they became the new bosses of the Marseilles Mafia.

Indeed it was Ricord – who was now called André by his friends – for whom François was waiting on this national holiday, at the ex-servicemen's club. Since his arrival he had been taken up by the 'Organisation'.

They were to meet other defectors, also sent by Mémé Guerini, so as to decide upon their respective roles in the heroin trade, whose further growth they shrewdly anticipated. Demands by American buyers were becoming increasingly pressing.

Two of these runaways, Michel and Raymond, had already arrived and sat down at a table in the restaurant. Michel was thirty-five. He was a small, slim man from Marseilles with thinning brown hair, fairly voluble, his accent conjuring up memories of garlic and pastis. His name was Michel Nicoli, but his Brazilian papers bore the name Miguel Dos Santos.

Having started life as a conscientious post-office worker, he had become a truck driver at twenty-five and then a taxi driver; he had begun to associate with drop-outs and took part in hold-ups. The Assize Court had sentenced him to death in his absence.

The Marseilles underworld harboured him from March to October 1962. A friend, Robert, who knew the Guerinis, gave him the address of a certain Raymond, Calle Libertad, in Buenos Aires. 'Just tell him that Mémé and I sent you. He'll look after you.'

As soon as he arrived in Buenos Aires, Michel went to look up Raymond and moved in with him. Raymond claimed to be called Mario Deniz. The police were to pursue him for years before they discovered that he was one and the same person as André Condemine, a known criminal wanted in France.

Raymond was not yet involved in drug trafficking. But he was thinking about it; in the meantime, the two new friends had turned their attention to smuggling American cigarettes, dispatched from Miami to Asuncion in Paraguay in the planes of the '*contrabandistas*', then to Buenos Aires via the Rio Parana.

* * *

Now groups of Frenchmen were going into the club rooms: small traders and industrialists, wives and daughters in summer dresses and, among them, the odd Embassy official. Everybody gave an ostentatiously wide berth to the 'bad lads', cutting them dead.

Gradually the club's atmosphere warmed up. François Chiappe, helped by Marguerite, filled endless glasses. He noted the diminutive figure of Ricord entering the room; after a conspiratorial glance, Ricord went into the restaurant to join the men whom he had arranged to meet. Two other escapees from France had taken up positions near 'Raymond' and Michel Nicoli; René Santamaria, also from Marseilles, who had already made several trips to Spain with Condemine, and Claude Pastou, sentenced to hard labour for life in France in his absence for his part in various hold-ups. He was mentioned in police records as dangerous and the previous year, in Paris, he had been lucky enough to meet Louis Bonsignour, Auguste Ricord's nephew, just as his departure was becoming a matter of urgency.

'I'm going to need everyone,' Ricord told them. 'I'm through with small deals, housebreaking and hold-ups which irritate local police. They don't care about drugs, because drugs are only in transit. If they are willing, Claude and Michel will deal with the deliveries. As Raymond will tell you, there's no great risk attached. One thousand dollars a kilo, thirty thousand for an air trip to Puerto Rico – it can't be bad. The Marseilles laboratories can provide us with unlimited quantities of the stuff.

'It's just a beginning. We'll be working with South Americans who've been smuggling cocaine for fifty years. We can use their networks and don't worry, I've got other plans. We'll all make a packet in this business.'

Pastou and Nicoli nodded. In any case, they were indebted to Ricord who had looked after them since their arrival. But now François les grosses lèvres appeared, looking embarrassed, followed by Naval.

'You'd better carry on elsewhere,' he said awkwardly. 'They're waiting for you to clear out in order to start the ceremony. There's no point in getting their backs up.'

'You're right,' agreed Ricord, rising to go. 'We won't spoil their fun.'

3

The Owner of the Grande Bastide

The villa 'La Roseraie' was in Aubagne, near Marseilles; on its terrace, paved with local stone, a suntanned three-year-old was pedalling figures of eight in his red plastic toy car. After skirting the swimming pool, a supple, sunburnt little girl walked towards some deckchairs where a woman was hemming napkins under a sunshade.

It was September 1964. The little girl and the toddler were the children of the owner of the villa, Joseph Cesari. The gentle, retiring-looking woman was called Renée Manoukian. She had been his companion since they met ten years before in a shoe shop on the Canebière in Marseilles.

Joseph, who had just arrived, walked briskly up to Renée and sat down on a deckchair. He cast a satisfied eye over his vast domain: his property included a hectare of land, a large house, a tennis court, a swimming pool and a building where Maman Nounou lived with her husband, Papa Nounou, who worked in a hospital in Marseilles. Young Mireille was hanging out the washing and Emilana, the gardener, was weeding the paths.

Renée was looking at Joseph with a worried enquiring expression. He took her hand; she thought yet again how thin his face had become, how tired he looked. She sensed his nervousness and noted the dark patches on his hands where the blood had come to the surface. They reappeared each time he resumed his activities in the laboratory. He reassured her.

'Don't worry. In a month it will all be over and I'll never touch the stuff again. We'll all move into the Grande Bastide and put all this out of our minds. I promised you we would and I'll keep my word. Tomorrow I'll go and see how the work is getting on.

Mireille's father telephoned to tell me that the Scalfatis have almost finished.'

The previous year he had bought an estate of 428 hectares near Rians in the Var, the Grande Bastide which consisted of two gentleman's residences, a farm, a lodge, outhouses, a sheepfold and stables. He had immediately engaged the Scalfati brothers to carry out certain alterations. They would be able to move in in a month. Cesari would have achieved his aim: to retire at fifty, devote himself to stock farming and forget about all the years spent making a product which had already undermined his health.

He had bought La Roseraie, in the Channel district of Aubagne, two years earlier. He hadn't skimped on the fitments there. He liked luxury. The drawing-room lighting, in marble and Venetian glass, cost thirty thousand francs per chandelier. His library included several rare works and some first editions, including Dantë's *Divine Comedy* illustrated by Dali. Each old master, each precious ornament, showed if not that he was a man of discernment, at least that he knew how to invest his money.

Cesari got up and brushed Renée's forehead with a kiss. 'Don't wait up for me tonight. I'll probably work very late. Now I've got some people to see.' He walked off towards where he kept his cars: a Peugeot 404, a Renault RL 4, a small Citroën station-waggon and a Renault van. His two other station-waggons were out, one in the garage for repairs and the other on the road, driven by the taxi driver Jean Galorini. It was to be loaded – if all went well – with drums of sulphur trioxide and acetone purchased one by one from wholesalers in Haute-Provence.

The 404 set off on the road running down to the plain. In the distance, the roofs of the small Provençal town of Aubagne clustered around the ruins of its medieval castle. Cesari slowed down and turned to take the road to Gémenos. Several peasants and workmen on their way home watched him pass. If they recognised him, they showed no sign of it.

He had never been accepted as a local notable despite his life style and his circumspection. There were doubts about the source of his fortune. When the locals heard that he fed his dogs on prime beef, they were suspicious. 'He must have made his money in something illegal,' people said.

On a nearby hillock, two hunters wearing tatty-looking caps, their guns leaning against a bush, were picnicking on a rock, their eyes on the car. One of them trained a pair of binoculars on the road. The other produced a notebook, looked at his watch and jotted something down.

'It's him,' said the first one. 'No point in hanging around here. He won't be back before dark.'

His companion produced a walkie-talkie from his hunting bag and pulled out the aerial. A conversation started up; a nasal voice gave out instructions. At sunset, the two inspectors from the Marseilles 'stups' were to keep a nearby farm, the Clos St Antoine, under surveillance.

Discreet surveillance of the movements of Joseph Cesari had been going on for a year. The seizure of a hundred and fifteen kilos of raw morphine hidden in a bale of kid skins on a Turkish cargo vessel in Marseilles harbour had brought him into the limelight. Investigations had led to the conclusion – though without definite proof – that the package was ultimately destined for him.

During the month of July, the police had discovered that Cesari often went to the Clos St Antoine. He had purchased it recently through an intermediary of a twenty-six-year-old Marseilles workman, Albert Véran, who lived there with his mistress, Anna P. The couple had carried out various conversions and then began raising poultry. They were assisted by Roger Caluzzi, a man of about forty who was well known in the Marseilles underworld as 'Petite Main'.

Investigations had confirmed Cesari's links with the inhabitants of the farm. 'He takes a variety of routes,' the surveillance reports stated, 'and also uses a number of cars. He is spending increasingly long periods of time there, and increasingly often. Sometimes he spends whole days and nights there, and on those occasions, the light on the first floor is on until dawn. Sounds of metal drums and containers being handled are also to be heard.' The investigators also noted a lot of coming and going by other vehicles, and loading and unloading of parcels and cases.

Later on Olivier, head of the police laboratory in Marseilles, made an inventory of the equipment stored in the laboratory and the farm outbuildings and estimated that it could produce six hundred kilos of heroin, at the rate of about a hundred kilos a week. The Marseilles clients dispatched it to the Puerto Rican and Cuban buyers in Miami or the Italo-American representatives of *Cosa Nostra* in New York.

The Marseilles section of the Central Office for the Prevention of Drug Trafficking was particularly eager to obtain rapid results because it was having to deploy its entire manpower on the affair and drop other less urgent enquiries. In 1961 the government was still relatively unconcerned about drug-trafficking. The necessary funds were allocated only very reluctantly. After all, the heroin made in the Marseilles region from the raw morphine delivered by the Turkish cargo boats was destined for the American market. France and the French were as yet untroubled by this social evil. The role of the Parisian Office was mainly a matter of administration and records. The few detectives who were pursuing investigations in the capital were well known to the traffickers, which meant that surveillance was unreliable. Sometimes they managed to pull off a coup thanks to information given by their American colleagues, who had a single representative in Paris: Victor Maria. Their car park at its fullest never held more than three cars: clapped-out Peugeot 404s which could be spotted a kilometre away and easily shaken off. The team consisted of a quartet of friends who called one another by their nicknames: Juju (Anglès), Bambois (Levergeois), Mumu (Mugnier) and Crucru (Crucifix). Their achievements may not have been spectacular, but they did build up dossiers which, several years later, enabled the senior crime squad to break up several important networks. 'An investigation may go on for years,' commented Inspector Carrère, who supervised their work. 'Our small group made it possible for those who followed after to achieve quite spectacular results. In some cases, all the spade work had already been done for them.'

Carrère gave them *carte blanche*. His tall slim figure, diplomat's elegance, polished language and fluent delivery made him an effective 'public relations' man for his subordinates. It was he who persuaded the various branches of police, CRS (the riot police) and *gendarmes* to participate more actively in the fight against trafficking. He tightened up collaboration with the Americans: Victor Maria and his boss in Rome, Michael Picini, 'the godfather'.

'At first,' Victor Maria was to say, 'we had difficulty in getting used to the French laws, which are so different from the American. But this didn't matter much, because in 1970 no one seemed to want to know anything about the drug problem.'

In reality the most active team was that of the Vice Squad of the Prefecture of Police, headed by Louis Souchon and Roger Voitot. They pursued small retailers and their clients in the hope of working up the chain to find the big suppliers from Corsica and Marseilles.

In this way the Marseilles branch of the Office had occasion to work more often in collaboration with the Vice Squad than with its own main Paris branch; this was bound to produce a certain amount of conflict and rivalry and prevented the growth of concerted action and overall strategy.

But the Marseilles 'stups' were not without their good points. There was a mere handful of them – fewer than half a dozen – under the command of Maurice Hug and supervised by Inspector Lavalette. They had a thorough knowledge of the Marseilles underworld and of those of its members implicated in heroin-trafficking. But they could not possibly have them all under surveillance at the same time, nor undertake any large-scale operations. For them Cesari's arrest, if it turned out to their advantage, would be the coup of the year.

The chemist's car drove slowly towards Roquefort-la-Bédoule. The detectives had long given up tailing all its movements. Each time it came out on to the road it would take new routes, new detours along by-roads. Cesari would check on the cars following him in the driving mirror, accelerate sharply, then brake and observe their reactions. If in any doubt, he would stop to let them pass or double back so as to meet them head on and take a look at their occupants. He always did this even on perfectly respectable missions.

This time, he was particularly cautious. He was going to visit his cousin Edouard Toudayan, a young Marseilles man of Armenian origin who had formerly worked for transporters of sea cargo the Messageries Maritimes, where he had been known as a 'sharp, quick-tempered and undisciplined employee'. The two cousins had joined forces several years later to run a restaurant on the Corniche, the Eden-Roc. The business had not been a success and they separated. Now they were once more jointly involved in a more profitable undertaking. Edouard Toudayan had at his disposal a very small-scale laboratory, which enabled Cesari to meet urgent orders.

Edouard was not an unknown quantity to the police. They already had a thick dossier on his activities, starting in 1955 with the seizure of several kilos of raw morphine delivered by a sailor from the Turkish cargo vessel *Ankara*. Incriminated in the affair, Edouard had disappeared and surfaced only six months later, accompanied by a lawyer who obtained his discharge before the county court.

In 1956 and 1957 he worked on the crew of a fishing boat, the *Sant'Anna*, whose owner, who went by the name of 'Jean-la-tache', was well known to the 'stups'. Edouard's catches, though rare, must have been miraculous, because he spent most of his time travelling in Turkey, the Lebanon, Italy and Switzerland driving about in cars which did not belong to him and using papers bearing a variety of names.

His activities were wide-ranging and he had probably not yet found his true vocation. In 1957 he was involved in a counterfeiting affair; in 1958 he found himself in court for carrying a weapon without a licence and infringement of currency legislation.

He was also charged with running arms from Switzerland to the Algerian FLN.

In 1960–61 he found his métier at last. He went to Turkey several times in an American car, in which he brought back consignments of raw morphine. As a retreat from his multifarious activities, he rented rooms in an isolated farmhouse at Roquefort-la-Bédoule in the Cadenets district; it belonged to a man named Vincent Pastore, a farmer and town councillor. He spent long periods staying there with his friend Irene P and their two children.

So that this apparent leisure should not appear too suspect, Toudayan was supposedly employed by a company, Méditerranée-Publicité, as a door-to-door salesman, at a salary of five hundred francs a month. This company belonged to Antoine Restori, a friend of Cesari known as 'Corduroy trousers'; his wife had two wine and spirit businesses. Like his friend Edouard, he had already been involved in an affair of counterfeit banknotes.

The manager of Méditerranée-Publicité was called Pierre R. He was a young man, about thirty, slim, smart, with handsome regular features, of average height and with short dark hair. He was Madame Restori's nephew. Furthermore it was 'Corduroy trousers' who had taught him, when he was sixteen, how to process raw morphine into heroin. Since then he had worked for all the big names in the trade: and in their opinion the purity of his white powder could bear comparison with Cesari's. He had two other points in common with Toudayan: he never went anywhere in his uncle's company and he had rooms, with his mistress Reine C, in part of the large house belonging to the farmer Pastore, at Roquefort-la-Bèdoule. Edouard and Pierre had been closely connected since 1961. They had been stopped by the police that year at Menton, when they were going to Italy in Pierre's Jaguar.

Pierre R led a life that bore little relation to his salary of six hundred francs a month. His Jaguar had been superseded by a Triumph Sport and a Mercedes 220. Reine C, a pleasant brunette whose handsome green eyes had engaged more than one heart, had bought a more discreet and utilitarian Renault 4L in 1964. Oddly enough, it consumed an enormous amount of butane-gas; she purchased two cylinders a week at the hardware store at la Bédoule. Pierre explained away his long stays at the Pastore's farm by saying that he needed peace and quiet because of his asthma.

He was alone at the farm when Cesari arrived. The two men waited until Pastore had driven off at the wheel of his tractor to go to the former dairy, now filled with coppers, carboys, cans and a whole range of hastily put together electrical equipment. Cesari eyed the assortment of gadgets with a sceptical grimace.

'In a fortnight,' he said, 'the Clos St Antoine period will be over. After this, I'm retiring. If you want to carry on, Pierre, you'll have to find bigger premises.'

When Cesari went back to Aubagne, night had fallen. The windows of La Roseraie, of the Clos St Antoine and the houses scattered over the neighbouring hills were lit up. The 404 drove through the gateway which Papa Nounou had just opened. He had already let loose the five Alsatians which patrolled the property and which now came to sniff at the chemist's ankles, tails wagging.

Heaving a carboy onto his shoulder, Joseph Cesari walked off under the trees. He had only three hundred metres of woodland to reach the Clos St Antoine. As soon as he was in the courtyard, the door opened. He passed Anna P without a word, walked through the ground floor in darkness and climbed the staircase. Then he entered the first of the four rooms that had been turned into a laboratory. Véran and Caluzzi were already at work, gas-masks covering their faces. The heat from the five butane-gas burners made the atmosphere as airless as a Turkish bath. Their clothing was impregnated with the strong smell of acetone. An electric motor fixed above a plastic dustbin drove a mixer, its blades plunged into the mixture of raw morphine and acetone. Caluzzi regulated its speed with the knob of a rheostat fixed to the wall.

Cesari put down the carboy. He too then put on a mask and an overall, and went over to the enamel basin, vapour from which was drawn off by a hood. He regulated the tap of the gas ring with a chef's skill. He then plugged in the suction pump which speeded up elimination of the impurities and alkaloids; it purred a descant to the noise of the mixer's motor. Véran was fixing another one on to another dustbin.

This was just the beginning of a laborious process which would last for almost forty-eight hours. The operation to dissolve the solid block of raw morphine entailed churning the substance for six hours. Cleansed of its impurities, the mixture would be treated with tartaric acid and bone black, then heated to ninety degrees.

This was the stage when explosions could occur. If it was underheated, the product would be ruined. If it was overheated, the laboratory would blow up. But Joseph Cesari approached this critical phase with the confidence of an expert. The success of the operation would depend more on his flair than on the thermometer. Silently, the three men continued their manœuvres among their instruments with the accuracy of seasoned lab assistants, amid the burning vapours and the din of the motors.

4

King of the Chemists

While Joseph Cesari was ruining his health and strength amassing a considerable fortune within a few weeks, the most famous of the clandestine chemists of the time, Dominique Albertini, was vegetating in a cell in Les Baumettes where he was serving the four-year sentence passed on him on 10 January 1963. Seriously ill, he had been taken to the prison hospital. Friends helped him escape a few months later.

The police of Venzolasca in Corsica were to find him, towards the end of the same year, in his parents' house at Lovetto di Cascinca, where he had gone to earth with his whole family. He was never to see his native village again but died in detention on 22 February 1970.

The new generation of traffickers had felt the mark of his strong personality. In 1964, the men who were making the tonnes of heroin in the Marseilles laboratories which were to be dispatched to the United States, were still his pupils. It was still the Lebanese suppliers who were providing the indispensable raw morphine; and the networks which he had helped to create were still functioning.

He had embarked on this profession in the early thirties, when the French clientèle was interested only in opium, which gave nostalgic pleasure to the old colonials, or else in cocaine, much sought after in the world of Paris night-life. But it was the American market that the gang leader Paul Venture Carbone had his eye on. When the measures taken under the aegis of the League of Nations prevented him from obtaining what he needed from obliging pharmaceutical factories, he organised his own processing industry.

The same methods of delivery were still being used forty years later. Sailors from the Turkish or Lebanese boats would throw watertight bags overboard before entering Marseilles harbour. Fishermen from Bandol or La Ciotat would fish them up in their nets after nightfall and deliver them at dawn to their partners.

It was then that Carbone suggested to a sailor who had already done him several good turns and who struck him as gifted, that he might devote himself to the processing of heroin.

'I can help you earn more in one year than you would earn in your entire career as a seaman. Of course, you'll have to learn the trade first. It can't be all that difficult to find a good teacher.'

The gifted sailor was Dominique; and the teacher was soon found. It might perhaps have been the chemist Fortin, an old drunkard who hung around Pigalle; or a Marseilles chemistry tutor; or possibly both. Either way, the new lab assistant justified Venture Carbone's trust. As the years went by, Dominique became a familiar and legendary figure in the Marseilles underworld; he loved food, drink and tall stories. He always drove fast cars with special panoramic driving mirrors so that he could keep a sharp eye on the road behind.

He travelled a lot, to Paris, the Lebanon, Milan, Genoa, Palermo. He also went to the United States. He was arrested there in 1952 for illegal entry and attempted bribing of an official. He spent a year there in prison, his only conviction prior to 1963. He then settled in a sumptuous villa in the St Julien district, Boulevard de la Cabane, with his wife and their four children. At the beginning of the sixties, it was being rumoured in the underworld that he supervised the production of three hundred kilos of heroin a month. Most of it was largely dispatched across the Atlantic by Italian sailors with Mafia connections.

The most gifted of his pupils was his half-brother Joseph Cesari, fourteen years his junior. He too had started out on the shipping lines of the Far East and had done military service in the Navy. After a dull period in his aunt's cheese shop near the Canebière, and having tried unsuccessfully to launch himself in various trades, he had seized the opportunity Dominique offered him. He had involved himself in his new activities doggedly and passionately, steeping himself in works on chemistry and improving the home-made procedures until he became the greatest expert on the clandestine market.

5

The Raid on Clos St Antoine

The eighth of October had been as close and muggy as a day in high summer. Towards the end of the afternoon the sun began to sink cautiously over the horizon and a breeze from the sea shook the shadows of the pines over the hot rocks.

The door of the Clos St Antoine opened. The solid figure of Anna appeared on the threshold. She crossed the courtyard carrying two pails and turned to look at the first-floor windows. One of the curtains was drawn back and a face gazed out, looking longingly over the hills.

The four rooms that made up Joseph Cesari's laboratory were like a furnace. An electric fan whirred without imparting the slightest coolness to the heavy air. The motors of the driers purred smoothly; the flames of the four gas burners fizzed under the coppers; pyrex flasks simmered in the water at a constant temperature of between eighty and eighty-five degrees. They contained a mixture of two kilos of acetic anhydride to one of morphine. The anhydride had been ordered in drums in Germany to avoid arousing unwelcome attention.

The necks of the flasks were topped by glass tubes extended with a coil; these were put through a current of cool air before returning to the flasks. Cooled, the vapours given off by this mixture had to go through this circuit for five hours, until there was nothing left in the container except for a soft paste whose colour would vary from brown to white according to its purity. Once treated with bone black and sodium carbonate and dried out, it would become the diacetyl morphine which, purified, would be converted into the chlorhydrate, which is heroin.

Naked under their overalls, noses hidden behind gas-masks,

Cesari and Albert Véran sat squarely in front of the burners, automatically wiping away the sweat which poured down their faces. Véran kept his eyes fixed on the thermometers which sank into the coppers, and operated the gas taps. If the temperature went below eighty degrees, the contents of the flasks might be ruined; if it went above eighty-five, an explosion could occur. In contact with air, the anhydride would start to sputter and could cause the chemists atrocious burns.

Cesari kept flasks containing soda, ammonia and sulphuric acid to hand. His job was to maintain the constant acidity of the mixture, adding either the acid or the base required. He also had a stock of litmus paper at the ready; this enabled him to check the acidity, but long experience meant that he could detect the slightest variation at a glance.

A sudden sound of footsteps, talking and barking coming from the outside and clearly audible above the drone of the motors, made them freeze. Caluzzi was in the process of taking the baker's trays containing the unrefined hardened diacetyl morphine from the driers; he put them down again hurriedly and ran to the window, pulling aside a curtain.

'It's nothing,' he said, 'just the Legionnaires coming back from training.'

Outside, the soldiers in fatigues and white képis plodded by unconcernedly, after a glance at the charms of Anna on her way back from the farm. They climbed the stony slope, skirted a group of trees and disappeared behind a rocky outcrop, followed by their Alsatians. Some seconds later, half a dozen hunters, rifles sloped, emerged from the bushes where they had flattened themselves on hearing the detachment approaching.

'This time,' said Inspector Hug, 'we can go ahead. If we wait too long, the birds may have flown.'

The surveillance had been going on for several months and was now drawing to a close. The siege of the Clos St Antoine had been decided upon two days previously. To obtain the desired surprise effect, the six policemen had rehearsed their elaborate scenario several times. Their colleagues were stationed around

La Roseraie, which Cesari had left the previous evening, and outside Galorini's garage in Marseilles. Chief Inspector Lavalette was supervising the operation.

Inspector Claude Chaminadas climbed onto the shoulders of one of his colleagues. Another fired a shot into the air. The would-be wounded man let out agonised shrieks while his companion, sinking beneath his weight, strode down the slope, crossed the courtyard and knocked at the door.

'Help! Help!' he shouted.

A first-floor window opened, above the door. Véran appeared. In his hand he was holding a plastic bag full of white powder. Chaminadas' groans redoubled.

'What's going on?'

'There's been an accident – my mate's been given a load of buckshot. We'll have to phone for an ambulance.'

'We haven't got a telephone. Go to the door on the right. We'll see what we can do.'

The two inspectors had caught the smell of acetic anhydride. Now they had located the laboratory. It was vital to gain entry before their quarry scattered. Following the instructions he had been given, the inspector – still carrying his mate – approached the doorway in which Anna had just appeared. She stood aside to let them pass. They entered the kitchen just as Véran came down the internal staircase.

Chaminadas now had his feet back on the ground. 'Police,' he announced. Quickly he grabbed the young woman's arm just as she was about to press the bell and give the alarm. Then he ran after his colleague who was going up to the first floor. He entered the laboratory just behind him and found himself face to face with Cesari, petrified, a packet of heroin in his hand, and with Caluzzi who was holding a baker's tray of diacetyl morphine at arm's length.

'Well done, gentlemen,' said Cesari sportingly. 'You've pulled it off.' They were then joined by Inspector Lavalette and his colleagues. The search began immediately. Thanks to the small transmitter Chaminadas had in his pocket, they were able to listen in on the successful outcome of their stratagem. His accomplices were cowed, but Cesari continued to play his part. He showed them his equipment with a certain pride, pointing out the stock of raw morphine – a hundred kilos of it – which he still had to treat and the two hundred five-hundred gram packets of pure white heroin, ready for delivery. The inventorying of the equipment and products housed in the outhouses was to occupy the police for a good part of the night.

As soon as Chaminadas and his colleague entered the farm, the second team was notified and entered La Roseraie. They crossed the lawn to find an already resigned Renée Manoukian. The furniture, the precious objects, the old masters, the bookshelves, the four cars lined up near the entrance, were all photographed. The process took an hour.

After nightfall, the customs men were joined by their police colleagues at the laboratory to make their own inventory. At daybreak, they went to La Roseraie and to their surprise found an empty house; all the furniture and valuables had vanished.

'We passed a van three kilometres from here,' exclaimed one of them. 'It might have been their removal van.' The cars shot out and managed to catch up with the van. In a few hours, thanks to the photographs taken the previous evening, everything was replaced.

The case was heard six days later. Cesari pleaded guilty, but the judges were never to learn anything either about the origins of the raw morphine or about the intended destination of the heroin. His accomplices claimed complete ignorance of his activities.

'I rented out the first floor to him,' stated Véran. 'I thought he was doing scientific experiments.'

Cesari was sentenced to seven years' imprisonment, Véran to three, Caluzzi to two, Galorini to one and Anna to a suspended sentence of eight months. Together they would have to pay Fr. 329,000 damages and over four million francs in fines. The chemist's fortune did not run to this. 'Friends' offered to help Renée and her children until Cesari was released. His freedom, when it came, was to be short-lived.

6

A Gifted Pupil

The police of the various countries concerned with drug trafficking still did not grasp its growing importance. But in Marseilles there were pointers which Inspector Hug's team recognised as ominous. The inspector prepared a report on the problem. After the closure of the clandestine laboratory at Clos St Antoine, the police knew that there would be repercussions in the world of the 'quiet men'.

Soon after Cesari's arrest, an informer told Inspector Hug's men that someone called Edouard Toudayan of Marseilles was the last link in a clandestine network which was importing raw morphine from Turkey. Over the next few months, Inspector Claude Chaminadas learned that it was being said in trafficking circles that heroin manufactured in 'Edouard's laboratory' was being sent to the United States. 'Edouard' had to be Edouard Toudayan.

The police followed Toudayan from bistro to bistro; he visited a great many. They included Le Michel on rue Ste Françoise, La Poste in rue de l'Evêché, the sailors' bar, the Fisher, in rue de la République, and the Bar Maritime in rue des Phocéens. Toudayan, who spoke Turkish, often hung around the harbour – particularly when the cargo boats *Akdeniz* and *Karandeniz* were in port.

Surveillance of Toudayan's movements continued throughout the latter part of 1964. Cesari had been behind bars for more than three months when the investigators learnt that Toudayan was having a villa built at Roquefort-la-Bédoule. By hanging around the village an inspector finally discovered that the future owner – who arrived from time to time to see how work was progressing – was staying at the Pastore farm under the name of M Edouard. The inspector also discovered that Reine and Pierre R were staying in the same house.

Pierre R had been chosen by the quiet men to assume the heavy mantle of Joseph Cesari, but his very primitive laboratory could not cater for the demands of a growing clientèle. As Cesari had foreseen, it was important to find premises and equipment quickly to make more intensive production possible. What was needed was a new Clos St Antoine and Pierre R had begun looking for a suitable house.

At the beginning of January, the young chemist at last discovered the perfect premises at Gémenos, in the Brigou district. It was a fairly isolated property of two thousand square metres. The house consisted of a large room and a kitchen on the ground floor, two bedrooms and a shower on the first floor and a completely empty room twelve metres square.

'This is where we'll have the laboratory,' Pierre said. 'Of course, we'll have to organise water supply and drainage and put in a bench – and improve the ventilation. There'll be quite a bit of work involved.'

'Bertolone will give you a hand with that,' said Toudayan.

Louis Bertolone was a man of about thirty. He had been a sailor and then a head waiter. He had returned from the Sahara a few months before and was living in Marseilles, in rue Ste Julie. He had already become an obliging and almost permanent guest at the Pastore farm. He set to work to help Pierre as soon as the contract had been signed, on 15 January.

While Bertolone was fitting out the Gémenos 'laundry', a new resident was moving into the Pastore farm. His name was Giuseppe Labate. He was wanted by the Genoa police for robbery, smuggling and conspiracy. He had been introduced by a colleague of Toudayan's who was responsible for the routing network for the Turkish raw morphine in Italy.

At the beginning of February the move began. On the ninth, one of the vans loaded up some of the equipment. On the tenth, it was the Renault 4L. The police watchers lost their quarry in the area of the Col de l'Ange. Only Labate was left at the Pastore farm.

Periès, the local examining magistrate, issued a warrant which gave the 'stups' the go-ahead to intervene.

On 12 February, Giuseppe Labate was arrested at the Pastore farm. He did not deny having been harboured by Toudayan, and this made it possible to arrest Toudayan the following morning. A search of the farm led to the discovery of traces of equipment which could have been used in the making of heroin. Samples of dust and waste water were sent to the police laboratory in Marseilles. Traces of morphine and heroin were detected.

This first operation caused quite a stir, and Pierre R and his uncle Restori were informed of it. A leak on the part of the local press confirmed their fears. Taking a wildly circuitous route in order to avoid being followed, the young chemist arrived at Gémenos where Bertolone was in the process of building the bench in the 'laundry'.

'The police are after us,' he said. 'Everything will have to go. And fast!'

'Everything' was a considerable amount: drums of acetone and acetic anhydride, pumps, motors and burners which were being stored on the ground floor until the lab was ready. The two men emptied the contents of the drums onto the ground, in the fond expectation that they would evaporate rapidly. But the pool of liquid spread, giving out its tell-tale smell. Various pieces of equipment were bundled hastily into the Renault 4L.

Meanwhile, the police resumed their researches at the point where they had lost sight of the van, at the Col de l'Ange. The whole region of Cuges-les-Pins, Castelet and Gémenos was combed. At last the property was located. The fumes of acetic anhydride left no room for doubt, and police reinforcements stood by.

At eight o'clock on the evening of 17 February, the police heard the sound of spades and pick-axes and the clang of containers and equipment being loaded into a vehicle. All the windows of the house were lit up, as well as the outer courtyard. Suddenly the gates were opened by Bertolone. The Renault, headlamps alight, set off down the road. Pierre R was at the wheel. He stopped to wait for his companion. Two policemen came into view in the beam of light, raising their arms and shouting 'Stop! Police!' R drove off, jostling them and dragging them with him for a few metres – they were clinging to the doors – and disappeared into the darkness. He passed a surveillance vehicle parked in darkness a little way further on and went off in the direction of the village. He was immediately followed.

The chase continued along the road to Toulon. The Renault forked off suddenly in the direction of Aubagne to join the motorway. The police car gradually gained ground. R braked suddenly. His car went into the hard shoulder; he jumped into the ditch and ran off, disappearing up the hillside into the night.

But the police were not left empty-handed. They held Toudayan, two of his accomplices and enough equipment to convince the judges. R meanwhile was taken in hand by the Marseilles underworld and given safe asylum. Instructions had reached him from Joseph Cesari in Les Baumettes prison. He was to lie low until judgement had been passed in the Clos St Antoine affair. Cesari had worked out a defence: he claimed to have been a beginner whose friends had done him a favour; friends whose good faith he had abused and whom he did not want to expose. Cross-examination of R might easily have compromised this fragile edifice.

When his boss had been sentenced, R was to give himself up to the police, on 29 June 1965. He was to claim complete ignorance of the production of heroin. He was one of the *bona fide* friends of whom Cesari had spoken, who had put the Pastore farm at his disposal and transported equipment whose purposes he had not known. He was sentenced to three years' imprisonment on 26 February 1966.

7

A Hundred Kilos of Junk Disappear

By midnight on 30 November 1964, a freezing drizzle that had been falling over Paris since early afternoon had stopped. The surface of Boulevard Suchet was still glistening wet.

A Citroën cabriolet, registration 458 PX75, coming from the Porte Maillot, slowed up as it approached number 45, drove onto the pavement and parked under the trees a few metres from the main doorway.

The driver turned off the headlights, switched off the engine, locked all the doors and started off towards his apartment. He then changed his mind, went back to the car, pulled off the sparking-plug leads, removed the distributor cap and slipped it into his pocket. He flipped the bonnet down again and disappeared into the building.

His name was Jacques Bousquet. He came from Lozère and was about fifty years old, solidly built, his hair slightly receding though only flecked with grey. He was smartly dressed and seemed quite at ease in this wealthy district. 'A very respectable gentleman,' his concierge was to say in evidence four years later, 'always pleasant and smiling.' He lived on the third floor in an expensive seven-roomed flat. All that his neighbours knew about him was that he was a dealer of some sort, married and father of three: a girl of eighteen and two younger boys. He was often away on business.

Very soon, the lights went out in the apartment. Bousquet was going to have to get up very early in the morning to collect his friend Eugène Malibert from the Gare d'Austerlitz. On 3 December Malibert was leaving for New York on board the *France*, with a Citroën. He was now coming back from Bergerac where his employers in the firm of civil service supplies had sent him on a course.

Before leaving, Malibert had signed all the relevant papers for taking over a car whose licence still bore the name of one of their friends and associates, Guirche. Bousquet had spent the previous week sorting out these various problems. Two days earlier, a telephone call from Marseilles had informed him that the goods would be delivered on the thirtieth. He had driven into the forest of St Germain in his Buick at the agreed time. A Citroën van with a Bouches-du-Rhône number plate had slipped in behind him near the Loges; then, one behind the other, the two vehicles had parked at a bend in a side-road. Glancing in his driving mirror, Bousquet had recognised Jean N, a Corsican from Paris and a leading figure in the underworld, who was replacing the usual carrier, a taciturn expressionless man from Marseilles.

Within a few seconds, four big cases had been transferred from the van to the boot of the Buick. Then the driver, who had left his engine running, drove off with a brief parting gesture. The Buick was back on the main road again a few minutes later, driving slowly towards Paris.

Victor M, an associate of Bousquet's, had rented a lock-up garage in Boulogne where he could load the goods into the hiding places that had been arranged in the Citroën DS in privacy. Previously the operation had been carried out on M's property at Croissy-sur-Seine, where the car would remain until the day it was put onto the boat, at Le Havre. But M had left unexpectedly for the south of France and had not even gone to meet his associate as arranged.

For this trip, as it happened, the suppliers had agreed to deliver a hundred kilos of heroin: two hundred transparent plastic packets containing a fine white powder. This load represented an investment of a million francs, and the American client would be paying about a million dollars for it. Precautions had not been taken for nothing.

It had taken Bousquet several hours, behind the doors of the garage, to stow these packets into the various hiding places created by an inventive coach-builder: inside the front and back wings, in the seat-backs and under the front seat, and also in a recess under the petrol tank, which now held about ten litres.

Jacques Bousquet left the building on Boulevard Suchet the following morning at eight, fresh-complexioned, wearing a suit of Prince of Wales check and a blue cashmere coat. He greeted the concierge with a beaming smile and stepped out onto the pavement.

Suddenly he stood rooted to the spot. A Peugeot 404 was parked just where he had left the Citroën the previous evening. He looked around him, went over in his mind his actions of the previous night and felt in his pocket for the distributor cap. No doubt about it: the car and its cargo had been stolen. It represented a loss of half a milliard old francs (just over £500,000). How the thieves had managed to select a car lacking the distributor cap, when there were hundreds of cars lined up along the boulevard which they could have started with a simple pair of pliers, was more than he could fathom.

The moment he stepped off the Bordeaux train at the Gare d'Austerlitz Eugène Malibert knew that a disaster had occurred. Seeing his friend's drained face, his first thought was of the police and he felt himself break out in a cold sweat.

'They've pinched the car,' Bousquet murmured flatly. 'With all the stuff. From in front of my place, last night. And I'd removed the distributor cap.'

He produced an ebonite cylinder from his pocket. 'I haven't told anyone. I wanted to see you first. We're going to have to cancel your trip, warn the guys in New York and try to calm down the fellows in Marseilles.'

'If they suspect you of double-crossing them, that might be the end of you.'

'And of you too, if they think we're in it together.'

They left the station and took a taxi to Malibert's, in the sixteenth *arrondissement*. This trip was to have netted the young courier Fr. 15,000. He was counting on this sum to pay some urgent debts. He was shattered. Clearly, if the police arrested the thieves and got back the car, they would discover the hiding places; and the documents had been in his name for several days.

'It was bound to happen,' sighed Bousquet. 'Everything had gone too well so far. Anyhow, it's still less serious than being caught by the American customs.'

He thought back to the many trips he had already made to the United States over the last three years, of luxurious crossings on the *France* or the *Queen Elizabeth*, of times spent in smart hotels in New York or Montreal, money extravagantly squandered. The first person to inform, he thought, was his associate Victor M who had organised the network with him and who had left him to run it on his own several months earlier, only supervising it himself from a distance.

The taxi drove through the streets of Auteuil between the wealthy stone houses. 'Only Jean N can get us out of this one,' remarked Bousquet. 'Provided I can convince him I'm not lying.'

When they arrived at their destination, he left Malibert and went to collect the Buick from Boulogne, from the lock-up garage where he had left it. Then he went to Passy, found a public phone-box in a *brasserie* and phoned Jean N at his home in rue des Belles-Feuilles; and guardedly brought him up to date with recent events. A few minutes later the Corsican joined him and listened darkly to an account of the theft down to the last detail.

'Well,' he concluded, 'let's suppose you're telling the truth. You wouldn't be so stupid as to play such a trick on us. If you've lied, I wouldn't give much to be in your shoes. I'm going to telephone Achille in Marseilles. But don't count on getting out of this scot free. Mark my words, those guys aren't fairy godmothers.'

He was unable to get through to Achille Cecchini, his immediate supplier and co-owner of the consignment, until 7 December at his home on rue Saint-Mathieu in Marseilles. Half an hour later they were talking on another, safer line. The conversation was long and stormy. Jean N needed all his powers of persuasion to convince Cecchini that the matter should be discussed 'between gentlemen' and without recourse to violence . . . for the moment.

During this time, Bousquet had gone to see Victor M in his Loiret property. He wasn't satisfied either. It was he who had specially asked the suppliers to raise this load to a hundred kilos.

'If they decide you've double-crossed them, they'll be convinced that I'm in it too. And if they impose any kind of penalty, they'll insist that I pay half and that I'm answerable for the rest.'

Back in Paris, Bousquet learned of developments from Jean N. 'I get the impression that their feelings for you aren't quite as warm as before,' he remarked. 'They're going to ask Big Charles to come up here and look into it. The decision will depend on him. In any case they'll ask to be reimbursed for the goods mislaid.'

'I'd be delighted to reimburse them, if they give me the means to pick up enough money. In all my bank accounts together, I haven't got a tenth of it.'

'Don't you think your exaggerating a bit? Well, we can always try. We'll just have to let things die down a bit and wait till Big Charles arrives.'

Big Charles, whose real name was Louis Jacques Douheret, who preferred to be called Lefranc but was known in Marseilles as 'Jacques l'Américain', and later as 'Big Charles' because he was supposed to resemble de Gaulle, arrived in the capital a week later.

The disappearance of Jacques Bousquet's car was the first serious stumbling block his suppliers had encountered. The chairman of this prosperous enterprise was Joseph Orsini. At sixty, he belonged to the generation of quiet men but his ideas were more modern. He realised that an age was drawing to an end and that only those who could adapt to the rapid growth in trafficking would survive. He had come back to Marseilles in 1958 after a few years in an American penitentiary. He resumed his privileged position in the local underworld without difficulty. As early as 1930 his police record referred to him as one of the first generation of traffickers who gathered under the banner of Venture Carbone.

After the Liberation – like his friend Spirito – he was prosecuted for hold-ups, attempted murder and, of course, collaboration with the enemy. Putting the Atlantic Ocean between himself and the French Government, he arrived in the United States on board the cargo vessel *Athos II*, with papers in the name of Joseph Casabianca. He settled in an apartment on West 85th Street in New York. He was forty-three years old; a stocky man, with heavy features, an imposing nose and watchful brown eyes.

He formed friendships with various members of the Mafia, and kept up his contacts with the men from Marseilles and Corsica who were reconstituting the networks broken up by the war. He was the close associate of two *mafiosi*, Schillitani and Giannini, who were to be shot in 1952 on orders from *Cosa Nostra*.

Arrested in 1951 by the US Immigration Department for possession of false papers, Orsini was interned on Ellis Island and charged with drug trafficking. Sentenced to ten years, imprisonment, he was sent to Leavenworth Penitentiary where he stayed until his deportation in 1958.

In Marseilles he was reunited with his brother Fernand, two years his junior; the same burly build, the same thick features, but in his case including a pair of surprising blue eyes. Officially he was running his café, le Bistrot Marseillais, in the Place de Rome just near the Préfecture. In reality, behind this façade he was closely connected with several veterans such as Marius Ansaldi known as 'le Matelot'; Dominique Reissent known as 'Nique-des-Carmes', and Spirito.

Now that he was approaching sixty, Joseph seemed to be aiming at retirement in his luxury villa in the Parc Borely. He lived a comfortable life and avoided excess of all kinds, even in dress. However, he did have a studio near the Piscine Vallier where he could lie low if things were to go badly. In fact, he had resumed the running of the team led by his brother Fernand.

He included Fernand in all his plans. Together they were looking for someone able and discreet to help them in their undertaking: to organise networks, find couriers and transporters, deal with suppliers and clients; in short, supervise the whole operational sector of the business. Their choice fell on Jean N.

His reputation in the underworld was that of a man you could count on; he had been born in 1913 in Sartène, in Corsica, of an irreproachable family. He had come to Paris where his obliging nature coupled with his circumspection very soon earned him the respect of the toughs of Montmartre. In 1950 he became manager of a bar in rue Notre Dame de Lorette, the Château d'If, where he was assisted by his devoted wife Suzy, a Jewess of Polish origin.

Seven years later, and still enjoying the esteem of the denizens of his chosen world, he was officially behind the bar of la Citrouille in rue de Douai. In the meantime, he had done a number of good turns, successfully handled several delicate affairs and proved that he was thoroughly trustworthy. 'When Jeannot gave his word,' people said, 'it was as if he'd signed a contract.' On 28 May 1957, his bar was severely shot up, causing some damage to the frontage and the clientèle. Questioned by the police, he feigned astonishment. He had been crouching behind his bar and had seen nothing. That evening, at la Citrouille, there had been no regulars and he had not been able to describe anyone. This reaction was much appreciated, except by the police.

Dispatched by Orsini, he began to travel around Europe, particularly to Milan, Rome, Genoa and Sartène. The *mafiosi* called him 'the man with the gold-rimmed spectacles'. He was often accompanied by his assistant, Jacques Douheret, alias 'Jacques l'Américain', alias Big Charles, who had been released from prison for good conduct two years earlier. He had been sentenced to fifteen years' detention in 1950 after the burglary of the station post-office in Montparnasse.

Jean N was in charge of the 'smuggling' section. 'Jacques l'Américain' was sent to New York by Orsini to make contact with one of his former prison mates, Beni Indiviglio. Indiviglio became his client, as did the brothers Romano, Arnold and Frederick; they actually worked for a boss, the famous *mafioso* Santo Trafficante.

Gradually, Douheret extended his stays on the other side of the Atlantic. Heroin reached him in small quantities: from six to twelve kilos at a time. It was often brought to him by sailors or couriers engaged by N.

These deliveries were always made by boat, in American ports. Orsini was not interested in the networks set up by the pioneer drug traffickers Ansan Bistoni or Jean-Baptiste Croce in the Caribbean and Mexico, or in collaboration with top Canadian *mafiosi* Giuseppe Cotroni's Canadian network. Nor did he wish to associate with competitors who used aeroplanes.

The Orsinis were also unwilling to set up laboratories in which they themselves would produce the heroin they exported. Their golden rule was always to keep clear of actually handling the white powder and to keep no written records. Joseph's own head was his calculator and computer.

They merely passed on orders to the various clandestine laboratories or to those who financed them. It was in this way – because they had a good reputation on the market – that they became the clients of the best chemist in the world in this field, until his arrest: Joseph Cesari.

The success of this cautious and efficient organisation encouraged them to take on competent partners. From 1961 onwards their choice fell upon an experienced technician, Achille Cecchini.

In Marseilles, it was said that Achille Cecchini had started off in life as a policeman. He might perhaps have made a successful career in the police force had an unfortunate matter of theft not resulted in his being sent to prison in 1943. He appeared as a docker, then, at the time of the Liberation, as a mason. Very soon he was driving around in sumptuous cars, Mercedes or Alfa Romeos.

Discreet surveillance allowed the 'stups' inspectors to get an idea of the range of his contacts. He mixed with notorious traffickers, meeting a Lebanese trafficker in Genoa, driving on to la Croisette at Cannes to dine with the chief supplier of raw morphine in the Middle East. But he always managed to avoid the traps that were laid for him.

He was a young-looking forty, brown-haired, thin-lipped, with a nutcracker chin in a plump but forceful face. He liked pretty girls and had a degree of success with them; he was open, hearty and generous. He was also married, and his wife kept a bar, the Carmen, on the Vieux Port. 'I do good business,' he would say to those who expressed surprise at his life style. 'Do have a pastis. It's on me.'

Cecchini had permanently entered the ranks of those whose prosperity was the reward of their conscientiousness and assiduity. Some devoted a part of their fortune to a passion or an ideal. Stockbreeding was Cesari's obsession. Others, like Croce, preferred gambling. Jacques Douheret – who had now settled in Spain – was a firm supporter of Algérie française. He gave financial assistance to former OAS groups in exile. At his trial, two professional killers from the organisation came from Madrid to testify in his favour. 'I carried out over twenty-four executions,' Michel Feischoz admitted. 'I couldn't say exactly how many enemies of Algérie française I shot,' added Georges Calle. And they both agreed that Douheret had been engaged in drug-trafficking on unofficial missions to fill the coffers of the OAS.

The majority of those successful criminals concentrated on enjoying life in the most ostentatious way possible. They set much store by the outward and visible signs of wealth. They kitted themselves out at the new male couturiers, St Laurent, Cardin, Lapidus, frequented luxury hotels and showered their less fortunate friends with gifts. An impressive number of jars of caviar and bottles of champagne were later found by the police in Sartène.

For all these people, Bousquet's mishap made a juicy talking point. The loss of a hundred kilos of heroin was not the most serious problem. The circumstances of its disappearance aroused suspicion. It was unlikely that it had been a matter of sheer chance, that young, small-time thieves would have picked on a car without a distributor cap. It might therefore have been underworld irregulars who were acquainted with the functioning of the network and could thus have guaranteed themselves a good start – with no initial outlay – in an expanding business. The idea of police provocation could not be dismissed either. By causing the junk to disappear, the 'stups' might hope to unleash rivalries among the various criminal factions. All they would have to do then would be to collect up the survivors in one vast haul.

Having become Jo Orsini's right-hand man, N began to aspire to a life style that suited his ascent of the social ladder. From 1960 caviar, champagne and foie gras no longer seemed adequate symbols of having made it. He discovered another interest which enabled him to join the élite: a passion for hunting. Four years before the mysterious vanishing trick on Boulevard Suchet, he was already dedicating himself to it with a plethora of special dress and equipment which enabled him to cut a dash in the most exclusive clubs.

He felt at ease with the fringe aristocracy and spent most of his weekends accompanied by the faithful Suzy, on the estate of one of his friends who owned several hundred hectares in the Sologne. It was called 'Le Petit Colmine' and was near Sully-sur-Loire.

His host was called Charles Martel; however, the only dynasty to which he could claim to belong was that of the brothel-owners, in which hierarchy he occupied an important place. At the beginning of the last war he had been the owner of the famous 'Sphinx'. After having subjected a flock of meek and well-schooled women to the bizarre desires of prelates, politicians, diplomats and industrialists during the roaring twenties, after the collapse of France in 1940 he devoted himself to the relaxation and delectation of German soldiers of all ranks. Adolf Hitler having decided to make Paris the knocking-shop of Europe, his undertaking could not fail.

Martel and N had known each other for a long time. Martel had been deported by some ungrateful clients shortly before the Liberation for having afforded some slight help to the Resistance and hidden arms on his Sologne property.

When the war ended, he none the less preferred to court oblivion and went to Canada to join his wife Blanche, who he had married in 1930, and the two children he had adopted and not seen since

1940. Shortly after the First World War, already owner of several hospitable brothels, Blanche had married a *sociétaire* in the touring Comédie française – a former partner of Sarah Bernhardt, Gustave Scheler. For the love of Blanche, he had given up a life on the boards and become converted to procuring. By his death, at the end of the twenties, the family estate had grown considerably.

In the absence of Charles Martel the chain of brothels and night-clubs – which had formed his fiancée's dowry fifteen years earlier – had enjoyed a new prosperity.

In 1947 Blanche's daughter, the heir apparent of this hedonistic empire, married a young French officer with a brilliant service record, a holder of the Légion d'honneur, the Croix de Guerre, the médaille de la Résistance and médaille des Evadés. He was twenty-seven; his name was Michel Victor M.

Memories of the Occupation having faded, Martel came back to France to settle at Viclain and work the property at Le Petit Colmine. Victor M and his wife also went to live there and joined in the running of the estate. At weekends, various local worthies were entertained at the shooting lodge, as well as American officers stationed at Châteauroux and various former contacts of the one-time owner of the 'Sphinx' – such as Jean N – who had acquired enough polish to pass as businessmen or rich dealers.

Victor M had charm; he was energetic and courageous and had led an eventful life. He came from Lorraine, had been recruited by the Germans and in March 1943 was currently a driver for the Wehrmacht officers in Sète. He deserted, applied to enter the police under the name of Maurice Valentin, was recaptured by the Germans, escaped again and after the Normandy landings found himself at the head of a *maquis* in the Limoges region, where he was known as Major Baptiste. It was said that he killed several dozen collaborators and Gestapo agents for Guingouin, the famous FTP leader of the region. Caught up with yet again by the Germans, he escaped this time by seizing the revolver and shooting the officer who was questioning him.

In 1946 he was in the Black Forest with the rank of captain.

He was commanding a company whose business was the protection and administration of the regional headquarters of the French counter-espionage. He was bored with his duties and applied to join the SDECE, the French equivalent of the CIA. He retained his rank in the army and seems to have been entrusted with several missions for the French Secret Service – though they refuse to confirm this – in Turkey, Germany, Morocco and . . . Canada.

In 1955, eight years after his marriage, he was once again in contact with Colonel Foucaud, who had commanded the headquarters in the Black Forest. The French army fighting in Algeria had commissioned Foucaud to supply them with engines and spare parts for armoured cars and trucks, from the American market. He asked M – a former officer in the Ordnance Corps – to help him solve the problems of distribution and adaptation of this equipment. In 1958, M put him in touch with a firm specialising in engine overhauling, called Leca-Tintignac.

Victor M was charmed by the cordiality and the elegance of the effusive Jean N at Le Petit Colmine. His wife had reservations: 'N's origins and his rapid rise to success are quite evident in his behaviour,' she observed. 'He thinks he can get away with anything.' It was true that the trafficker was all the more self-assured because Martel was thinking of going back into business and taking part in the expanding clandestine trade. 'During 1960,' N revealed later, 'he talked to me about the opportunities he might have of transporting drugs through his son-in-law, who had "official" means. And indeed a first transport was effected through Victor M.'

Between visits to the Sologne, Jean N was working on the organisation of the network with his Marseilles associates. Of course, Victor's 'official means' of which Martel talked, consisted of his collaboration with Colonel Foucaud, who had retired two years previously but continued to keep an eye on the American motor market. That year he sent M to Ohio, to make a selection of some 'Hercules' engines which had been offered him.

In Marseilles, the idea of using Victor M gained ground. The suggestion of using a saloon car to conceal the load of heroin had been accepted by Jo Orsini. Achille Cecchini, assisted by Jean N, was to oversee the operation. For the first trip, it was decided that only a limited quantity of heroin, sixteen kilos, should be sent, by way of dress rehearsal.

Everything was ready by the beginning of 1961. On 1 March Victor purchased the saloon car, registration number 3419 FL75. It seems unlikely that any special alterations were carried out, since by the tenth it was already on board the *Liberté*. It went through the customs without difficulty and Jacques Douheret took it over in New York. 'The first "carrier" I met was Victor M,' Big Charles later admitted. 'That dates back to March 1961.' The goods safely delivered to the American buyers and payment effected, M returned to France.

It was then that a rather remarkable episode occurred. Like many unattached agents, M was invited to resume activities by the Services Spéciaux (Special Services undercover operations). Algeria was in chaos. The OAS was at its most active and was compromising government policy. All the faithful who had proved themselves during the war were called in to help.

At the beginning of April, our hero was a paratrooper in Algiers. His job was to infiltrate the OAS. Back in mainland France in June, he was arrested for distributing OAS propaganda leaflets in the Paris streets, and interned. The flimsiness of the pretext seems to indicate that it was a manœuvre on the part of the Special Services.

It succeeded. During his detention, Victor M learned from another prisoner, Armand Belvisi, that an attempt was soon to be made on the life of General de Gaulle on the way to Colombey-les-deux-églises. The plotters wanted to set off a gas container full of explosives as his car went by.

The attempt did indeed take place and the head of state escaped without a scratch. Official version: the charge did not explode properly. Generally accepted version: the 'Services Spéciaux' had infiltrated the terrorist group. They allowed the attack to take place, but defused the home-made bomb to strengthen the impression that the General led a charmed life and to reduce the sympathy the OAS inspired, at least among a portion of the public. As for M, in October he was taken discreetly to Orly and put on board a plane for Canada. Whether this was to keep him clear of possible OAS revenge or whether it was deportation pure and simple, is unclear. In any case we know that by 24 November, he was back in Cherbourg where he and Bousquet embarked on the *Queen Elizabeth* for New York.

This first voyage together was mainly to observe the formalities of the port and customs authorities, and to make contact with Jacques Douheret, who was to take delivery of the merchandise for the American client.

Two months later, on 12 January 1962, Bousquet set off again on the same liner, but this time with a consignment of sixty or so kilos which he handed over to 'Big Charles'.

Before leaving Cherbourg, Victor M had introduced Bousquet to Jean N.

'Welcome to the club,' he had said with a broad smile which concealed any appraising glance. 'Victor is a good judge of character. I'm sure we'll work well together.'

A regular series of trips was to be made during the next three years.

Although Joseph Orsini and his friends had not been unconciliatory, the reimbursement they demanded for the lost heroin did pose a difficult problem for M and Bousquet. In the end it was Charles Martel – now in bad health – who helped them solve it. On two occasions he gave his son-in-law a parcel of shares in the Laboratoires Bellon so that he could negotiate them and pay off his debt. An old offender, he knew that these were obligations one could not escape in the underworld. He also felt partly responsible.

Some days later, Victor handed Jean N a bundle of forty thousand dollars. He would pay the second instalment on the date agreed. Bousquet was to settle the balance during the summer.

To make up for this drain on their resources, there was only one solution: to make another delivery. Bousquet had new heroin suppliers in Nice. During his numerous trips to the US, through Douheret, M had met the agents of the American buyers – the Orsini group. There was nothing to prevent him from dealing directly – and discreetly – with them. There was no more talk about the hundred missing kilos.

8

The Citroën Cabriolet's Last Trip

Before being loaded on the liner *France*, at Le Havre, the vehicles accompanying passengers on their Atlantic crossing were thoroughly washed and their petrol tanks emptied. Sometimes Transat employees had to wash as many as fifty cars in one day. On other occasions they might do as few as five or six.

One of these employees, who had worked for the company for several years, had noticed that a certain car had done a considerable number of crossings, in both directions, under different registrations: it was a Citroën cabriolet with bodywork by Chapron, metallic grey in colour. The model was fairly uncommon and its lines pleasing enough to attract attention.

'Well, here's our old friend coming back for a spell of French air,' he remarked as the cars were put on board the *France*.

At the same time André Levergeois of the Paris 'Office' was pondering over a slim but well-thumbed dossier – that of a network which had been active for several years and had been brought to police attention by an informer, who had specified that the trafficking was taking place between France and the US in private cars. It was not much to go on. If all the cars crossing the Atlantic were to be searched, sea traffic would grind to a halt.

Once again, he sent a note to the customs and to Transat, to ask them to notify him of any vehicles which struck them as in any way suspect. The observant employee mentioned above drew the attention of his superiors to the *wanderlust* of the Citroën cabriolet.

Immediately the various bodies concerned – including the Service des Mines, which dealt with car registration – set to work. The lengthy analysis of thousands of official documents finally pointed to two Citroën vehicles. One of them, with the serial number 4236082, made in 1959, had done five return trips to the US under five different registration numbers and had had four successive owners. The other, serial number 4200373, after having belonged to various owners since 1962, had begun the same shuttle service in 1966. Their successive registration numbers naturally revealed the names and addresses of their numerous owners.

'These two vehicles, fairly old models,' concluded Levergeois in his report, 'would have been poor ambassadors for the French car industry. They were undoubtedly used for the clandestine dispatch of substances or matters to the US. And the only substance that immediately comes to mind is heroin.'

These Citroën users were certainly only incidental couriers. If their employers as well as the suppliers and their American clients were to be apprehended, it was vital to avoid alarming them. A note was therefore sent to the Service des Mines, asking for notification of any possible new registration for either of these two cars. The reply reached the Office at the beginning of April: a new registration for the DS that had belonged to Gilbert Froger had been asked for by a certain Bernard Guerrier on 4 April.

'Big Bill,' said Guerrier's neighbours, 'was a decent chap who knew how to enjoy himself, and was very obliging. He was involved in various businesses, including car-washing. He didn't seem to have any financial problems.'

But Big Bill was being watched all the same. Transat informed the police that he had a booking on the *France* and that the car he had just brought was to accompany him to New York. The *France* sailed on 19 April.

On 18 April, Guerrier, still under surveillance by 'stups' inspectors, met Bousquet in his Buick on the Esplanade des Invalides at ten in the morning. Together they went to the Chateau restaurant at Maisons-Laffitte where Malibert was waiting for them. A few minutes later Bousquet and Malibert set off again in the Buick. They came back, each driving a DS Citroën cabriolet. 'For the first time,' Levergeois observed, 'we had the two absolutely identical cars we were looking for, before our eyes.'

The three accomplices immediately set off in the direction of Le Havre, followed by police officers Levergeois and Anglès. They stopped at Rouen for lunch, had their petrol tank filled twice en route and at ten past five in the afternoon Guerrier's car, in driving rain, drove up the ramp at the Transat terminal.

Duty before pleasure: without having had a bite to eat, Anglès and Levergeois called Inspector Carrère, their superior, in Paris, to give him a report of their progress.

'Well,' said Carrère, 'you know what's next. You've got a cruise on board the *France*, on the house. Make the most of it! You won't have much spare time once you get there. We'll notify our American colleagues.'

All the impromptu tourists now had to do was hastily to go through the various formalities before embarking on the *France* the following morning. Sailing went ahead as scheduled and the two policemen, after having ascertained that Guerrier was indeed occupying his cabin, prepared to make the most of their unexpected holiday.

On 22 April, Bousquet and Malibert met at Orly, to fly to Geneva There they boarded a Swissair plane and landed a few hours later at Kennedy Airport. Completely relaxed – these trips were routine matters for them by now – they took their places in the passenger queues and went through immigration controls. Then they went into the customs hall, reclaimed their luggage and waited for the crowd of passengers to disperse a little before going through customs.

Malibert wandered around the hall for a moment and went up to a rattling teleprinter. He bent forward, stared at it absent-mindedly and suddenly stiffened: in a partially read message he had just caught sight of his and Bousquet's names. He pulled himself together and went back to his companion.

'I think we've been spotted,' he said. 'I saw our names on the teleprinter.'

'We'll soon know,' said Bousquet, paling visibly. 'There's only one way out.'

He pulled Malibert towards the customs counter. The official looked at their passports, stuck a green label on their luggage and waved them through. Half-reassured, they walked rapidly through the exit, hailed a taxi and asked the driver to take them to Manhattan, En route Bousquet changed his mind, suggested another itinerary, changed his mind again and finally gave the Belmont Plaza as his destination. During all this, Malibert kept his eye firmly on the rear window. At last he turned round, teeth clenched.

'A black Buick has been following us ever since we left the airport.'

They paid the taxi and went into the hotel. At the reception desk the clerk, who knew them, handed them a key.

'Two gentlemen came yesterday and asked if you had made reservations,' he told them in a low voice.

On entering the bedroom. Malibert turned on the television. Nothing happened. In silence, they went over to the window and pushed it open. The noise from the street was deafening.

'They've put in a microphone,' murmured Bousquet. 'The TV has been unplugged so that there won't be any interference. Let's get rid of anything that could be incriminating.'

In the bathroom they emptied their pockets and tore up various pieces of paper, throwing the bits down the lavatory. Still in silence they left the room, leaving their luggage, went out of the hotel, took the Hertz car they had booked in advance from the carpark, turned into the avenue and then down a number of side streets.

'Now,' observed Malibert, 'there are three of them following us.'

Two of the vehicles following them, passed them. Bousquet suddenly locked over to the left and accelerated. Two minutes later they left the hired car in a car park, took a taxi to Kennedy Airport and sent the car keys to Hertz with a brief note, then booked seats on the first plane to Montreal. From Dorval they flew to Frankfurt and then to Geneva, abandoning Guerrier to his fate.

On 24 April, the *France* entered New York harbour. The passengers on board were preparing to disembark. In his cabin

Bernard Guerrier was going over the advice Bousquet had given him before leaving him at Le Havre.

'Don't forget to mention the car on the customs form. It simplifies the formalities. When they put in the gallon of petrol, prime the pump for it to start. If we're not there, ask Arthur Benvenuto to help you. He'll have been notified. He's in charge of luggage and freight for Transat.'

Anglès and Levergeois, who had no luggage, had been on deck since six a.m. Before the stately ship sailed into the Hudson River, a customs launch moored alongside it and federal officials went aboard, accompanied by 'narcs' agents. They and their French colleagues went down into the hold. They saw that it would be impossible for them to search for the drugs hidden in the Citroën cabriolet before the liner docked.

'A pity,' said one of the American agents, 'We've spent two days at the Citroën agency training to dismantle a DS in record time.'

When the boat had docked, Bernard Guerrier was discretely followed by the customs men. They saw him talking to 'Arthur', whose job was to solve Transat's passengers' problems.

'M. Bousquet phoned me yesterday from Europe,' 'Arthur' said to Guerrier. 'He's sorry he couldn't be here on time. He asked me to look after you.'

Arthur Benvenuto had known Bousquet for seven years. He had also known Victor M at the beginning of the sixties. He knew nothing about the traffic in which the men and their friends were engaged, but the tips they gave him – anything from twenty dollars – were big enough for him willingly to see to it that administrative procedures were facilitated for them.

'Give me all those forms,' he said, 'and come back tomorrow morning. By then I'll have it all sorted out.'

In the middle of the following night, while Bernard Guerrier was sleeping peacefully in his hotel room, the Citroën was put on a truck and taken to the garage of the New York City Police, on C Avenue. Levergeois and Anglès accompanied their American colleagues, who were at last going to demonstrate their recently acquired skills. In less than an hour, the vehicle was dismembered.

Two hundred and twenty-five packets each containing five hundred grams lay in rows on the floor. There were some hidden under the false floor of the boot, under the petrol tank which had been reduced to a third of its original volume, and under the base of the back and front seats.

In accordance with tradition, the contents of all the packets except one were replaced by flour. The cabriolet was reconstituted and taken back to the dock shed on wharf 88. The next morning when Guerrier came back, Arthur told him that all the formalities had been dealt with and that he could take the car. He sat down at the wheel after working the pump handle by hand, turned on the engine and tried to get into reverse. Impossible. Very probably, during the previous nights hasty dismantling and reassembly, some screw or pin had been overlooked.

'Don't worry,' said Arthur. 'I'll see to it. Come back tomorrow.'

He knew nothing of the manipulations that had taken place during the night, but his knowledge of the docks enabled him to scent the unusual atmosphere that surrounded the car: the constant presence of customs men, the comings and goings of men in civilian clothes who clearly belonged to the police. He went to find his superior and said: 'I'm having problems with the vehicle belonging to the passenger Guerrier. I get the impression there's something fishy about it. I don't want any more to do with it.'

The next day when Guerrier reappeared, Arthur took him aside and whispered: 'Your car is under surveillance. If I were you, I wouldn't come back. Personally, I don't want anything more to do with you.'

For four days the unwilling tourist wandered around New York, his every movement followed. Finally, at the end of the month, he set off again by plane for Paris. For a few more weeks the Citroën stayed on wharf 88 with its cargo of flour, until the 'narcs' decided to seize it officially.

On his return to France Bernard Guerrier became seriously ill and went into hospital. On 14 June he was arrested, as was Bousquet, at their first meeting since he had left Le Havre. Malibert soon joined them, followed by the successive drivers of the DS 19.

Meanwhile investigations went ahead, bank accounts were scrutinised and the file thickened on the desk of the examining magistrate, Roussell. Victor M was charged the following year.

The affair had unexpected repercussions in May 1969. The investigators' attention had been drawn to a friend of Bousquet and Malibert, Maurice Mary, who had an account in a Lausanne bank and who had probably helped the two associates in their transfers of funds. His income was relatively modest, but together with his mistress Régine he spent very considerable sums. He had seemed edgy and worried since the beginning of the year. He wore dark glasses, skulked around and would wheel about suddenly in the street.

On 18 May, shortly before midnight, he was going up Boulevard Victor at the wheel of his turquoise 'Dino' when a Fiat passed him and drew in suddenly, forcing him to stop. A man in shirt-sleeves leapt out and went up to Mary. Two passers-by heard an animated discussion punctuated with sudden outbursts. Suddenly the unknown man pulled a gun from under his shirt, pointed it at the driver and pulled the trigger. Maurice Mary collapsed and the killer drove off in the Fiat.

A kilometre down the road, it stopped. The unknown man got out, poured petrol over the car, set fire to it and vanished into the night.

Who had killed Mary and why? The only likely hypothesis was the following: he was the holder of the sums amassed by Bousquet and Malibert during the previous years. When all the members of the DS gang had been arrested, he had thought he could keep the remaining money for himself. He had then found himself in disagreement with the network's suppliers, who were probably interested in the profits. Certain of impunity, he tried to be too clever and paid with his life.

He had forgotten that in the underworld, nine reprisals out of ten are not caused by the flouting of the unwritten law of silence, but by a far more serious crime: misappropriation of the profits. As in many similar cases, the cause of Maurice Mary's death has never really been explained.

9

Warrant Officer Conder's Freezer

It was daybreak one morning in February 1964, and the town of Melun was sunk in mist. Behind the walls of the country gaol, the three hundred and seventy prisoners were beginning to file out of the dormitory buildings and into the workshops. They dawdled around in the yard, still half-asleep, waiting to be dispatched by the warders, who were quite as numbed by the cold as the men they were shepherding.

Suddenly one of the prisoners produced a revolver and struck a warder with the butt; the warder fell to the ground and the prisoner immediately shot at another, but missed. The chief warder, who had witnessed the scene, came running to the spot. He too fell; a bullet had gone through his leg just above the knee. Another armed man held his co-prisoners at a respectful distance. This was Nonce Lucarotti, nicknamed Zé, a model prisoner, who talked of becoming a monk. He had even published a booklet, *The Men in the Abyss*, dealing with the rehabilitation of prisoners.

Four men had now moved away from the general crowd and run down the central passageway towards the kitchens. Two of them were carrying a twenty-foot ladder, which they had just taken from the tool cupboard. They put it against the kitchen wall, climbed onto the sloping roof and managed to reach the first surrounding wall. The ladder was promptly pulled up, then swivelled over above the wall walk. The other end landed on the top of the outer wall. One after the other the escapees climbed onto this fragile improvised bridge.

A warder, alerted by the sound of shooting, came running into the wall walk below them and fired in their direction. The escapees returned fire. Another warder from his observation post at the angle of the outer wall, fired in his turn. One runaway had already jumped down into the street, then skirted the edge of the prison. Nonce Lucarotti collapsed on the ladder, twice hit and badly wounded. His mates pulled him to the wall and slid him down onto the pavement where one of the group broke his fall.

The others joined him. They carried Nonce to a black Pontiac parked at the kerb. When the warders, in hot pursuit, turned the corner of the outer wall, they saw the dark mass of the vehicle drawing away and disappearing into the mist. It knocked down a passer-by before driving off in the direction of Paris.

Nonce was accompanied by his half-brother Ange, by Armand Charpentier, sentenced for murder, and by Albert Bergamelli, sentenced to twenty years' hard labour for theft. Two days earlier Albert had received a visit from several members of his family who probably managed to slip him the revolver.

The Pontiac stopped on the road before arriving in Paris. The door opened. Two men got out and vanished into the morning gloom. The car drove on. It was found two days later, abandoned and damaged at Bagnolet, the back seat drenched with Nonce's coagulated blood.

At the end of January 1964, ten days after these events, a policeman stated: 'At all events, Nonce had had it. They took aboard a dead man. His mates have presumably already buried him in some out-of-the-way wood.'

The dossier of the former leader of the 'Savings Bank gang' was filed in the record under the heading 'presumed dead'. His record resembled those of so many Corsican gangsters of his generation. Born at Bastia in 1915 and orphaned at a young age, he was taken in by a family from Lyon. It was after the war that he began to be noticed. He took part in various hold-ups. He was arrested for theft in 1948 and did eighteen months in prison. In 1950, after an attack on a bank, he was back in the cells for four years. He already knew some of the big names in the Lyon and Marseilles underworlds. He had a past history which spoke in his favour; furthermore, he was the nephew of the much-respected Jo Orsini. Among his contacts he counted leading names in clandestine trafficking, such as Cesari and the Aranci brothers.

In 1959, after a series of four hold-ups, he was arrested in a hotel in Villeurbanne – whose entire staff had been replaced by policemen. 'He was completely lacking in any moral sense,' psychiatrists noted. His greying hair, thick glasses and quiet middle-class appearance impressed the jury. Once again he got away with his life. 'By arresting me,' he said, 'you are depriving France of the honest citizen I wanted to become.'

Shortly before his arrest, he made the acquaintance of Jacques Douheret in a Lyon Bar. The two men had warmed to one another. When Lucarotti learned that his new friend specialised in drugs, he thought that perhaps the moment had come to re-orientate himself. From prison, he had written to the address Big Charles had given him in Madrid, that of his mistress, who received all his correspondence.

Towards the end of February 1964, an emissary came to inform Douheret who was staying in Marseilles at the Hôtel d'Arbois, that Nonce was still alive and had recovered from his wounds. A meeting was arranged, in a café in Aix-en-Provence. Behind the dark glasses Douheret recognised the face of his friend, thinner now and lined by all he had been through. Quickly, the experienced trafficker took stock of the situation:

'People think you're dead. That's a piece of luck you mustn't spoil. Go to South America. In Brazil there's no danger of extradition. Your half-brother Ange is already there. Later, we'll find ways of making use of you. I'm beginning to be too well known in New York since I've been meeting sailors and their parcels. Thanks to you, I'm going to be able to withdraw from the limelight.'

Before his departure – which could be for good – Nonce Lucarotti took the risk of going to Marseilles, on a pilgrimage by which he set considerable store. He went to the monastery of Ste-Marie-du-Désert, where several criminals who had paid their debts to society had retired to devote themselves to the service of God. He had a long conversation with Father Marie-Grégoire, his cell-mate in 1947. He shed a few tears. When he left, the monk said to him, crossing himself: 'Nonce, I will pray for your happiness.'

From Orly, equipped with a false passport, he flew to Buenos Aires on an Iberia Boeing. A few days later, he arrived at São Paulo, where he settled under his new name, Lucien Duval. He soon set up house with a young Frenchwoman of about twenty who came to join him: Thérèse B.

Life was not easy for the couple during those months of waiting. Nonce received occasional sums of money from Douheret, who asked him to be patient. During the summer of 1964 his patron proposed joining him in New York. Nonce went there with his false passport and the two friends dined together in an Italian restaurant El Bambino (sic) on University Place. Two other guests joined them: one was Major Samuel Desist and the other was a young woman, a mistress of Douheret's, whom he called Sandra. She lived in New York and was called Suzanne C.

'I'll probably need you before the end of the year,' Jacques l'Américain said to him as soon as they were alone. 'A big load, about a hundred kilos. Then I'll introduce you to our clients.'

'Meanwhile, I could deal with the sailors' parcels, the ones you mentioned before I left.'

'That scheme is in abeyance for the moment. Two or three guys have got caught. In the future the stuff will have to be sent to Jamaica, and M. Paul will have to get it to his clients from there. But old Joseph hasn't made up his mind yet.'

Lucarotti set off again for São Paulo with a wad of dollars that Jacques had given him, enough to last for a few weeks. They met again at the beginning of December, once again in El Bambino, together with a young sailor of Corsican origin. From this Nonce concluded that deliveries had started up again.

'Your uncle doesn't trust networks with too many links,' Big Charles explained. 'He's dropped M. Paul. He prefers to work with just a very few trustworthy people.'

They were awaiting news of the promised load, a hundred kilos due to arrive on the *France* on the tenth, hidden in Malibert's

Citroën. Two days later they learned that the car containing the drugs had been stolen on Boulevard Suchet. Nonce set off once more for São Paulo with enough money to survive until the next time.

Once again, the months went by. In Brazil Nonce met up with a former cell-mate, Didier Barone, who had settled in São Paulo with his mistress Ghyslaine. One day at Barone's place he met another prison acquaintance whom he had met at the Palais de Justice in Paris when they were both waiting, sandwiched between policemen, to be questioned by the examining magistrate. The man was Edouard Rimbaud.

'It so happens,' he said, 'that it was you I was coming to see. I've got some money for you from Jacques l'Américain.'

During the years that followed Edouard Rimbaud was to become one of the most astonishing personalities in the drug trade. A swindler with a riotous imagination, he was pathologically unlucky and his schemes regularly took him straight to prison.

After Rimbaud's departure, another event encouraged Nonce to bide his time. His girl-friend told him that she was pregnant. This was his most exciting affair to date, and he was going to be needed, almost a year after the disappearance of the hundred kilos in December 1964. Douheret advised him to adopt a better thought-out identity than that given him by the phony passport which had enabled him to flee from France. 'Best of all would be if you could become Brazilian.'

Thanks to an acquaintance, Nonce got himself the birth certificate of a certain Francisco Morraes de Almeida. Armed with this official document, he made the rounds of the administrative departments and finally found himself in possession of a voter's card, a service record and an identity card which enabled him to get a passport. None of the officials to whom he spoke seemed surprised to hear this established Brazilian uttering, only with the greatest difficulty, the odd word of Portuguese.

At the beginning of September 1965 the regular guests at Charles

Martel's shooting lodge on his estate Le Petit Colmine had come together to celebrate the opening of the new hunting season. Jean N was being exquisitely urbane.

This year, their host did not join them. It was Victor M who had taken over the organisation of the party. The health of the former owner of the 'Sphinx' was declining rapidly. He was confined to bed and, in so far as he concerned himself with his affairs at all, he could hardly see the papers he was signing. He had spent some time with his daughter in Las Palmas at the beginning of the year. He was to leave the estate, two months later, to go into a clinic in Paris. When he came out at the beginning of 1966 he was in a coma most of the time and he died in his bed shortly afterwards.

While the servants handed round drinks, one of the guests called Jean N away from the group he was haranguing. He was an exceptionally elegant American who spoke almost perfect French, and who had settled in the region after leaving the army in 1964, with the rank of major.

'I've got some news which may interest you,' he said. 'A warrant officer who lodges in an apartment next to my house at St Jean le Blanc is going back to the US. As you know, military regulations allow him to take his furniture and car with him without having to go through any customs checks or pay any duty.'

'You haven't said anything to him, I hope?' asked N nervously.

'Not yet. I've helped him out on several occasions. If I ask him to take a parcel to the States for me as a personal favour, he won't have the nerve to refuse. But we must act quickly. He's leaving at the end of the month.'

The two men arranged to meet the following week. On his return to Paris, N contacted his friend Cecchini who in his turn alerted Orsini. As expected, they immediately saw the advantages of the proposition and gave their agreement. They had a stock of a hundred kilos of heroin at their disposal. All they had to do was find the ideal packaging.

It might be wondered whether this was the first time Major Desist had offered the network the opportunity to profit from his privileged position. After the break with the Bousquet–Malibert team, the Orsini organisation urgently needed to find a comparable dispatch system if it did not want its turnover to sink rapidly. The investigations carried out a few months later used an analysis of the moves made by the persons concerned to confirm the hypothesis that two important deliveries were made during the spring of 1965.

Samuel Desist's life style was in itself somewhat suspicious. The son of a modest miner from West Virginia, of Italian extraction, he made a career in the army. He was a lieutenant in 1947, and was posted to Orléans in the third division of the General Staff from 1950–53. He returned there in 1958. In 1962 he married a young Frenchwoman from Lyon and was decorated with the Ordre général du Mérite for his devotion to the cause of Franco-American friendship. In 1964, unwilling to follow the US army to Vietnam, he decided to return to civilian life.

At this point the officer promoted from the ranks went to live at St Jean le Blanc, where he bought a *manoir*. He was then commercial adviser to an enterprise called Chromax. He was in evidence at all official receptions; he was a friend of the *préfet* and other leading citizens of the district; he became a member and then vice-president of the Rod and Gun Club; he entertained his friends regally in his *manoir* and spent lavishly.

In the grounds, beautifully equipped greenhouses produced exotic fruit and vegetables which he distributed generously to his friends. He had a reputation as an expert in French wines and his cellar justified this reputation.

A week after their conversation, N confirmed that his associates had agreed to the plan and passed on their instructions to him. The next day, Desist went to visit his tenant, Warrant Officer Herman Conder, in his flat on rue St Dillon in St Jean le Blanc. 'As you're going back to the US,' Desist said to him, 'there's something I'd like you to do for me. I'd like you to take a freezer of mine along with your furniture.' Conder was surprised at the request. What could be the point of taking such a gadget to the States when another could be purchased for a few dollars. Desist explained that packets of small diamonds would be concealed in the insulation material between the two layers of casing. The risks were minimal.

'You don't have to do anything. I'll send someone to take delivery of the freezer when the furniture arrives at your place. This person will give you ten thousand dollars . . .'

Conder was in a difficult position. It was the first time he had been involved in such an enterprise. Competent and well thought of, he was only thirty-five and could expect further advancement. He lived a modest life; he had three children, got on with his wife and had no debts. But his former commanding officer had smoothed over certain aspects of life for him in France and he felt he could not refuse. He asked to be allowed to think it over for a few days.

'I didn't like the sound of it. I didn't say anything to my wife, but the affair obsessed me. At last I said yes, although instinctively I knew I ought to say no.' Two days later, the freezer was delivered and stored at the base. It seemed absurdly heavy. In fact, all of the insulating material had been removed and replaced by two hundred plastic bags, each containing five hundred grams of heroin.

The removals took place that same week. Conder was using the Berkins Van Line. All the furniture, freezer included, was put into crates which were piled into three containers. On 17 September the lot was loaded on to the cargo vessel *American Hurricane* which was sailing to New Orleans. Its ultimate destination was the warrant officer's new posting: Fort Benning, in Georgia. He was to arrive there in the third week in November.

During September, Inspector Hug in Marseilles learned – through an informer whose identity remained a secret – that Jean N, Orsini and Cecchini were preparing to send a hundred kilos of heroin to the United States. An informer cannot know everything; this one did not know that the consignment was already on its way across the Atlantic on the *American Hurricane*.

Hug alerted his American colleagues Anthony Pohl and Victor Maria, so that they could contact the Bureau of Narcotics in Washington and New York. Then – a year after Cesari's arrest – the handful of policemen from the Marseilles branch began the thankless and often unpleasant process of investigation and surveillance of hide-outs which would enable them to seize the goods, those selling them and those buying them at one fell swoop.

The delivery of a hundred kilos of drugs – a load worth a million new francs – was bound to be a large-scale operation. Everything would take place according to a minutely detailed plan which implied a lot of comings and goings. Carrère's men in Paris were also mobilised to monitor the doings and movements of the Orsini team.

The 'stups' men soon realised that their informer had not misled them. Jacques Douheret returned to Marseilles and stayed at the Hôtel d'Arbois on 19 September. On the twenty-first, he met Joseph Orsini and Achille Cecchini there. Then Jean N – who had been in Corsica – arrived on the twenty-second and had a confabulation with Douheret and Orsini.

Unfortunately, the police could not hear what they were saying. Any remotely rash action on their part could well jeopardise the whole undertaking. For this reason they did not know that during the course of a conversation with Joseph Orsini, Jacques Douheret had suggested using the services of Nonce Lucarotti. 'We owe him that at least. Last year, the business of Bousquet's hundred kilos slipped through his fingers because the idiot had his car stolen.'

His suggestion was accepted. Douheret left for Madrid where, in the days that followed, he engaged in almost daily correspondence with Cecchini. At this point, Warrant Officer Herman Conder's freezer – its owner having reached Fort Benning – was about to round the 'keys' to the south of Florida and enter the Gulf of Mexico on board the *American Hurricane*. Cecchini and Douheret corresponded regularly between Marseilles and Madrid. At the beginning of November N confirmed that Major Desist would go to New York on 22 or 23 December. Two days later, Douheret announced his departure for Rio de Janeiro.

On 15 November, a telegram sent from the Brazilian port of Santos informed Cecchini of Big Charles' new address. Messages were to be sent to him at the Atlantic Hotel. The following day he received N's instructions: 'We hope to sign the contract on 25 November. We'll let you know the exact date of the meeting. Yours, Jean.'

Naturally, a copy of the message was immediately transmitted to the Evêché at Marseilles. The information was sent from there to Paris, then to New York, via Washington. A further letter addressed to 'dear cousin Josephine' reached Orsini. It was signed 'Pilar'. Pilar was asking for various further details. 'Are we to hand over all our shares to these customers? Can they pay a third of the total in a first instalment, i.e. 200 and the rest in successive instalments?'

While awaiting the answer, Douheret dined with Lucarotti. Around a paella prepared by the expectant mother, the two men planned their appointment in New York.

'On Tuesday 14 December you'll take the plane to Kennedy Airport. I'll introduce you to the buyers as soon as we get the goods. There may be two of them. Every day at midday you'll go to Grand Central Station and wait in front of the car showroom. That's where we'll meet. Here is a list of hotels. Contact them in that order and take the first available room. Don't forget it's Christmas. We'll also make another appointment under the big clock in the foyer of the Waldorf Astoria. It will be cold outside.'

He gave his protégé a thousand dollars for him to buy his ticket. At the Varig office Nonce learned that he would now need a visa from the American Consulate. Seeing that he had difficulty in expressing himself in Portuguese, the helpful hostess accompanied him to the Consulate and sorted out the formalities for him. Once again, neither the Consulate official nor the young woman seemed surprised at the sight of a Brazilian who was totally ignorant of his native tongue.

On 3 December Cecchini received a message that Douheret was on his way to New York. Big Charles insisted that N – who was taking a few days holiday at Sartène – should join him as soon as possible. He would be travelling under the name of Jean-Claude Lefranc. He gave his address, or rather, Sandra's; she was the young woman Lucarotti had met with him at El Bambino the previous year.

To receive people as important as Jean N and his friends, the New York Bureau of Narcotics pulled out all the stops. More than fifty agents were called out with sophisticated monitoring equipment at the ready. The Customs Department had been notified and the city police were standing by. During that week, the police of Miami, Atlanta and Columbus Ohio were to step in in their turn under the guidance of local 'narcs'; even the CID section of the American army were to be drawn on.

On 14 December, the information received – though it held out hope of success – was none the less slight. According to the report of the Marseilles agent – installed in the US Consulate General – during the last month a certain Jean-Claude Lefranc had been in contact with the Orsini brothers and had gone to São Paulo. Someone called Jean N was to join him in New York. A consignment of ninety-five kilos of heroin had left Marseilles, two months ago, in a Citroën van, bound for an unknown destination. That same morning, the mysterious informer who had alerted the French police in October confirmed that Jean N had left for New York on 11 or 12 December, probably under a false name.

All agent Michael Antonelli and his men had to do was to check the immigration forms of all travellers who had arrived in the city during the last few days and count on their flair to find Jean N. They began with Kennedy Airport. They had been at work since eight in the morning, downing beers and sandwiches when, at two in the afternoon, Antonelli exclaimed: 'This is him, the bastard.'

N had arrived two days earlier under his real name and given Waldorf Astoria as his address. The reception desk confirmed his presence in room 1602.

'Go about it quietly,' advised the clerk. 'He's a very distinguished guest and always spends at least two thousand dollars a stay.'

Two agents immediately settled into an adjacent room. Two others, with binoculars and a walkie-talkie, took up positions on the terrace roof of the nearby Sheraton, from where they could see into the room. Its occupant was observed to be about to go out, so they alerted their colleagues. Surrounded by a restrained but attentive throng, the natty little Corsican was going out to do some shopping: ties, cashmere overcoat, assorted gadgets.

Meanwhile, an expert was installing a microphone under the communicating doors between 1602 and 1600; it was linked to an amplifier and tape recorder. Everything was ready when N returned. At eight, a visit from a young woman he called Suzanne allowed the quality of the monitoring system to be checked. She telephoned various hotels about the whereabouts of a Brazilian traveller, Francisco Morraes de Almeida. The name was immediately noted down and another team set out on that trail.

The painstaking sorting through of the immigration forms had also made it possible to track down Jean-Claude Lefranc. He had arrived on the 12th, on Varig flight 854 from Brazil, and in the morning of the 14th had left for Miami, where he landed at 12.40. The Miami Narcotics Bureau caught up with him during the afternoon at the Bel Air Hotel.

'He telephoned to someone called Frankie Dio,' the chambermaid told them. 'They arranged to meet this evening.'

This was important information for the police. They knew Frankie Dioguardi well; he was a *mafioso* of the Profaci–Magliocco family, regarded as one of the ten most important drug distributors in the US. He had been in Florida for ten years, managed three companies and ran a night-club, Dore's, on Sunny Isles Boulevard; his brother-in-law, Johnny Sutera, was the barman there. No doubt about it: the investigators had come straight up against the buyers of the consignment.

That evening, they witnessed the conversation between the three men in a bar near Dore's. Dio was wearing a sky-blue shirt and trousers and a navy sweater; Sutera was wearing grey trousers and a royal blue shirt and pullover; Douheret looked unimpeachable in his city suit with a tie matching his green eyes. An hour later, the Frenchman went back to his hotel and booked a seat on the plane to arrive in New York in the late morning two days later.

At the end of the day, the Narcotics Bureau could admit to being well satisfied with the results obtained. They had located several people involved in the affair, and the sensitive tape recorder had faithfully picked up all N's conversation; he seemed to be the brains behind the undertaking.

The following morning, 15 December, at dawn, the 'narcs' were on a war footing. The tape-recorder was switched on in the hotel room next to N's and registered several irrelevant telephone conversations. Then the little Corsican left the Waldorf Astoria. He made a few more purchases, still under police surveillance, and then received a new visitor, Major Samuel Desist. That evening they ate together at the restaurant Quo Vadis. A telephone call from Miami informed the investigators that Dio and Sutera would be in New York on the 17th and would leave again on the 18th.

On Wednesday the 16th, the return of Douheret, alias Lefranc, created a certain stir. That very morning Lucarotti – alias Senor de Almeida – had also arrived and checked in at the first hotel on his list, the Summit, on 55th Street. He had not yet taken any steps to meet Lefranc.

In the early afternoon, after having strolled round the Rockefeller Center, observed the antics of the skaters and bought the *Figaro* at the Librairie de France, Jean N met Douheret at 63rd Street. The agents Telb and Lee Hughs noted down the time: ten past four.

The two Frenchmen walked down Fifth Avenue together.

'My word, they're indefatigable,' mumbled Telb, 'the amount of pavement they can cover in a day.'

They arrived at 42nd Street. There was a long session at the counter of Eastern Airlines.

'They're going to Atlanta,' the clerk informed the police.

'They're intending to hire a car to go to Columbus for two or three days. Then they're going straight to Miami by air.'

'Well, it'll make a change,' commented Lee Hughs. The policemen rejoined their quarry in front of the Waldorf Astoria and followed Douheret, who took them as far as 54th Street, to his friend Sandra's, where he was staying and which he was using as a postal address. There he found a letter from 'Cousine Josephine' in Marseilles. He was told that he could hand over all the shares to these clients, 'though you are to give them only half at the moment, and tell them that the other half will arrive in ten or fifteen days. I'll write to them to this effect.' In plain English, old Orsini was willing to give credit, but preferred to string out deliveries so as to limit the risks.

At the Waldorf, in the bathroom of room 1600, sitting on the lavatory seat, agent Jacques Kiere was listening to a tape, a pair of headphones over his ears. In the next room, N was talking to Samuel Desist, who told him that he was going to Atlanta the next day.

'Conder will come and meet me at the airport. I've promised to take him two thousand dollars. We'll meet the following day at the Black Angus Motel. Everything will be thoroughly worked out.'

After Desist's departure, N went down into the hotel lounge, where he met Douheret. Together they went to the nearby 'brasserie' to eat. Then in the sleety drizzle, they talked in the street, walking round the block for two good hours, to the despair of the police who could not return to their quarters and write their reports until late that night.

On the morning of Thursday 17 December, Police Constable Telb was given the job of tailing the Brazilian Morraes de Almedia, whose role was still a mystery to the 'narcs' and who had not yet emerged from his room in the Summit. Towards midday, having hung around the hotel lounge, he at last decided to face the cold and damp. He went to Grand Central Station, ruminated over the cars on display in the shop window, went to the Waldorf Astoria, cooled his heels for half an hour under the big clock, and finally took a taxi to University Place. He sat down at a table at El Bambino in front of an ample Italian meal. The proprietor and his wife treated him as a regular.

A strange man, this Brazilian! He then returned to the Summit, shut himself up in his room and did not emerge again for the rest of the day. As to Samuel Desist, he had left New York at eight in the morning. There was nothing to be done now but await the report of the 'narcs' agents who were lying in wait for him at Atlanta Airport.

Luckily, agent Hughes and his three colleagues had spent a more eventful day than Telb. They tailed Douheret – Jean-Claude Lefranc to them – and found that he too hung around at Grand Central Station and under the clock in the Waldorf Astoria – but not at the same time as Lucarotti; they saw him get into a white Ford, in front of the Royal Scott's Grill on Lexington Avenue. Frankie Dio was at the wheel and Johnny Sutera at his side. A few minutes later, the trio were gathered round a table at Adano's Restaurant, on 18th Street.

Hidden in the cloakroom, behind a row of coats, Constable Grunden listened intently. He caught snatches of general reflections on the wretched New York weather, the Miami sun, and traffic jams. Two of his colleagues had then come in, put their coats in the cloakroom and taken their places at the bar. Dio went to the telephone booth. PC Smith promptly slipped into the neighbouring booth and overheard the following.

'Lefranc and N will be in Atlanta tomorrow. They hope to be in Miami by Monday or Tuesday. Lefranc will phone me to let me know the day and time of arrival.'

The conversation ended and the *mafioso* went back to his two friends. Thanks perhaps to the bottle of Valpolicella which had accompanied the escalope Milanese, further details were vouchsafed. 'To save time we could go to Atlanta with you and take delivery of the goods there,' suggested Sutera.

But the Frenchman insisted that they should keep to the agreed plan. It was N who had all the information. Lefranc did not even know how the goods had arrived, nor who was going to get the merchandise to them. This compartmentalising was crucial for everyone's safety. 'If we alter our plans now, we might make mistakes and then anything could happen.'

The two *mafiosi* agreed and the three men left the restaurant about midnight, arm in arm. At one in the morning, the lights went out in Sandra's flat, where the two Italo-Americans had deposited their companion.

The Eastern Airlines plane from Atlanta landed on the runway of Muscogee Airport, Columbus, at 12.30, on 18 December. Black clouds streamed across the sky, a bitter wind lashed the tree-tops; fine rain had been falling grimly since early morning.

The few passengers hurried towards the entrance hall. Among them were Douheret and N and, a little apart from them, two unremarkable men who looked like commercial travellers, the New York 'narcs' Kiere and Thompson. The two Frenchmen were joined by a squat man with close-cropped hair and a thin black moustache, his suntanned face glowing above the collar of his putty-coloured raincoat.

Samuel Desist, who had arrived the previous evening at nightfall had been met by Herman Conder, who was eager to conclude this worrying business.

'The freezer is there all right, is it?' the Major immediately asked. 'Is it in good shape?'

'Don't worry, everything's fine. I put it safely in a shed near our caravan. It's still in its box. My wife keeps asking me what on earth I'm going to do with it, because we've got a brand-new one of our own. When are you going to collect those diamonds?'

'In two days' time at the latest my client will come and get the box and you'll get your ten thousand dollars. Don't worry.'

So after a night at the Black Angus Motel, the Major met his associates, who were equally eager to conclude this deal which had occupied them for more than three months. Idlers and officials, apparently ambling around the airport, kept a close eye on them. They were in fact members of the local police and city 'narcs'.

The three men went to the Avis agency, hired a new yellow Plymouth and drove off towards the city.

On the road, the flow of traffic was slight. It was not the kind of day for a drive. The three police cars tailing the Plymouth found it difficult to maintain contact without making themselves apparent or else losing sight of their quarry; all the more so since N was at the wheel and the policemen sensed his nervousness. 'He would slow down and then accelerate suddenly,' Kiere noted. 'Then he would go round the block, his eye firmly on the rear window.'

At last, Desist got out at 12th Street and walked back to the Black Angus Motel where Herman Conder was waiting for him. The two Frenchmen drove on to the small town of Opelika. In a succession of shops, they bought two blue suitcases, a tin trunk and two kit bags. Then at nightfall, they went back to the Black Angus and met Desist in the bar.

Tailing began again an hour later. It took the policemen, who lost the Frenchmen's Plymouth several times en route, to the Atlanta Waldorf Hotel. The day's work appeared to be over. A telephone call to New York informed Kiere that the Brazilian in the Summit had set out on his habitual round again: Grand Central Station, Waldorf lounge and El Bambino, and that he had returned to his room without having met anyone.

The meeting between Desist and Conder meant that Conder could be added to the list of suspects and that a new observation post could be set up near the Bill Miller Mobile Trailer Homes where he and his family were living in a caravan at 3310 Victory Drive.

Feeling that he had been spotted the evening before, Kiere and his colleagues changed cars when they resumed their tailing on the morning of Saturday 19 December. They need not have bothered. The Frenchmen knew quite well that they were being followed. They stopped the yellow Plymouth in an empty street, strolled about for a few moments, looking in shop windows, then set off again and joined an expressway. Suddenly, with a violent screech of brakes, N created a pile-up and took advantage of the incident to take the Birmingham road.

'He's got me stymied,' said Kiere over the radio. 'He's driven off down the Birmingham road. Keep in touch. We're going back to Columbus.'

His colleague Rice accelerated. The Frenchmen were once again ahead of him on the expressway. Five minutes later, another of N's manœuvres enabled the Plymouth to dodge its pursuers once again. The police gave up the pursuit.

In the middle of the night Douheret and N took the plane to New York under false identities, without returning to their hotel.

Surveillance was then concentrated on the Black Angus Motel. The policemen moved into room 7, from which they could see the interior of 108, Major Desist's room.

'He told me he was coming here to spend two days with his son who was doing a training course at Fort Benning,' the hotel manager told them.

This 'son' was clearly Herman Conder. That evening, the two men sat down opposite one another in one of the restaurant booths. Through the insubstantial wood partition, agents Waters and Salvaggio at a neighbouring table listened to their conversation.

'We've had a slight hitch,' said the retired Major. 'My clients have been called back to New York on urgent business. I'll send you someone tomorrow, in the afternoon at the latest.'

They parted a few minutes later. Conder went back to his family caravan, and Desist to his room where the light went out almost immediately. It was the end of a tough day for the 'narcs' agents, but tomorrow might well be worse. The men they were shadowing knew that they were under surveillance; their reactions were totally unpredictable.

The next day, a Sunday, after a problematic tailing, as foreseen, when they twice lost track of Desist, the policemen at last passed him on the road sitting next to Conder in the latter's VW. They caught up with them in the carpark of Gaylords stores, and followed them to the travel goods department where Desist showed his friend some suitcases.

'You yourself will have to get the goods out of the freezer and put them in the suitcases. These will do fine. Keep them somewhere handy, so that they can be delivered at short notice.'

Conder was given a wad of dollars; then he drove Desist back to his motel and returned to the Gaylords stores. Shortly afterwards, Conder returned to his caravan with four red suitcases which he deposited at the door of the shed. He removed the freezer from its packing case and then began to unscrew the lining.

Now, through their binoculars, the Federal Police who had relieved their colleagues that morning were able to witness the look of amazement and dismay with which Conder contemplated the bag of white powder that he had just removed from its hiding-place. His obvious astonishment was brought up later to confirm that he was unaware of the nature of the traffic in which he had become involved, when he pleaded extenuating circumstances.

While Conder was retrieving the one hundred and ninety packets from the freezer, one of the policemen crossed the avenue and phoned from a service station to notify his colleagues. A search warrant had to be issued and submitted to the Federal judge. Meanwhile, Samuel Desist had flown off to New York, and that same evening he took a Pan Am Boeing to Orly. Before leaving, he telephoned Conder. 'You're going to have to hang on a bit longer. Something's not quite right.'

At the time when Samuel Desist was driving towards St Jean le Blanc mulling over the consequences of the setback, twenty or so policemen had already surrounded the service station on Victory Drive, Columbus. Two of them hid in the caravan park. Another team still had its binoculars trained on the door of the shed, closed with a combination lock, into which they had seen Conder put the four suitcases of heroin the previous evening.

At twenty past twelve, Conder arrived from Fort Benning and went into his caravan. Five minutes later, Salvaggio and Waters knocked on the door. A young boy opened up and called 'Daddy! Daddy!'

Herman Conder appeared. He was walking on tiptoe and put a finger to his lips. 'My wife is ill. She's asleep.' Waters asked him if she knew what was going on. He shook his head and took them to the shed.

They were immediately surrounded by other policemen. The suitcases were opened. There had not been enough room in them for the ninety-five kilos of drugs. Conscientiously Conder had put some packets in two suitcases of his own.

In New York, after the return of N and Douheret and while waiting for news from Columbus, the various surveillances had been resumed. The police knew they had reserved seats with Air France for that same day. In the morning, before going out, Lucarotti had asked the hotel porter to send a telegram addressed to cousin Josephine: 'Arrived 16th. Haven't met fiancée Pilar as arranged. Can't wait indefinitely. Need money. Love.'

When he entered the main foyer of the Waldorf Astoria, Lucarotti was so convinced that he was wasting his time that he sat down in an armchair under the clock and began to read the various French newspapers he had just bought, while Douheret was pacing up and down on the other side of the clock. The only people to make contact at this failed rendezvous were the policemen who were shadowing them.

After a few minutes Douheret emerged into Lexington Avenue and hailed a cab. Three policemen got in with him and gave an address to the driver: 'Ninety-six Church Street.'

This was the headquarters of the Narcotics Bureau. Half an hour later Morraes de Almeida, who had gone to get information about flights for South America, was about to go back to his room, forgoing lunch at El Bambino. He saw agents Antonelli and Telb coming out of the escalator.

'Police,' said Antonelli, 'you're under arrest. You're not Francisco Morraes de Almeida, you're Joseph Nonce Lucarrotti.'

The Corsican turned pale. Tears poured down his cheeks. 'It's true,' he murmured, prostrated.

Hardly had they left the hotel than a telegram from France arrived at reception: 'Have informed Miss Pilar of your problems. Am cabling you five hundred dollars. Letter follows. Love, Cousine Josephine.'

At the same moment, Jean N was being arrested in the lounge of the Waldorf Astoria.

An hour later, six thousand kilometres away, near the *manoir* at St Jean le Blanc slumbering beneath the grey sky and gaunt bare trees, a Peugeot occupied by Inspector Anglès of the 'stups' and Victor Maria of the BNDD drew up on the verge for a long night's vigil. On Tuesday, at nine o'clock, as the grille opened to let Major Desist's Citroën through, they went up to him.

'Major Desist, we must ask you to come with us to the Orleans police station for questioning.'

'I know what it's about,' the American answered calmly. 'I demand to go back to the United States to account for myself.'

The constant shadowing of Frankie Dio and Anthony Sutera the previous Saturday had meant that they were followed to Kennedy Airport where they took the plane back to Miami to await the delivery promised by Douheret. On Monday evening, it was not the Frenchman who called Dio, but an employee of Dore's who told him that some plain-clothes policemen were outside the door. He excused himself from the customers he had just shown to a table, buttoned up his wild silk jacket and went to greet his visitors with a smile on his face: 'Gentlemen, I was expecting you.'

Sutera gave himself up a week later. The arrest of Achille Cecchini, on 29 April 1966 at Sault, in the Vaucluse, concluded the 'American sergeant's freezer affair'. 'Cousine Josephine's' post arrived at the address of a night watchman living in rue Lanthiers in Marseilles. The night watchman and his post had led the policemen to Cecchini's sumptuous villa where, it was rumoured locally, 'even the bath taps were gold'.

10

Reorganisation of Gangsters and Burglars

Their affair had begun like those holiday romances which usually end as soon as you put away your bikini. Simone was a quiet clerk in a Parisian Post Office Bank. When she was not at her office, she led an uneventful life in a girls' hostel. In June 1965 she had gone to the south of France for her fortnight's paid holiday, more because it was the done thing than out of any real desire for new horizons.

In Marseilles, at first, she went along with the crowd; it was a round of fun: bathing, walks, a small family *pension.* One day she and some friends had gone into a bar on the Vieux Port, Chez Papa. 'A young man who knew one of my friends came to sit at our table. He was introduced to me as Serge. He was good-looking and I felt attracted by him.'

The next day, Simone went back to Chez Papa alone. She wanted, to see Serge again, but perhaps she also felt an idle desire for adventure. As she hoped, the young man was there. He invited her to his table, introduced her to his friends, whose dubious manner made her feel pleasantly nervous. One of them, who seemed particularly intimate with Serge, was called Fanfan. The two young people began to see each other every day.

'I became Serge's mistress. At that time he had a white car which belonged to one of his friends. He said he had a smarter one of his own which he would show me later. At the end of the holiday I went back to Paris and left him my phone number, but I never thought I'd see him again.'

A fortnight later, he telephoned her and arranged to meet her. They met on the terrace of a café on the Champs Elysées. As they watched the tourists go by, he took her hand. This simple gesture moved her.

'Listen,' he said. 'I've been thinking. I like you. We get on together. It would be silly to lose touch. Why don't we live together? Give up your job. Considering what you earn, it'll be no great loss.'

A week later she had packed her bag, given in her resignation and moved into a studio he had found for her on rue d'Armaillé, in the seventeenth *arrondissement*.

'He explained to me that he couldn't live with me all the time for the moment, because of business problems.' When they went out together, they went Dutch. Simone soon found herself penniless. Serge was very sorry about it. His current projects would not net him any profits for a couple of years. Then they would have no more problems.

'You'll see, we'll be rolling. We'll be able to marry, have a child, take a big apartment. You can be a lady of leisure. We'll travel. But meanwhile . . .'

Meanwhile it would be ridiculous for her to slave away in an office for a pittance. By walking the streets, on Avenue de la Grande Armée in a single day she would make the equivalent of her monthly salary at the GPO, just with one or two clients. Pretty as she was, there would be no problem. He was a broad-minded man.

Of course she refused, wept, begged. He comforted her and tried again. She could not imagine life without him, the prospect of going back to her grinding loneliness. When he went away – on business again – a fortnight later, she was resigned. For two months she walked the streets, or rather the Avenue de la Grande Armée, with a beginner's relative luck.

When Serge came back, in December, he found her discouraged, disgusted and gloomy. He comforted her again, reassured her. Everything was going to work out. She would just have to be brave for a few more months. He suggested that she might prefer to work in a hotel near Les Halles. He knew the owner; he would look after her and introduce clients. She would be on call only from six until midnight.

He took her to rue des Lombards in his Mercedes. The deal was done.

'I began to work regularly in that hotel. The proprietress was a big fat woman. I got together a wardrobe with the money I earned. Serge never asked me for a penny. He phoned me every day. From time to time he came to see me but we weren't going out together any more. Except once, when he took me for a ride round Paris in his car.'

She still did not know where he lived. She did not even know his surname. Nor did she know that he had another mistress, Mireille. If he had told her his real name, Christian David, it would not have meant anything to her in any case. He had not yet earned the notoriety he would later enjoy. Officially, he was still just a petty crook.

'Le beau Serge', as he was known in the underworld, had been born in Aubervilliers. As soon as he was through adolescence, just after the war, he served his apprenticeship in car-stealing and procuring and took part in some burglaries, before launching into fraud and hold-ups. Convictions mounted – twenty within fifteen years – but Serge changed identity with ease and managed, despite various setbacks, to become the owner of a bar in Bordeaux, the Whisky à gogo.

In 1960 he managed to escape from prison in Besançon. He was recaptured on an embankment in Bordeaux, in February 1961, as he was preparing to steal a car with a 11.43 gauge rifle on him. He feigned madness and was transferred from Fort du Hâ to the psychiatric hospital in Cadillac; he escaped again after a few weeks.

He found himself at large in a France torn by dissension over affairs in Algeria. Some of the underworld had been deployed in the various 'special services' whose job was to counteract the OAS rebellion. A friend guided him in the direction of the units which were operating in the region of Oran and which, thanks to the use of torture, were obtaining remarkable results. It seems that, after Algerian independence, his new employers sent him to black Africa to carry out a number of missions of a rather special nature. He was in France again when the leader of the Moroccan opposition, Medhi Ben Barka, was kidnapped and executed, with the collaboration of several members of the secret service and their bully boys.

These last events had taken place at the time of Serge's idyll with Simone. It was understandable that he should not have had much time to spend with her. But on 2 February, towards midnight, the young woman received a phone call in her studio on the rue d'Armaillé. Her lover informed her that he was coming to visit her for the evening. She obtained permission for the proprietress of the hotel in rue des Lombards to leave work before midnight.

While she was beginning her irksome plod between the entrance corridor and the room where she conscientiously tried to satisfy the requirements of the passing trade, le beau Serge was in a bar on the rue d'Armaillé, the Saint-Clair, playing cards with an unattached sub-prefect whom he had known in Algeria, Belkacem Mecheri.

It was a quiet, secluded bar. Three customers were playing dice, perched on the red bar stools, four others were chatting in the inner room, sunk deep in armchairs around a small table. The proprietress, Sylviane, a statuesque strip-tease artist from the Crazy Horse saloon, was on the floor above with her daughter who had measles.

In the street, a man of about thirty was pacing up and down, occasionally glancing in the direction of the bar window with its closed curtains. This was Inspector Maurice Galibert, recently appointed head of the Serious Crime Squad. A few minutes later, he was telephoning the Quai des Orfèvres.

'I've been told that Le Ny, who was involved in the kidnapping of Ben Barka, is at the bar St Clair, in rue d'Armaillé. I'm there now. Can you send me reinforcements?'

It was his first big job, and virtually his first contact with gangsters. When two other police officers, Pick and Couzier, joined him, Galibert and his colleague Gibaux told them that it was not Le Ny after all, but Christian David, who was also a wanted man.

Immediately, leaving the driver at the wheel, they went into the bar.

One after the other, the surprised customers were asked to show their papers. Finally the police came to the table occupied by David and Mecheri. Mecheri expressed indignation and flaunted his official papers. Le beau Serge produced a red, white and blue card.

'I must ask you to come with us to the police station,' announced Galibert, 'for an identity check.'

Christian David stood up. One of the inspector's assistants patted his clothing to check that he was not carrying a weapon. Once outside, he asked for permission to go back and collect the raincoat that he had left on the bar coatstand. Inspector Galibert then committed the fatal mistake of granting this permission. The five men moved down the street towards the car.

David protested his innocence, 'It's not me. You've got the wrong man.' Suddenly, he backed away. The hand which he had just thrust into his raincoat pocket reappeared armed with a 7.65. He shot 'because he was in a tight corner', he said later. Gibaux, then Galibert and finally Couzier fell to the ground. Pick threw himself flat on his stomach. Taking advantage of their surprise, the murderer rushed towards rue du Colonel Renard. The driver whipped out his revolver and fired, hitting no one. Pick leapt up and rushed off in pursuit. But David was already out of range. Inspector Galibert was dead. The other two officers were wounded, one in the thigh and the other in the wrist, leg and hip.

Simone waited for her lover all night in her room. She had heard nothing. The next day, she noticed a bustle in the street, though still without real concern. At one o'clock, watching TV, she learned of the events which had taken place the previous evening, though still without connecting them with her friend Serge. A few moments later, the telephone rang: it was Serge.

That evening she returned rather gloomily to rue des Lombards. One of her companions handed her the paper she had just been reading. This time she did recognise Serge from the photo, and learned his real name. She began to read the article, but her first client arived. Slowly, blankly, she went up the stairs before him.

A few hours after the murder of Inspector Galibert in Paris, Belgian police constable Albert de Leener was on his lone beat in the empty streets of Brussels. There were mounds of snow everywhere. He noticed a car carelessly parked near an island in a way all too likely to add to the traffic problems of tomorrow morning.

De Leener went up to it, took down the number and put his hand on the bonnet. It was still warm. A glance at his notebook informed the policeman that its owner had reported the car's disappearance two days previously. It was possible that the thieves had not yet abandoned it. De Leener decided to withdraw to a nearby *porte cochère* and wait.

A few minutes went by; the silence was almost total, scarcely broken by the distant muffled sounds of the sleeping city. Then a group of men carrying suitcases appeared. They went up to the car and were about to open the doors. De Leener emerged from the shadows and accosted them.

Immediately the newcomers scattered, sinking their hands into their pockets and taking cover behind parked vehicles. De Leener drew out his gun at the same time as they did. Two shots rang out: flashes of light seared through the darkness; then silence fell again. In the middle of the street the policeman tottered, dropped his weapon, collapsed onto a heap of grimy snow and lay motionless.

'That's him done for,' said the man who had just shot him. 'Let's get out of here before it gets crowded.'

'He might have had time to photograph us,' said one of the group. 'How stupid to have fired.'

He walked slowly up to the recumbent body, revolver at the ready. De Leener, still unconscious, moved his head and groaned. Deliberately, the man aimed his revolver at the wounded man's temple and pulled the trigger.

The whole thing had taken only a few seconds. Quite unruffled, the murderer gestured to his accomplices. 'We'd better get him on board and dump him somewhere. Get moving!'

The body was lifted up: the boot of the car opened. During the operation, a small piece of cardboard fell from the pocket of the man who had fired the final shot. The investigators found it on the pavement, a little later. It was a fake identity card bearing the name Lucien Sabatier. The photo was of a known French criminal, aged about thirty, who had a record under that name at the Quai des Orfèvres. He was called Lucien Sarti. He had been arrested and imprisoned at Les Baumettes, in Marseilles, for theft, violence and illegal possession of firearms on 8 May 1960. Twenty months later he was conditionally released.

The car had driven swiftly off into the darkness with its grim cargo, in the direction of Knokke-le-Zoute. Huddled together inside, the gang were silent. It was their first serious encounter. They had come together the previous year and had specialised in hold-ups abroad, in Germany, Belgium and Holland. The gangsters, who all came from the south of France, were going back across the border.

The car drove into the sand dunes and came to a halt in a hollow. The men got out. Two of them poured the contents of a drum of petrol onto the seats. The policeman's body was left in the boot. A match was lit. Flames leapt up, lighting up the dismal surrounding countryside. The men fanned out into the darkness. Each was to make his own way across the frontier.

The following evening, arriving in Paris, Lucien Sarti read the newspapers and learned that he had been identified. There was an account of De Leener's murder plus a photo and description: 'one metre seventy-six in height, brown hair and eyes'. He was now a hunted man. There was only one thing for him to do: go to South America. Two of his past contacts had gone there before him: Claude Pastou and François Chiappe.

He would have to proceed with caution. The manhunt was already on. His friends and his usual meeting-places were undoubtedly being watched. He would have to abandon the idea of seeing his wife and two-year-old daughter, Véronique. He had married

Liliane, a young woman from Marseilles, in April 1963. The couple had bought a house in the Ardèche, just down the road from Lucien's parents, in the village where his father had retired to become gamekeeper and town councillor.

Lucien had been on the wrong road for some years now. His marriage had not quietened him down and indeed he returned home only to catch his breath between jobs. His family had no inkling of the object of his frequent journeys.

He was not short of contacts; he knew people in Paris, Lyon or Marseilles who would harbour him while he waited to get out of France. Indeed he could choose between several networks: Mémé Guerini and the sailors of the *Provence* or *Bretagne*, after a short stay at La Ciotat; or Constantin and his 'ranch', Le Kentucky, before sailing from Genoa. He preferred a third solution – Spain. His friends Roger Bocognani or Sauveur Pironti, known as 'Loule', often crossed the Spanish frontier to supply the bridge-heads of veteran Auguste Ricord's organisation with heroin. They would find him an interesting recruit.

Hunted by police throughout France, Christian David was directed, in short stages – thanks to the solidarity of his procurer friends and their links with the special services – to Le Kentucky ranch on the Etang de Berre; here he waited for several months for an opportunity of sailing to Buenos Aires on board an Italian vessel.

His stay was by not unpleasant. He was the guest of Constantin, a gang leader who had been a friend of Carbone and then of Guerini, and who was to die some years later in a reprisal action. A cautious yet ambitious career had enabled him to create the Kentucky out of several hectares of parched, uncultivated land. It was like a leisure centre with an Olympic swimming pool, night-club, motel and restaurant. It was there that Chiappe and Condemine had gone to ground and that Lucien Sarti had got to know Liliane.

Before leaving Paris, a week after the murder of Inspector Galibert, Christian had once again phoned Simone in her studio on rue d'Armaillé and told her of his departure.

'It's all fine! Don't worry. Some friends are looking after me. I'm going to have to leave France. I can't take you with me right away but I'll send for you as soon as I can. Keep on working as before. I won't forget you.'

'He didn't make any comment about the murder he'd committed,' Simone recalled later. 'He said, "Someone informed on me." And also, "I was in a tight corner. It was instinctive." He didn't say where he was phoning from. I had the impression that he was terribly overwrought and nervous.'

His first stop had been in Neuville-sur-Ain, at the 'Fetich Club, a brothel which was to enjoy a certain notoriety a few years later and which benefited from the joint protection of a chief of police and of a deputy. Simone had sadly resumed her activities in the hotel on rue des Lombards and put aside some savings against a happier future.

Towards the end of April she received a phone call: 'This is Fanfan. Do you remember me? Come to place de l'Opéra at three o'clock tomorrow and wait for me there.'

She knew only one Fanfan: the one she had met in Marseilles, in the bar Chez Papa with Serge. She did not know that his real name was François Orsoni and that he already had a fairly impressive track record as a gangster. Her heart in her mouth, she went to the rendezvous, and patiently paced up and down. At last he appeared and whisked her into a *brasserie* on the Boulevard des Italiens.

'I wanted to make sure you weren't being watched. Serge sent me. He'd like you to know that he's thinking of you and that you must be patient. And carry on working.'

'Is he still in France? Tell him I'd like to see him again, just once, before he goes.'

Fanfan promised to give the message. When he left the café, two plain-clothes policemen followed him to his car and began to tail him. The two months' surveillance devoted to Simone seemed to have paid off at last. This trip took them to Boulogne, where they discovered that Fanfan lived with his mistress Jeanine in rue du Chemin vert, then to Clichy where another of his protégés was harbouring Christian David's mistress, Mireille, who was also wanted by the police.

Meanwhile, while they waited for the arrival of Lucien Sarti and Christian David on the shores of Rio de la Plata, François Chiappe and André Condemine continued to oversee the South American network from Buenos Aires. It was still having teething troubles. It was only when these four strong underworld personalities came together that it really took off and achieved legendary dimensions, progressing from the cottage industry of small-time couriers to the level of big multi-national enterprise. Together with Lucien Sarti, André Condemine was to be the chief architect of this transformation. He had already been in Latin America for several years. His name was not mentioned in any police records, but that of Mario Deniz, his alias, was found there with increasing regularity during the sixties; like so many of his *confrères*, he progressed from procuring to trafficking during those years.

He was born in February 1933 in Larbresle, near Lyon, where his father worked on the railways. He was two when his mother separated from her alcoholic husband, and took the child to Lyon, to her sister's. Shunted from pillar to post, he went to live with grandparents, then to a Swiss family. After a brief period of technical studies, he entered a Lyon foundry as a moulder, did his military service in the air force, then worked as an unskilled labourer in Vanissieux, married and had a daughter, Jocelyne, in 1955.

He then teamed up with a friend, Henri de Barros, of Portuguese origin, who was to achieve a degree of ill-fame in the heroin trade under the name Guigui; together they set up as scrap merchants. Their association ended the following year when they were arrested for theft and receiving.

André Condemine was sentenced to two years' imprisonment. On his release, he decided definitely that the underworld was for him. Tall, athletic, dark-haired and blue-eyed, with his oval face, languid walk and self-confidence, he was both immediately attractive and somewhat daunting. His wife was in a sanatorium;

he lived with his mother, but she rarely saw him. He began to earn his money by procuring and associated with several criminals from Alsace who specialised in armed robbery.

On 12 December 1958, a car from the Mulhouse Crédit Commercial de France stopped outside the offices of the Sécurité Sociale on rue des Trois-Rois. A bank messenger got out, holding two money bags containing eighteen million francs in notes. Suddenly he found himself confronted by two armed men who grabbed the bags and ran off towards a grey Peugeot 403 parked at the roadside.

Hearing his colleague's shouts, the driver leapt out, weapon in hand, and fired in the direction of the Peugeot, which drove off while its occupants replied in kind. The bank messenger fell to the ground. The 403 disappeared down the rue du Raisin.

The men involved were 'Ded' (Condemine), 'le Rasé', 'Jacky' and 'Gros Pif'. Two of their women, Marlene and Marcelle, put the police on their trail. Three of them were arrested, but 'Ded' was nowhere to be found. Protected by the Lyon underworld, he followed the itinerary used by numerous other criminals before and after him, and like them ended up at the restaurant El Sol in Buenos Aires. He was subsequently seen in Venezuela and Brazil.

After the gathering organised by Auguste Ricord on 11 November 1964, Condemine formed his own team. Alfredo Mazza, who introduced him to Colonel Aguilera, became his deputy. They had adopted the same methods as François Chiappe and Michel Nicoli, re-selling Bolivian cocaine in France in order to purchase the heroin they sent to the US. Condemine – whom everyone called Raymond – cynically christened this technique 'the death triangle'.

The activities of François Chiappe and André Condemine's carriers did not entirely escape notice. It was Inspector Le Mouel's Serious Crime Squad which smelt a rat. During their activities, the investigators discovered that the hold-up men and burglars under their surveillance were buying large quantities of sticking plaster. At first they linked these unusual purchases with an American news item: some house-breakers in Los Angeles had wrapped up a safe in adhesive tape before blowing the door out with a bazooka, so as to muffle the noise and prevent the scattering of debris.

But this hypothesis was never substantiated by any actual crime. On the contrary, since the end of the Algerian war the level of armed aggression had fallen considerably. The massive purchases of sticking plaster remained a mystery. On the other hand, the hypothesis of a redeployment of certain gangsters into a more remunerative activity was gaining ground. Several of these men had gone into the twentieth *arrondissement* with a load of sticking plaster. After trying to shake off possible tails, they had disappeared into a shabby building from which various old timers who had supposedly left France years before then emerged. In addition to these events attention was focused on the sudden rise in the price of heroin on the Marseilles black market.

A fortnight later news reached the Buenos Aires *grupo frances* that Etienne Carrara – who was also a deputy of Mémé Guerini, apart from his involvement in cocaine trafficking – had been arrested on Boulevard des Capucines after an eventful car chase.

Next it was the turn of Pedro Caballero-Linares and another courier to be questioned at Orly Airport just as they were leaving for the Argentine with their consignment of heroin. Finally, Jean Bouillon, a regular at the ex-servicemen's club and a courier for the Madrid network, was imprisoned.

This raid was the result of deductions made by Inspector Le Mouel and his team. The sticking plaster had been used to attach the packets of heroin to the small-scale couriers' bodies.

11

Simone Sees 'Le Beau Serge' Again

At the beginning of May 1966 Simone was still patiently waiting for news of le beau Serge. Day followed dreary day, as did one client after another. She climbed the stairs more than twenty times a night, with a man at her heels. The banknotes slipped into her *corsage* were added to the modest hoard already laid by in the rue d'Armaillé studio; for Simone still hoped to accompany her beloved into exile. One morning the telephone rang. She recognised the distant voice of the man she still loved.

'Book a seat on the Marseilles plane for tomorrow. As you come out of Marignane airport, someone will come and tell you what you've got to do. Bring some money, if you've got any. I'll need it.'

Two other passengers took their seats along with Simone on the Air Inter Caravelle at 17.15 hours: police officers Venier and Siano. They had been clearly briefed as to the restricted nature of their mission.

'Real tailing would be too risky. Make do with noting whom she contacts on disembarkation and try to discover where she's really going to.'

When she emerged from the plane, Simone crossed the almost empty arrival lounge. In the distance the police officers recognised Fanfan among the few people strolling about. He went up to Simone and murmured, 'Take a taxi and ask to be dropped at the motorway exit.'

Then, ten minutes later, he walked sharply out of the building, set off at the wheel of a beige DS and disappeared before Venier and Siano could take down the number.

At the motorway exit, Fanfan parked by the roadside, the

young woman got in beside him and the DS drove off in the direction of Cannes. 'During the journey, Fanfan kept on looking in the driving mirror to see if we were being followed. We made just one stop, in a café restaurant. After Cannes we came to a supermarket. Fanfan turned down a side street and dropped me in front of the supermarket.'

A few minutes later she caught sight of Serge, dressed in a polo-necked jersey and ducks, his face discreetly hidden behind large dark glasses. He came up to her, hugged her and dragged her off. Chattering eagerly, they arrived in front of a large modern building on the sea front, went up to the first floor and disappeared into an unfurnished studio.

Proudly, Simone produced from her bag the eight thousand francs she had put aside over eight months. He took the bundle and slipped the lot straight into his pocket.

'You're a good girl,' he said. 'I think I'm going to be able to go in a few days' time. Anyhow I'll let you know before I leave.'

This final tête-à-tête lasted twenty-four hours. The next day, the young woman left the building and walked two kilometres before finding a taxi to take her to Nice airport. She was back in Paris that same evening. In the months that followed she waited in vain for news from Serge. When she had asked him if she would see him again, he had shrugged his shoulders and said: 'It is in the lap of the gods.'

An Italian tough, imprisoned in Turin in 1969, was to inform Inspector Anglès that he had met Christian David in San Remo at roughly the same period. He carried two revolvers, one on his person and the other in a briefcase from which he was never parted.

In June, le beau Serge landed in Buenos Aires, where he was met by François Chiappe and André Condemine.

'You've arrived just at the right moment,' they said. 'There's a job for you.'

When Auguste Ricord once again called his closest colleagues together in the restaurant El Sol, the team was almost complete.

The decor suggested a cross between Provence and the Pampas. During these last months Ricord had been travelling through 'Creole' America: the Argentine, Chile, Uruguay and Paraguay.

After the last customer had left, the curtains were drawn, the tables pushed together and El Sol became the boardroom of the *grupo frances*. The bosses were there: Louis Bonsignour, François Chiappe, Jean-Paul Angeletti, black hair plastered down onto his skull, Michel Nicoli, Christian David the newcomer (whom everyone called Jean-Pierre), Luis Calabrese, the gangster Joannes Muñoz from St Etienne nicknamed 'Peluquita', and finally the man everyone knew as Raymond or Mario Deniz, André Condemine.

There was also William Perrin. Arrested in Italy the year before for a double murder and released for lack of evidence, he too had taken the road to Buenos Aires. At thirty-five he had a long and brilliant record behind him, but his speciality was safe-cracking, a field in which he had worked for Jean Penserani, known as 'Jeannot-le-triste'.

Auguste Ricord's position as chairman of the enterprise was unchallenged. He had taken up a commanding position at the head of the long, improvised table. He had fined down over the years, and his ex-boxer's muscles stood out beneath his now wizened skin; his hair had receded and what was left was now white; his face was shrunken and his cheekbones protruded; his drawn features betrayed his uncertain health but his expression was still alert and mobile.

Drugs poison not only those who use them, but also those who trade in them. For them, drugs are what gold was for the *conquistadors*; and the prospect of fabulous fortunes made within a few months or years was the only bond between these men.

Auguste Ricord was not only the undisputed leader of this South American network, he was the inspiration behind it. It would never have occurred to him to rely on the gratitude of all the fugitives whom he had received here, nor to count on their obedience. But the glittering future he held before them guaranteed their adherence to his plans for the moment.

The composition of the various teams was the result of circumstances and not of a pre-established scheme. Their general pattern emerged during this meeting. On either side of Ricord were Jean-Paul Angeletti and François Chiappe, the management. Jean-Pierre (Christian David), the newcomer, sat a little behind them: he fulfilled the modest function of bodyguard, but everything pointed to the likelihood of imminent promotion from this subordinate position. He was living with a young woman connected with the Uruguayan Tupamaros and he had made contact with representatives of the Argentine Liberation Front, who were interested in his experiences as an agent of the French 'Special Services'. It was not long before he built up his own team, which gradually moved out of the orbit of the 'Organisation'.

Two further teams had formed during the past years, that of Domingo Orsini and Louis Bonsignour, which had just experienced various setbacks, and that of André Condemine. 'Peluquita' and René Santamaria had joined him, while William Perrin appeared to lean in the direction of Christian David. 'Marcello' – François Rossi – was ready to take responsibility for a fourth group and was already making his authority felt. The last team was represented by François Chiappe; Michel Nicoli, who was one of the most experienced elements of the network, had become its manager.

All these men were still beginners. Ricord-Bonaparte had not yet become Napoleon. The ex-procurer did not for the moment see beyond the technique of concealing drugs on individuals, which limited each consignment to two and a half kilos, and required a considerable number of volunteers but had the advantage of restricting loss in case of seizure.

'Development in this industry,' explained Ricord, 'requires an increase in manpower. There aren't enough French exiles to meet this demand.' They had turned to local labour, and already recruited Alberto Gurini, a thief and smuggler, Laura Ŏses, Ricardo Rosales and Maria Luiza Buzio.

'We're going to need a number of passports. Our couriers must be able to change identity from one trip to another, to avoid being noticed. Nicolai Ajachinsky and "Pico Cobo" are going to get them for us.'

Louis Bonsignour then described the result of his labours. The Argentinian couriers would be able to go to Marseilles where they would be contacted at the Bristol by a mysterious Monsieur François. Some would receive their consignment at the Balmoral in Barcelona. The goods would be stored in a house on the Campo Sagrado. Their agent was called Imenez.

The prospects opened up by the 'death triangle' so dear to André Condemine were also considered. Gurino knew a member of the Bolivian embassy in Uruguay who could route considerable quantities of cocaine from La Paz in Montevideo and take over from the network of the late General Aguilera Gomez.

Ricord had also made contact with Chilean smugglers, Jewish in origin, former thieves or pickpockets who dispatched cocaine to the US via Panama. They agreed to put their network at the disposal of the French. The Marseilles sailors on the boats serving the Pacific ports on the South American coast would be able to effect deliveries to Valparaiso, Antofogasta or the Chilean free port of Arica.

In this way, some of the heroin would use the cocaine routes for which a solid infrastructure already existed. The sailors on ships flying the Panamanian flag also delivered it to the US ports on both coasts. The network had representatives in Bogota, Mexico and Tijuana on the Californian border. Various companies had already been officially set up. They had offices in New York which could safeguard the repatriation of money paid out by the American clients.

Ricord set forward his ideas with conviction and obtained the support of his associates, who cared little about the particular nature of the trade into which circumstances had drawn them, or about the misery drugs could bring in their train. Heroin trafficking involved fewer risks than the illegal activities which had brought them into exile and it offered an opportunity for making fabulous fortunes very quickly and satisfying their wildest desires, including the appearance of respectability which fortune brings.

But Ricord kept a part of his plans back from his audience. Some projects were not yet ready for exposure, and some he was keeping exclusively for himself. His aim was to maintain his supremacy over his team-mates by divulging his best ideas to them only gradually.

The one he set most store by – and which he would put into operation when the European laboratories were in a position to supply him with sufficient quantities of heroin – was to make use of the *contrabandistas*.

Over the years the *contrabandistas* had become almost an institution. Since the war, they had criss-crossed the skies of Latin America aboard aircraft of every description: Cessna 210s, Piper 25s, Twin Beech Bonanzas, Fairchild 22 C 70s, old DC3s which had done tens of thousands of hours of flying time, and even old wartime B25 and B26 bombers.

Pilots of astonishing virtuosity, the *contrabandistas* flew from Florida with cargoes of cigarettes, transistors, jeans and whisky, purchased legally from American firms, all perfectly above board. Their planes were registered in Florida, Louisiana, California or Illinois, in the Bahamas or Panama, Buenos Aires or Asuncion. They belonged to legitimate companies or to individuals who chartered them; sometimes the pilot himself was the owner of the plane.

Their profits were enormous: jeans were resold for three times their original price, cigarettes four times – all on the black market, of course. The goods were loaded on in the full light of day, but delivery took place on private or clandestine airstrips in the various Latin American countries to the east of the Cordillera, which most of the planes could not cross. Airfields were improvised on route for refuelling.

Several New World millionaires owed their recent prosperity to the daring of these aviators: Babe Ricardo and Simon Saida in the Argentine, Jaime Garlich in Paraguay. The latter's assistant, Elio Varela, was to become Ricord's partner, Paraguay was in fact the most important centre of this traffic. The *contrabandistas* were sure of total impunity thanks to the complicity of two high ranking officers from the entourage of the dictator-president Stroessner: Generals Patricio Coleman and André Rodriguez.

Coleman had a private aerodrome on his huge estate near the town of Santa Elena. Rodriguez controlled a clandestine landing strip – a thousand metres of dirt track in an inaccessible region to the east of Asuncion, Hernandarias. Dozens of planes landed and took off from there each week. The general's right-hand man, Carlos Barretto, levied two dollars per crate of cigarettes transported. Thanks to these obliging military men, within the space of a few years Paraguay became the biggest consumer of American cigarettes in the continent.

Auguste Ricord's idea was therefore to utilise the planes of the *contrabandistas* to dispatch his future cargos of heroin to the US. Hitherto, after landing their contraband cargo, the planes had set off again empty for the US. Sometimes, the pilots would swell their coffers by ferrying a few handfuls of Colombian emeralds or Brazilian rubies, or the remnants of vanished Indian civilisations so sought after by collectors.

Thousands of aircraft plied the skies above the southern states. Most private flights were not checked. The *contrabandistas* could easily land one or two suitcases of heroin at carefully chosen spots before going on to their official destinations. Ricord was proposing to devote the next few months to the solution of this problem. The time would soon come when he could transfer his headquarters. to Asuncion.

12

A Novel Use for Oscilloscopes

For a year, Louis Bonsignour had journeyed endlessly from Buenos Aires to Madrid, Paris to Puerto Rico, Marseilles to New York. 'In the United States, under several identities, in New York, Miami and even Los Angeles, he had various addresses and bank accounts which enabled him to carry out his various operations,' noted Inspector Mugnier in one of his reports. He also had a pied-à-terre in Paris, in the Place Emanuel Chabrier, and a title: export manager of the Cabanas Congeladas company.

On 2 May 1966, the Washington Narcotics Bureau received a message from one of its agents in Paris. An informer had told them that an industrialist, Paul Chastagnier, was planning to send a certain quantity of heroin to a client in New York. The heroin was to come from Marseilles and to be transported by a courier.

Investigations made by the French police revealed that the industrialist had had numerous contacts with Louis Bonsignour and Emile Beze. They also led to the discovery that Chastagnier had been the object of discrete surveillance by the French police for a year now.

A few months earlier, the kidnapping of the exiled Moroccan leader Mehdi Ben Barka, kidnapped outside the Lipp restaurant in St Germain des Près, had highlighted the activities of some 'Special Services' agents and strong-arm men working for these services. The house where Ben Barka was taken, in the Paris suburbs, belonged to a notorious gangster, Georges Boucheseiche.

Boucheseiche had settled in Morocco but often returned to France; he owned two hotels in Paris under his wife's name, one used for prostitution on rue Blondel and the other on Boulevard de Montparnasse, the Unic-Hotel. After the Ben Barka affair, regulars of these establishments had been the object of police investigations. It was thus that a dossier had been built up on a friend of Boucheseiche, who had taken up official residence in the Unic, namely, Paul Chastagnier. Originally from Marseilles, he had numerous contacts in the underworld but was himself considered something of a fringe figure.

He was involved in shady businesses, often verging on the illegal. Among his contacts was the director and sleeping partner of a firm called Young Electronics: Paul Lacour, known as 'Polo', who had, according to a police officer, 'a horse at Barbizon, a forty horsepower boat at Ste Maxime and an Alfa Romeo worth twenty thousand francs, half of which he had had to borrow, a life style being well above his means'.

At the time, Lacour was earning about ten thousand francs a month. He was tall, well dressed and often seen with attractive women. In May 1966, when Inspector Mugnier resumed the lapsed investigations after the information imparted by the BNDD, he found the two men in a café in the fifteenth *arrondissement* where they were regulars. Lacour always drove up in his red Alfa Romeo and joined Chastagnier at the back of the room, where they talked at length.

Inspector Mugnier, known as 'Mumu' then became a regular himself. Every day he met Chastagnier at midday, apéritif time which, for him, coincided with breakfast time. Chastagnier dropped his guard and vouchsafed that most of his nights were spent in night-clubs. He was fond of female company but never formed a lasting liaison because he admitted, 'I'm not much of a Don Juan in bed.'

Young provincial police officers had been called in to take part in this tailing, but several months were to go by before the enquiries bore any fruit.

During his conversations with 'Mumu', Chastagnier was careful not to mention another of his contacts, Philippe Chaboche, the sales manager of a company in difficulties. But Chaboche had been tracked down by other detectives involved in the operation.

Chaboche was a former journalist with *France-Dimanche* who, while he had seduced and married a rich heiress, had signally failed similarly to conquer her father. He none the less managed to extract quite considerable sums from him by playing his fatherly concern for a daughter whom he did not want to see in any kind of straits. Much of this money was diverted into dazzling of Philippe's friends; he tended towards the megalomanic. One of his contacts revealed that he liked to wander through the state rooms at Versailles dreaming of the splendours of the past. 'Louis XV's life style would have suited me,' he sighed.

During their outings in night-time Paris, Chastagnier and Chaboche had on several occasions touched on the financial advantages that heroin could bring them. Chastagnier's contacts in the underworld meant that, if he wished, he could count on the co-operation of Marseilles suppliers. They had even considered various ways of concealing the drugs so as to foil the American customs.

'I know a piece of apparatus that would do the trick,' Chaboche had said. 'It's the "Cardiotest". It is so complex to put together that no one would think of dismantling it to find out what was in it.'

At last, in November 1965, Chastagnier visited New York. He had gone to see a friend with whom he had lost contact for some time, Georges Varsa. Fifteen years earlier they had been partners and opened a French style restaurant, Chez Maxim's, in the Ecuador port of Guayaquil; its speciality was *poulet à la crème*. Paul did the cooking and Georges received the clientèle. The business had lasted two years.

'It couldn't go on,' Chastagnier had admitted to 'Mumu'. 'We were passionate football fans and every time there was an important match anywhere in Latin America we'd go there by plane, leaving an old Indian woman at the stove.'

Since then, Georges had settled in the US and, over the years, had become the sales director of a New York company called Foreign Trade Representation, of 90 West Street, whose annual turnover figure was almost a million dollars, enough to satisfy the

Hungarian émigré who had tried his hand at most things since the end of the war.

He received his friend with a smile which froze when Chastagnier asked him to take delivery of some Cardiotest apparatus destined for American clients. He knew Chastagnier too well to think it was genuine.

'Sorry, old chap,' he said, 'but my business is concerned with exporting, not importing. I like my job and I don't want to compromise it by any fancy business. But I can give you the address of various importers who specialise in electronic equipment.'

So Chastagnier went back to Paris having achieved nothing. He met Bonsignour a few months later; Bonsignour was willing to supply him with quantities of heroin he needed and to find him a client in New York. Paul Lacour's discovery of the ideal packaging to dispatch the drug to New York gave a new impetus to the plan. The apparatus in question, the oscilloscope, was made by an electronics firm based in the Savoie. It was a very sophisticated precision instrument, the size of a portable television, which made it possible to spot the slightest variations in electric voltage and translate them into graphs on the surface of a cathode ray tube. It was also much simpler than the 'Cardiotest' that Chaboche suggested using.

Lacour was a shareholder in a small-scale enterprise, the Société de fabrication d'accessoires électroniques (Electronic Fitments Company) run by an ingenious technician, Jacques Courbet. Towards the end of the summer of 1966, after the holidays, the three associates, who were later to be called the 'Chairman', began to put their plan into action. Lacour took it upon himself to persuade Courbet.

'What we'll be doing is sending home the capital belonging to certain *pieds noirs* living in Africa. We'll replace the transformers of the oscilloscopes with steel cases which will be identical and which I shall design. You'll get five hundred francs for each piece of apparatus handled.'

Meanwhile, Chaboche got in touch with the oscilloscope manufacturer, calling himself Champelle. He presented himself as the general European agent of Foreign Trade Representation; Chastagnier had got hold of some of their headed writing-paper for him. The apparatus would be paid for in dollars.

'We anticipate the purchase of a hundred and fifty oscilloscopes over the year,' he explained over the phone. 'But six will be enough for next month.'

There were no hitches. The industrialist was so enthusiastic that he proposed mentioning the name of his transatlantic client in advertising brochures. The parcel arrived a few days later at the manufacturer's Parisian office. Louis Bonsignour's supplier sent the twelve packets of heroin that made up the first consignment from Marseilles. Their courier put them in a luggage locker at the Gare de Lyon and Chastagnier collected them. He settled the first order of oscilloscopes with a cheque drawn on the Geneva branch of the First National Bank under a false name.

As soon as the parcel arrived from the Savoie, Chastagnier brought an oscilloscope to his workshop on the banks of the Marne. With Courbet he dismantled the transformer, and Lacour took this as his starting point to draw up the plans for the case which was to replace it. Then, considering that his mission was accomplished, the 'Chairman' went off to travel the world, leaving his accomplices to finish off the details of the operation.

Chaboche and Chastagnier put the packets of heroin in the case which Courbet had provided for them (later Chaboche's finger prints were found on the remains of the metal seized in the workshop). Then they were fixed inside the oscilloscopes. Naturally, Courbet suspected that Lacour had lied to him and that he was involved in something more than met the eye. A cautious man, he worked at night and on his days off, then threw the incriminating transformers into the Marne. He used Lacour's return to ask for an increase in his share of the profits, and indeed in the following consignment it was raised to 750 francs per instrument transformed. Lacour's secretary typed the customs documents accompanying the two first parcels, which Chaboche and Chastagnier took to Orly themselves.

Chastagnier still wanted to make use of Georges Varsa, but now he had a better idea of how to approach him. He did not ask him to enter into a partnership of any kind; he simply informed him that he was sending Varsa two parcels which he himself would take delivery of in New York. The Hungarian could not refuse this; he wrote a note of assent to the address his friend had given him, that of his tailor.

On 22 December 1966 an Air France Boeing 707 came to a standstill in front of the international airlines block, and the hundred odd passengers who alighted formed a queue to go through customs and immigration formalities. Among them was a personable fifty-year-old holding an expensive leather suitcase, a businessman, one of thousands the customs men saw filing past every day; it was Paul Chastagnier.

No cable had alerted the authorities of his arrival. So far he was only one of the host of multiple suspects being subjected to sporadic surveillance. He may perhaps have seemed slightly nervous; he knew that he had passed the point of no return. His behaviour attracted the attention of the customs men who came to examine his luggage.

The fatal words were uttered, 'Would you be good enough to follow me?'

But a more thorough search proved unproductive. His papers were perfectly in order; his name did not figure on the list of individuals wanted or watched by the American authorities. He was allowed to leave. But during the incident he had attracted the attention of an agent of the Narcotics Bureau, Albert Garofalo, who decided at random to tail him.

As soon as he was released, Chastagnier went to a phone booth and phoned Georges Varsa. 'We'd better cancel the appointment we made by letter, and meet at five at the bar of the Taft Hotel.' The previous rendezvous in a bar on 51st Street, had been noted in a notebook that the customs men had leafed through.

Chastagnier hailed a taxi. He was promptly followed by a Narcotics Bureau car. One behind the other the two vehicles drove to Manhattan amid the cheery bustle of shoppers laden with gaily-coloured parcels and the shops lit up and decorated. The policeman soon lost Chastagnier from sight; they then went to 51st Street but saw no sign of him; finally they gave up. They had plenty of other things to do.

As soon as he had met Varsa, Chastagnier pulled him out onto the pavement. They vanished into the crowd and reached 57th Street where the Frenchman had another appointment: at number 135, where there was an apartment that had been rented by Louis Bonsignour and occupied for several months by Larrain-Maestre, a small-time Cuban trafficker.

'A parcel of four oscilloscopes arrived two days ago,' explained Chastagnier, 'and another one of six should be arriving today. We're going to see the person who is going to take delivery of them.'

After being introduced to the Cuban, Varsa went back to his office where the oscilloscopes had been delivered five days previously, shortly after the Christmas holidays. He phoned Larrain-Maestre, who came round and put the two bulky parcels in a taxi.

The following day Chastagnier and Varsa – who was still a little nervous – went back to Larrain-Maestre's apartment. With a lordly gesture, Larrain-Maestre opened a huge money-bag full of hundred-dollar notes, took out two wads and handed them airily to the surprised Hungarian, who accepted them. He realised that he was now irreversibly caught up in machinery which could lead him to his doom. Many recruits, torn like Varsa between greed and fear, did not dare to back-track, convinced that they were already too compromised to pull out and certain that no one would believe their innocence.

'We've unpacked the parcels,' explained Chastagnier casually. 'Ten kilos of heroin at ten thousand dollars a kilo. Our Argentinian friends will bring the money back to France. You don't have anything to worry about. They'll deliver the parcels to your firm and we'll come and get them.'

Varsa said nothing, but an image flitted across his mind: that of the label on the parcels. It bore the name of the recipient: 'c/o

Georges Varsa'. At the first sign of danger, he would be the first to be incriminated. Gloomily he received the friendly slaps on the back administered by his delighted companions, and listened to debates about the procedures for further delivery as though in a daze.

In France, the police were keeping the three 'Chairmen' under increasingly close surveillance. The detectives who were helping Mugnier had been led to the tailor's shop where Chastagnier received his mail.

On 26 June 1967 Chastagnier met Paul Lacour – identified by the registration number of his Alfa Romeo – at a bar, the Petite Rotonde, in Montparnasse. In his turn Lacour led the investigators to Boulogne, to the annexe of Young Electronics. The step from there to Courbet was easily made.

On several occasions Chastagnier had been sighted in The Claridge; there he had met one of the hotel guests, Emile Beze, a former cook who had become a bar owner in Venezuela; he had sold out at the beginning of the sixties to settle in the US, where certain entanglements he had had with the law had at last been sorted out. Beze therefore set off again for New York during the month of January and returned at the end of February with Louis Bonsignour, in whose apartment he took up residence. Twelve kilos of heroin from Marseilles were delivered to Chastagnier at the beginning of March.

Lacour went skiing at Serres-Chevalier, then travelled to Hong Kong, San Francisco and finally New York. He had to do some groundwork for the Gadgets Department of Young Electronics. But above all he had to see Georges Varsa to whom he announced the imminent arrival of two parcels of six oscilloscopes.

Varsa was not the only one – apart from Larrain-Maestre and his accomplices – to be informed of this consignment. The collaboration between the French 'stups' and the Parisian section of the Narcotics Bureau made it possible to reconstruct almost completely the puzzle of the gang's activities. A telex informed Washington that a certain number of oscilloscopes had been ordered from the Savoie firm. Twelve were to be sent at the beginning of

March 1968, ten a little later and twenty-five the following month. An examination of customs records at Orly confirmed the existence of the two December parcels. This time the police were positive they were on the right track.

The tailing of Emile Beze during his stay in New York had not been fruitful. A young woman with flaming hair had come to meet him at Kennedy Airport and they had holidayed together at length apparently as carefree tourists, visiting the city, the night-clubs, frequenting the French restaurants of Manhattan and passing part of their time in a flat on 67th Street.

At the beginning of March, the French and American police were poised for intervention, to put an end to the 'Chairmen's' activities. Several points were still unclear in the organisation of the network, but the haul, if it succeeded, would help to elucidate them. It was vitally important not to arouse the suspicions of Chastagnier and his accomplices before the next consignment.

This consignment posed a problem. If the whole network was to be broken up, it was crucial that at least one of these parcels should cross the Atlantic. It would make it possible to lay hands on and arrest the American intermediaries and buyers. The others would be kept at Orly and would serve to indict the senders and their suppliers. This plan required a degree of synchronisation between the two operations so as not to arouse the suspicions of either party. The French and American customs were kept informed of the situation. All that remained was to await Chastagnier's first move.

On 20 April, a cable arrived at the New York branch of the Narcotics Bureau. It announced the departure of Louis Bonsignour, now calling himself 'Felipe Spadaro', for the United States and stressed his probable role in the trafficking. The next day, Chastagnier and Lacour went to Orly and deposited two big packages containing the oscilloscopes; Lacour filled out the customs forms.

Immediately after their departure, Inspector Mugnier, his assistants and two 'narcs' agents opened one of the parcels, took out an oscilloscope and set about dismantling it. Half an hour later, they had laid their hands on two plastic bags whose contents, for form's sake, they hastily analysed. They then decided to send the second parcel off the following morning. It would be accompanied by Inspector Anglès of the 'stups', whom the American agent Garofalo would meet at Kennedy Airport.

In the few days before this, two new events had completed the pattern of information gathered by the police. Chaboche himself had taken the sheet metal needed to make the cases to his Chennevières workshop and on the 17th he had gone with Chastagnier to take delivery of the oscilloscopes at the Savoie firm's Paris depot. Finally, on 19 March, a postmaster had given Mugnier two envelopes addressed to Chastagnier's tailor. They made it possible to identify his correspondent in New York positively as Georges Varsa.

On the morning of the 22nd, immediately after the departure of Anglès and the parcel, Chastagnier, Chaboche and their accomplices were arrested and discreetly imprisoned. No information was given to the press. The police were waiting for the green light from New York. But news travels fast in Paris. The midday edition of one paper published a paragraph which gave no names, but mentioned the use of oscilloscopes.

In New York, the time difference caused the parcel and Inspector Anglès to land at Kennedy in the morning, under a leaden sky. The parcel was immediately delivered to a customs office where experts dismantled the apparatus it contained. The twelve packets of heroin they discovered were opened, the white powder analysed and replaced by yeast, with the exception of five hundred grams which had, as usual, to serve as evidence. Then all the equipment was reassembled so that no trace of interference remained. The parcel was then handed on to the freight service of Air France who informed the consignee of its arrival.

But a message announcing the publication in a Parisian paper of the six arrests made by the French police upset the planned procedure. It was vital that the parcel should reach Foreign Trade Representation as soon as possible, before Varsa learnt of the fate of his French friends. A delivery van was immediately chartered, the various forms for the consignment were hastily typed out. A customs man and an agent from the Narcotics Bureau disguised themselves as driver and warehouseman respectively.

Meanwhile, in Paris, in the offices of Agence France-Presse, a conscientious journalist leafing through the morning's papers came across the ill-timed paragraph. He knew his job and sent a telex to the New York office to get information about the events which had taken place at the other end of the network. Several telephone calls won him the name of the recipient of the parcel.

At three in the afternoon, the telephone rang in Georges Varsa's office. 'Hallo, this is Agence France-Presse. We would like to ask you for a few details about the arrest in Paris of one of your clients, Paul Chastagnier, for drug trafficking.' Varsa hung up immediately, his hand trembling. It had to be a hoax. How come his buyers had not informed him? What should he do in such circumstances?

Before he could recover himself and try to get hold of Larrain-Maestre, a delivery van stopped in front of the building at 90 West Street. The incriminating parcel was put into the lift. On the eleventh floor, the bogus warehouseman knocked on the door of Varsa's office. As to the manner born he handed Varsa the receipt and assorted papers to be signed. He gave him the carbon copies and rejoined his mate, leaving the disconcerted Hungarian with his parcel.

Several customs agents and 'narcs' had already surrounded the building and were concealed on the various floors. Several minutes later an innocent Foreign Trade Representation employee was pursued as far as Broadway. At Trinity Church, he quickened his step and saw three unknown men bearing down on him. Naturally enough, not a grain of heroin was found on him. Still in his office, after a few moment's hesitation Varsa decided upon escape, and took the elevator in his turn. Two floors down, he was joined by a 'narc' agent. One behind the other, they set out along Broadway. Suddenly Varsa darted into a building and ran to the back of the hall. The policeman ran in behind him and arrested him. The

Hungarian let himself be led meekly to a car which had just drawn up at the kerb. A few minutes later, in one of the offices at 80 Church Street, he revealed everything he knew about the traffic and his relations with Larrain-Maestre.

He was shown sheaves of photographs and recognised Louis Bonsignour – to whom his buyer had introduced him a few weeks ago and in whose company they had dined at La Grenouille. After this initial questioning, Varsa went back to the Foreign Trade Representation's premises, accompanied by several policemen who proceeded to make a minute search. During the operation, the telephone rang.

'Hallo Varsa? This is Phillippe. Have the parcels arrived? I've just landed and I haven't been able to get hold of our client.'

Obeying the police instructions, the luckless Hungarian tried to sound casual, reassured his correspondent and asked him to come and collect the goods as soon as possible. 'Spadaro' said that he would be there in the morning when the offices opened. But he was not to fall into the trap which was promptly laid for him.

The search of Varsa's office, his confession and the investigations which followed made it possible to reconstruct the workings of the traffic with a few hours. That same evening, the police knew that Larrain-Maestre had checked in at the luxury Drake Hotel towards the middle of the month. His room had been reserved by the luscious redhead with whom Emile Beze had spent several pleasant days a month earlier.

Searches in the hotel and the flat on 57th Street produced nothing. Larrain-Maestre's mother had seen a programme about the affair on television and immediately telephoned her son, who promptly fled. The only consolation for the police was the chance arrest of a Puerto Rican trafficker, Raymond Lomabardero Ramirez, in the building where Bonsignour had rented an apartment.

The haul had not been as fruitful as the Narcotics Bureau had hoped. Airports were watched, but Larrain-Maestre managed to slip through the net and reach Buenos Aires.

Louis Bonsignour preferred to lie low; he stayed in a Manhattan hotel using a new identity. He was arrested there a month later and his bail fixed at seventy-five thousand dollars. His family links with Auguste Ricord gave the Federal Agents a fuller insight into the ramifications of the most important contemporary drug-smuggling business: the Latin American network.

The results obtained by the French police were more satisfactory although, as was too often the case, the clues leading to the suppliers stopped at the gates of Marseilles, where the law of silence was still respected. However, one of the 'Chairmen' was to escape justice: Philippe Chaboche, hospitalised in the Hôtel Dieu, managed to escape. He committed suicide several months later.

13

Plying Between Manhattan and Buenos Aires

At the beginning of 1967, Jack Grosby knew no more of drug trafficking than what he read in newspapers or heard discussed in the bars he frequented. Nor indeed did he have any reason to take the slightest interest in it; his business was good and offered plenty of scope. He imported thoroughbreds to the United States and sold them to various breeders. These horses came from the Antilles and various Latin American countries where he had friends.

His success was the outcome of ten years of assorted effort and failure. In 1956 he was still called Jacob Grodnitzky. He was an Argentinian citizen and was already involved in horse-breeding in Buenos Aires. After a series of setbacks he and his wife decided to leave the country and to try their luck in the United States. He had also had a spell as a representative for an industrial lighting firm in Puerto Rico, and as an employee of International Cash Register.

One of his childhood friends had settled in Manhattan in 1954. His name was Luis Stepenberg. After having started the South County Export Company, he had gone into the car trade. According to Grosby's immigration papers, one of his guarantors was a Brooklyn trader, Joseph Magliocco, an influential member of the Mafia.

So with the assistance of Stepenberg and his associate Juan Ricardo Fernandez, Jack Grosby tried his luck in New York. For a year he worked with the sales department of a record business, then opened a travel agency on Amsterdam Avenue, the Buenos Aires Travel Service. Finally he became manager of the Blake

Hotel on 44th Street. In 1962 he became a naturalised American and the following year he went into horse-dealing.

He gave up the hotel and, until such time as his new-found activities brought him wealth, he sold used cars for Luis Stepenberg. 'At the time,' he claimed, 'Stepenberg was not yet involved in the clandestine drug trade.' During his numerous trips, Grosby met people from every walk of life, some of whom made use of his services. Among these were Luis Calabrese and Carlos Mercado, an associate of Condemine's.

They would go to Puerto Rico for short sessions at the Hotel Flamboyan, or the Regency, on the other side of the avenue in San Juan and run by Dean Martin's brother. They came from Corsica, Marseilles or the Argentine and were mostly Italian in origin; they gambled away thousands of dollars in casinos on each trip, then carried on to Buenos Aires, Madrid, Paris or Frankfurt. Grosby forged links which were to strengthen as the months went by and, when the opportunity arose, he did various minor favours for the friends Luis Calabrese sent him: hiring cars, making reservations in hotels or at Madison Square Garden, or finding furnished apartments.

Still, he was anxious to preserve the patina of respectability which he had slowly acquired. In his own street he was regarded as a rich foreign 'sportsman' and he took particular trouble with his appearance. His towering figure was always highly distinctive, attired in suits of tweed or Prince of Wales check; he had lack-lustre fair hair, dark blue eyes and a slightly fleshy, blotchy face.

Towards the end of 1966, he made the acquaintance of Louis Bonsignour, alias Felipe Spadaro. It was Luis Calabrese who introduced them, during one of his spells in New York. After this meeting the two men saw one another almost every day. On 23 March, they went together to the Cassius Clay–Folley fight in Madison Square Garden. Jack found an apartment for Susan N, his new friend's mistress, and undertook to furnish it. He hired a car for them and acted as their driver, since Spadaro had no licence.

The Frenchman – whom Grosby still believed to be a South

American – also took an interest in horses and wanted to invest in a racing stable. He suggested to his companion that they should go into it together.

Grosby, Spadaro and Calabrese sometimes met Alberto Larrain-Maestre at the Rincon Argentino on Broadway over a *parrillada* washed down with wine from Mendoza. Gradually, without knowing it, the law-abiding South American sportsman found himself drawn into the orbit of the chief members of the South American network whose existence was still entirely unknown to the Narcotics Bureau.

One evening in April 1967, after leaving his childhood friend Luis Stepenberg, Jack Grosby sauntered up Sixth Avenue and settled himself behind a bar window where he was to meet Spadaro. He gazed at the fountains reflected in the glass façade of a skyscraper. In a few days, he was to leave for Puerto Rico to select the thoroughbreds for their projected racing stables.

Minutes passed, then an hour. It was the first time the Frenchman had been late. Grosby waited a little longer, then, puzzled, started back home. On his way he bought a paper which he opened as soon as he had installed himself in an armchair in his living-room. On the third page he came upon a short article which informed him both of the haul which had made his friend's arrest possible, and the important part he played in the drug trade.

Jack was not too amazed, but he was worried. The Narcotics Bureau might well discover his dealings with the accused and ask him some awkward questions. Of course he himself was in the clear, but his activities might well suffer from any unwelcome curiosity on the part of the authorities. A bail of seventy-five thousand dollars was asked for the Frenchman, a considerable sum to raise at the time, even for drug traffickers; this meant a long period in prison.

Two weeks passed. No policeman came to the door of the apartment on 72nd Street. Grosby had almost forgotten his erstwhile colleague when, one evening in May, he returned home to find an attractive young woman on his landing; he immediately recognised her; it was Susan N, Felipe's friend, for whom he had found an apartment a few months previously.

'Louis asked me to come,' she said. 'I've been to see him in prison. There's something he'd like you to do for him.'

Somewhat surprised, Grosby ushered her in. He did not know anyone called Louis in prison. A few moments later, he learned that the man he had always known as Felipe Spadaro was in fact called Louis Bonsignour, and that he was counting on his contacts to get him a lawyer and to help him regain his freedom.

'The judge wants the bail to be paid in cash. He won't accept a first instalment of ten per cent and the guarantee of a "bondsman" for the balance. Louis would like you to go and see his family in Buenos Aires and bring back the sum needed.'

'And does he intend to stay here in New York for the case?'

The young woman gave an ambiguous smile. 'We can think about that once he's out. Now about the travel expenses . . .'

Grosby interrupted her. He would not hear talk of money as long as his friend was behind bars. He sensed that he was about to come into contact with an organisation which turned over hundreds of thousands of dollars. He was certainly not thinking of taking part in the trafficking, but he could do small, well-paid favours without incurring risks. Indeed he had done so already, on a modest scale, for his friend and his friend's friends.

Three days later he landed at Buenos Aires, a European city stranded on the American continent and seething with descendants of Basques, Spaniards, Italians and German émigrés; sunny casual and hot-blooded, its broad avenues lined with imposing stone buildings, remnants of the economic boom of the beginning of the century.

On the terrace of the *confiterias* on Avenida de Mayo he met childhood friends who apparently had not left their café tables for a decade. After playing the role of the prodigal son, he took a taxi to the Olivos district where, according to Susan, he would be welcomed with open arms by the mother and uncle of the unfortunate Louis – Maria Traversi Bonsignour and Auguste Ricord – in their restaurant El Sol.

He was received, in fact, with guarded cordiality. Auguste Ricord's gaunt figure, long horse face and balding forehead, framed by greying side-whiskers, gave no clue to the eminent position he already occupied in the trade. The debris was cleared away from the table with its patterned cloth, and around it conversation gradually got going. Brother and sister listened to their visitor's tale in silence.

When she heard the figure in question, Maria Bonsignour burst out, 'Seventy-five thousand dollars! Do you think I can just hand over a sum like that? You'll never convince me that the American judges will release Louis for money, now they've got him. Even for that sum!'

Grosby and Ricord – who had already heard talk of release on bail – tried to instill some notions of American law into the incredulous Maria. But she closed her ears to argument, torn between her concern for her son and her fear of parting with her money.

'Furthermore,' Grosby persisted, 'as soon as he has a lawyer – and you will have to give him an advance of several thousand dollars – this bail can be considerably reduced.'

'I'll accept the bit about the lawyer,' Maria finally conceded. 'We'll see about the bail when it's reduced. But what proof have I that it really is Louis who is sending you?'

Pastis was served and the discussion continued, more cordially now. In conciliatory vein, Grosby told of his relationship with the young Frenchman. He talked of his girl-friend Susan, of their plans for partnership and of their mutual acquaintances. When he rose to go Maria, half-convinced, hugged his huge frame; they arranged to meet again the following day.

After downing an enormous fillet steak under the massive beams of the restaurant La Cabana – 'the best meat in the world' – and experiencing the pleasure of 'Buenos Aires by night', Grosby went to sleep in one of the vast rooms of the Hotel Bristol, convinced that he would have no difficulty in conquering the peppery and unforthcoming Maria. But the next day, at the arranged time, he found himself in front of a positive tribunal. Maria Bonsignour introduced him to his judges: Jean-Pierre (Christian David),

François-les-grosses-lèvres, Marcello (Rossi) and his lawyer Dener Pelossi.

He was made to understand, amicably enough, that they were all only too eager to trust him, but that they had to be cautious. Pelossi would go with him to New York with enough money to engage an American lawyer. They would see later about the bail. Of course, these delays were inconvenient for the hapless Louis who was languishing in gaol, but he knew the value of money and would appreciate his mother's farsightedness.

Less than a week after his original departure, Jack Grosby was once more walking the pavements of Manhattan, lawyer Pelossi on his heels. Pelossi took a dim view of his reception in free America. Hardly had he found out about the conditions of the payment of bail, than he was interrogated for hours by agents of the Narcotics Bureau, then summoned by the District Judge of New York. They wanted to know where he would be getting the bail money from.

The lawyer they finally found, Paul Rao Junior, succeeded in reducing the bail to fifty thousand dollars. 'If your friends can wait a bit,' he said optimistically, 'I'll get it reduced further.'

'Don't worry,' said Grosby philosophically, 'they'll wait.'

In June, he made another trip to Buenos Aires and came back, this time having won the confidence of the Bonsignour family and their associates, who were satisfied with the results already obtained. He was now regarded as their indispensable collaborator in New York.

On his return from this second trip to Argentina, Jack Grosby began to concentrate on his business once again, though he kept in touch with lawyer Rao. Louis Bonsignour waited patiently in his cell. He knew that wheels were being put in motion for his release.

At the beginning of August, taking advantage of the fact that a number of judges had gone on holiday, Rao requested a third reduction of the bail before a new magistrate. It was fixed at thirty thousand dollars. The moment for action had come. Once again Grosby had a visit from Susan.

'Louis thanks you for everything you've already done. Now he'd like you to take the matter up with his partners. His stay in prison means lost business opportunities ten times greater than the bail figure. He knows that you're involving yourself out of friendship but he says you won't lose out, quite the reverse.'

Thus encouraged, Jack took an Aerolineas Argentinas Boeing and met his friends' partners in Pelossi's office, at 1880 Calle Lavalle. There it soon became clear to him that he was involved with real professionals. The lawyer Pelossi was determined never again to set foot in the United States after the disagreeable experience he had had at the beginning of June. One of his colleagues would therefore accompany the traveller.

'The thirty thousand dollars,' as Christian David explained with a 'chairman's' aplomb, 'will be paid here to a foreign exchange office, the Pereira, which has a branch in New York. They will give you a cheque which will be guaranteed on your arrival and which you will give to Louis' lawyer.'

One week later Rao, together with Grosby and a new Argentinian lawyer – whom we shall call Alfonso – appeared before the Judge of the Southern District of New York and obtained the release in bail of the accused Louis Bonsignour. He hugged Grosby effusively, and the two friends then went to Susan's apartment in Sutton Place, where Louis was to stay until appearing before the court.

The next day Jack, Alfonso and Louis met to discuss the future. The Frenchman renewed his promise to enable his faithful friend to earn considerable sums of money without risk. The Argentinian lawyer informed him of the measures taken to allow him to leave the United States. Louis broke in, 'I promised Paul Rao that I'd be at the hearing. He feels that the evidence obtained by the customs and BNDD is insufficient to secure a conviction. Tell my friends down there that everything is fine, and to hold out.'

The lawyer went off again the next day. During the following weeks, Louis apparently concentrated on exploiting his newfound freedom. He went out with Susan and Jack's girl-friend;

they were to be seen in fashionable restaurants and night-clubs. Then one evening, arriving in Sutton Place, Grosby found Susan both furious and distressed. She had just discovered a letter from her lover telling her that he had left the country.

14

Meetings in Madrid

Within the space of a few weeks the Royal Bus, in Madrid, had become the fashionable night-club for those traffickers who were going through or meeting one another in Spain. Among its occasional French clientèle was a 'quiet man' of the trade who had kept a very low profile during the previous years. This was Ange Simonpieri, and the last affair in which he had been incriminated dated right back to 1958. Then he had been dispatching modest consignments of heroin to the United States via Brussels, and had enjoyed the good opinion of his Marseilles colleagues.

He was a heavy fifty-year-old with a coarse face and a weak heart. In 1960, like many of the men who were later to make a career in clandestine trafficking, he was mobilised by the special services to fight the OAS in Algeria. The work he did for them ensured him a degree of immunity for several years and he was not convicted until September 1971.

Algeria gained independence. Simonpieri came back to France and settled at Marsangy in the Yonne, in a luxurious villa which he had bought through his mistress Noémie F, who also owned the bar My Sin in the sixteenth *arrondissement*. The 'Château', as it was known locally, very soon became the meeting-place of a number of mysterious men who arrived by car after nightfall, loading and unloading suitcases and disappearing before daybreak; comings and goings which did not seem greatly to worry the local police. But then, Simonpieri had become a local notable.

Towards the end of spring 1967 he turned up in the Royal Bus in Madrid, together with a middle-aged Swiss who had just emerged from a Swiss gaol; he called himself Robert Mori. He too had contacts in the Paris underworld – men who had come to prominence at the time of the Ben Barka affair.

One of Mori's friends was a compatriot whom he had known in prison, Willy Lambert, aged thirty-five. When Mori went into the heroin trade, he suggested to Lambert that he might enter the network as a runner. As soon as this was agreed, Mori telephoned Simonpieri, in Marsangy. Another Swiss, the banker André Hirsch – already being sued for fraudulent financial dealings – was part-backer of the affair.

At dusk one evening at the beginning of July, Mori and Lambert arrived in Marsangy. They slipped into the garden and went into a sort of cave which Simonpieri had equipped with a bar, electricity and a fireplace. There they took delivery of a consignment of four kilos of heroin. Lambert hid it in the car, crossed the Swiss frontier without difficulty and flew off the following day to Vancouver, with eight packets hidden in his clothing.

From Vancouver in Canada he went to Seattle in the US by road. There, on 18 July, he met Mori. He handed over the consignment and received the promised four thousand dollars, plus travelling expenses. He was not the network's only runner; Robert Mori just had the time to return to New York to meet a shirt-seller from Boulevard des Batignolles whose shop was used as an accommodation address and who was also bringing him a consignment of four kilos. Mori and Lambert met several days later in Geneva, then in Madrid, well satisfied with the success of their undertaking and determined to improve output in the course of future trips.

At the beginning of the summer of 1967, a mysterious blonde woman had made an appearance at the Royal Bus, and became a regular. She was eccentric and lively, and often sat with Ange Simonpieri and Robert Mori. All that was known about her apart from her name, Paulette Follai, was that she was a riding instructress at the Constantine Riding School.

It did not occur to anyone to connect this lively blonde with the slightly twisted nose – 'a tumble during a race at Chantilly' –

with Josette Bauer, the dusky brunette who had incited her husband to kill her father and who had been sentenced to eight years' imprisonment by the Geneva assize court in 1961.

Her photo had brightened the front pages of the newspapers on several occasions. The daughter of a Geneva industrialist, she had married the son of another such, the retiring and insipid Richard Bauer, by whom she was pregnant. Little Dominique was born in 1955 in a modest suburban villa. However, the young couple did not have to labour under the burden of poverty for too long. Bauer senior died, leaving his son twenty odd million Swiss francs.

Then they splashed out: parties, sports cars, fur coats, nothing was too good for the young woman as she led her dazed husband after her in a mad sarabande. He swallowed everything, even her lovers. He was subjugated, totally enslaved by her madness. The fortune was soon spent. But Josette refused to give up her waking dream.

It was then that the hideous plan was born. Old Mr Geisser was even richer than old Mr Bauer had been. If he were to die . . . On 8 November 1960 he was found lying on the steps of his villa, with eight stab wounds in his body. The weapon was lying near him, together with a rudimentary club made from a broom handle. The press referred to it as the 'Délices' murder, this being the name of the district where it had been committed. Josette and Richard moved into the villa. They offered a reward of a hundred and fifty thousand francs to anyone with information which might lead to the identification of the assassin. The dance began again almost immediately. The frightful pair travelled the world, staying in luxury hotels, with an airline pilot, Josette's acknowledged lover, in tow. While the Geneva police patiently pursued their enquiries, the young woman was carrying off the Coupe d'elégance Automobile at Juan-les-Pins.

Eighteen months had gone by since the death of Leo Geisser when police compared a broom with a sawn-off handle found in a cupboard in the villa with the club found near the corpse. Summoned before the examining magistrate, Richard admitted his crime and tried to exculpate Josette. He did not succed. In April 1960 he was sentenced to fifteen years in prison and Josette to eight.

She spent three years in a cell in a prison in Hindelbank, a model prisoner awaiting her conditional release. It was not forthcoming. She wounded herself deeply in the stomach and was admitted to the hospital in the canton of Berne. The newspapers claimed that she then embarked upon an epistolatory idyll with another noted prisoner, the tearaway Jaccoud. One Sunday in September 1964 in the chaos of visiting time, Josette mingled with a group of visitors and with them went out through the gates.

She managed to reach Paris without trouble. A surgeon remodelled her face. At Philippeville, in Algeria, she completed the transformation process by dying her hair. Gradually time brought out a new personality. She aroused new passions, in particular that of a Jewish doctor, but he was soon forced to leave the country. Once again the young woman was available for new adventures.

When she met Ange Simonpieri and Robert Mori, she knew nothing about their activities. During her chequered career she had learned the art of speedy character assessment and she suspected that the pair lived a shady life. But she was ready for anything.

When Robert Mori reappeared in the Royal Bus and introduced his friend Lambert, it was not love at first sight. But Josette and Willy were prepared to get on well enough to team up together and enjoy easily earned money.

At the beginning of August the trio went to Paris. Paulette had already used her false passport on several occasions to go and see her daughter Dominique who was being brought up in France. Once they were there, her friends took the train for Sens where they met a paunchy little red-headed man called Max Bernard, who brought them their four kilos of heroin from the Ali Baba's cavern at Marsangy.

Back in Paris, Lambert arranged the eight packets around Josette's waist with sticking plaster. That same day, 14 August, she took the plane for Boston where Mori had gone before her. She came back with forty thousand dollars, four thousand for her and ten thousand for Lambert, who gave sixteen thousand dollars to Bernard the following day, as his share in the two kilos which belonged to him.

On 31 August 1967 a small Italian steamer, the *Federico*, sailing towards the Caribbean, docked at Port Everglades, not far from Miami, in Florida. The passengers jostled down the gangway, laden with cameras and beach bags and went off along the quay to discover the New World. The weather was close and damp; the overworked customs men followed the file-past somewhat listlessly. At this time of year, tourists were the chief merchandise to land in this drowsy port.

Their gaze scarcely brightened when, amid the crowd of retired folk, they glimpsed the youthful outline of a blonde with a mini-skirt, a Twiggy haircut and long tanned legs who was making her way towards the taxi rank. Despite the heat, she was primly buttoned up in a white suit which seemed to hide abundant charms.

'Hotel Carillon, Miami,' she said to the driver.

When the car disappeared down the palm-edged avenue leading to Fort Lauderdale, a delayed passenger appeared on the deck and went towards the gangway. He was tall, young well groomed and sunburnt. He would have been eminently attractive had his back not been deformed by a hump. Perhaps the raincoat he wore had been donned to disguise this fact. He proceeded hesitantly, his hand trembling on the rail; a sympathetic customs man came forward to help him.

Suddenly the hunchback, who had come to a halt, seemed to get a second wind. He made a feint at the customs man and charged off, head lowered, towards the port entrance where he was met by a group of intrigued officials, swerved sharply and disappeared behind the depot. Such suspect behaviour was tailormade to set off a manhunt. The gates were closed; the hunchback was trapped.

A quarter of an hour later, he appeared at the entrance of the depot with a customs man on each arm. They took him to an office, where he showed them a Swiss passport bearing the name Willy Charles Lambert, born 29 September 1930 at Orbe; profession: salesman, address: 41 rue des Clochettes, Lausanne.

He made no objection to removing his jacket and then his shirt to reveal a rudimentary harness made from an old corset and holding eight packets. Each contained five hundred grams of heroin.

On the quay, a man moved away from the group of loiterers who had witnessed the arrest. He went off towards the gates, got into a taxi and was taken straight to the airport. He embarked on the first Eastern Airlines plane for New York; he was Robert Mori.

Ignorant of these events, Josette Bauer, the mini-skirted blonde, had arrived in Miami. She crossed the foyer of the Carillon and asked at reception for Robert Mori.

'There's no one of that name in this hotel,' said the receptionist after consulting the register.

Somewhat at a loss, the young woman walked up and down the foyer for a few minutes. This possibility had not been foreseen in the detailed instructions given her by her friends. The *Federico* was to set sail that same evening. Her experience of the trade was too brief to offer any solution. Since she had been employed, she had done only one trip, which had been uneventful. At last she made up her mind, went into a shop on the avenue and bought a travelling bag. Then she went to the lavatories in the Greyhound Bus Station and removed the three kilos which Lambert had arranged around her waist. She put the packages in the bag, which she then put in a luggage locker.

She went back to the hotel, asked for an envelope at reception, put the key of the locker in it and gave it to the receptionist, asking her to give it to Robert Mori when he arrived. She left the hotel, hailed a taxi and went back to Port Everglades, nostalgically eyeing through the porthole the images of the good life for which she still yearned.

During her absence, the customs men had searched the cabin occupied by Lambert on the *Federico*. They had discovered that he had shared it with another passenger, Paulette Follai, and had found fourteen hastily concealed packets of heroin.

So the ambitious couple had tried to introduce fourteen kilos of drugs into the United States. These had been handed over to Lambert by Max Bernard. Seven belonged to the Mori–Simonpieri team and seven to Bernard and his associates. Willy had then rejoined his girl-friend, who was waiting for him in a Cannes hotel. The next day they had embarked on the *Federico*.

Their cruise ended at Port Everglades. The customs men were waiting for her on her return to the ship, and Paulette Louise Follai, riding instructress, appeared the following day with her accomplice before a judge who fixed their bail at a hundred thousand dollars for Willy, ten thousand for his companion. But the enquiry continued. It was discovered that Paulette Follai had a false passport; her fingerprints were sent to Interpol in Paris but she had no record. Her true identity was revealed by the Geneva police two days later.

Josette did not give up the struggle. There was no other evidence against her except the fact that she had shared a cabin with Willy Lambert. The latter tried gallantly to clear her. She herself was thinking of the three kilos still hidden in the luggage locker at the Greyhound Bus Station. She mentioned it to her lawyer. He hired a private detective who was to go and claim the envelope at the Carillon Hotel, retrieve the travelling bag and scatter the contents in the ocean; or so he stated.

Josette Bauer appeared in court together with Willy Lambert, one autumn day in a room at the Miami law courts. On the advice of their lawyers, the two accused had pleaded guilty. Their revelations made it possible to identify and track down their accomplices in Europe. But they were insufficient to incriminate them.

The young woman was shivering. She was still wearing her mini-skirt and white jacket, which had become somewhat shapeless over the weeks. It was in this pathetic outfit that she heard the verdict: seven years for each of the accused. Her past had weighed heavily in the scales of justice.

Two years later, on 10 October 1969, she was to escape from Alderson Federal Prison in West Virginia, as easily as she had left the hospital in Berne on 13 September 1964.

15

The Horse-Dealer Sticks his Neck Out

Louis Bonsignour's misfortune was only a temporary setback for the 'bad lads' of Buenos Aires.

From the terrace of the Copacabana, Jack Grosby gazed at the lively groups of *cariocas* who were preparing for the Carnival along the sea front. Beside him, Louis Bonsignour and Susan, stretched out on deckchairs, savoured the sea, the sun, a well-whipped coco-fizz and . . . freedom. Grosby had left New York two months previously, for the Christmas festivities which he had spent *en famille* in Buenos Aires. Thanks to his friends in the restaurant El Sol, he had met Louis, who was about to leave for Brazil and had promised to join him there. Grosby already had some idea of the sort of propositions that his grateful friend was going to put to him. After lengthy consideration, he had decided to accept a share in the gold-mine that the South American network represented; on condition that he did not have to run too many risks.

'The thing is,' Louis said to him, 'I need someone in New York whom I can trust. My compatriots can't stay there too long without the danger of being tracked down. You've proved your reliability. Your horse business is the perfect cover.'

'It takes up a lot of my time and doesn't involve any risks.'

'With me there won't be any risks either. In exchange for a few hours' work each month you can earn tens of thousands of dollars. You don't even need to handle the goods, if you're well organised. All I ask you to do is to find a buyer. We'll discuss the price later.'

'And if I don't find any clients?'

'We'll put you on the trail. It's not difficult, and there's no urgency. Go to New York; I'll go back to Europe to organise the suppliers. When I'm ready, I'll let you know.'

Before they parted Louis handed Jack a wad of hundred-dollar notes to cover the expenses of the various trips he had already made as well as the first outgoings.

After two months' absence, Grosby was pleased to see the skyscrapers and the uncaring crowds again, to feel the wind howling down the avenues. Over the years New York had come to feel more reassuring for him than the combination of brazen wealth and sordid poverty that characterised the tropics. But now he was aware of a new sensation, that indefinable sense of fear which dogs those who have decided to live beyond the law.

He was still undecided when he arrived at the comfortable apartment where he had experienced all the pleasures that a man without principles or conscience can indulge in. But boredom and old age were so near at hand, ready to pounce if he did not react. His association with Louis would help him to shake off the torpor that was creeping over him; to help him experience again some of the heady excitement of youth.

The very next day, a taxi dropped on the corner of Broadway and 136th Street. He threaded his way among the rows of second-hand cars towards the prefabricated building which rose above them. He went up the stairs, and at the top he encountered the imposing bulk of Luis Stepenberg. The two friends shut themselves in the office and Jack explained his problem.

'Look no further,' said Stepenberg after a moment's thought. 'I know quite a few people who are interested in junk. If you want, I'll be your client. It'll be less risky for you and we'll both make money.'

They did not go into details, since they did not know the quantities they would be dealing with nor how often deals would take place, nor indeed the price their suppliers would ask.

'The first problem,' concluded Stepenberg, who seemed well acquainted with these matters, 'is to find someone to transport the stuff. That way, even if you're watched, no one will ever be able to prove anything.'

This someone was employed two days later. He was called Daniel Metnik and Jack had known him for a long time. He was no genius but he was prepared to transport suitcases anywhere, without worrying about what was in them, provided he was well paid. All that now remained was to inform Louis Bonsignour of the development of their plan, and to tell that the car-dealer was willing to buy any quantity of heroin at ten thousand dollars a kilo, and also prepared to settle within twenty-four hours.

In reality – as Jack was to learn later – his friend had been involved in trafficking for some time. He had a small shop near a site with used cars; in this shop an Argentinian, Fernandez, whom Grosby had known in Puerto Rico, sold tobacco, cigars and sweets. He was helped by another Argentinian, Eduardo Poeta, a recent arrival. Fernandez received mysterious parcels in the shop, which he promptly delivered to no less mysterious recipients.

A letter addressed to Jack Israel arrived in Stepenberg's New York office. It was sent from Buenos Aires and signed 'Yoyo'. It requested Grosby to go to Barcelona in a few days' time. He would be expected at the Hotel Presidente.

At the beginning of March, Jack and Daniel Metnik were seated at a café terrace on las Ramblas in Barcelona together with Louis Bonsignour. 'Everything is ready for delivery.' He was evasive about the way the drugs would be dispatched. His runner was to make contact with Jack as soon as he arrived in New York. The matter of price was also approached and Louis proved amenable.

'Basing myself on the going rate for the merchandise in Marseilles, I'll sell it, as delivered to New York, at between eight and eight and a half thousand dollars the kilo. What your client proposes is no concern of mine. You found him. You'll also pay Daniel Metnik. Naturally, if your client agrees, we could send larger quantities: a couple of hundred kilos. By boat.'

'My client will almost certainly agree,' answered Grosby. 'But a hundred kilos is too much for me. For the moment, six to ten kilos per consignment is more my line. Any more than that, and I'd have to set up a whole organisation.'

Agreement was reached on this basis. Daniel Metnik arrived in the United States while Grosby extended his stay until 7 March. Then he flew off to Paris where he spent three days at the races before returning to the US to await the first delivery.

A week later, he received a letter from Bonsignour. 'My friend Bille has to go to New York about 22 March. He would be pleased to meet you at the bar of the Hotel Manhattan at midday, any day you like.' In the envelope, he found half a hundred peseta note. The courier would produce the other half.

On the 23rd, Grosby went up Eighth Avenue, entered the hotel, crossed the foyer and climbed the few steps leading to the bar. He was looking around the room when he felt a hand on his shoulder. Its owner was a fifty-year-old whose slightly vulgar air of a successful horse-dealer was toned down by an over-careful elegance.

'I'm Bille,' he said.

He produced his half note and immediately explained that he had a six-kilo consignment he wanted to get rid of. He wanted to leave again as soon as he had the money. Grosby telephoned Stepenberg who gave his agreement.

Two hours later, the Argentinian stopped in front of the Commodore Hotel at the wheel of a hired car. Bille, a suitcase in his hand, got into the front seat. As they were going up Park Avenue he suggested another meeting the following day, at the Manhattan. He got out a few streets further on. Grosby continued towards Stepenberg's office.

After putting the suitcase in the boot of one of the second-hand cars which his friend had pointed out to him, he went home. The next day, during the afternoon, he gave Bille the fifty-one thousand dollars which Stepenberg had brought him. That same evening, the courier flew off to Switzerland.

This operation earned the new trafficker nine thousand dollars. A year had passed since the day he promised Susan to help Bonsignour escape from prison. His devotion was beginning to bring in the dividend he had hoped for.

16

Speculations of a Swiss Banker

During February 1968, a prisoner from a Federal American gaol asked to see the governor; he had something to tell him. Among his co-prisoners were several drug traffickers.

The informer had overheard one of his co-prisoners telling his cell-mate that if, after his release, he ever wanted considerable quantities of heroin, all he needed to do was to go to Geneva and telephone the number he then gave him. He was to ask for Louis, André or Léon.

The spy had noted the number. When notified, the Swiss police replied a few days later that it corresponded to Mori's telephone line, which was being used in his absence by three people: Louis Brique, André Hirsch and Léon Rossignelli. A parallel enquiry revealed that they were in constant contact with two other individuals: Jean-Louis Cevolli and Rolf Small. The latter's real name was known only later: it was Ange Simonpieri.

The ideal solution for the police would be to send the trio an undercover agent who would pretend to be from the Mafia. But, in the meantime, Mori had been released on bail from the Florida prison and had flown to Geneva, stealing a march on them.

He immediately gathered his friends together to inform them of a new plan he had worked out: to send heroin to the US using a method that had been developed during the previous few years for the smuggling of watches. The technique was simple; it involved TWA planes arriving from Europe in the US, landing at New York or Washington. Passengers and aircraft went through customs control. Then, with a new crew, the plane would carry on into the interior, landing at cities where the customs men had no reason to intervene.

It was therefore sufficient to hide the merchandise so that it would avoid the preliminary searches. During the flight, a passenger who came on board had plenty of time to retrieve the consignment without arousing suspicions, particularly if it was concealed behind the laminated wall of the toilets.

Hirsch was a shrewd businessman. He immediately saw the plan's potentialities. He had customers. At the beginning of the fifties he had taken part in the smuggling of aircraft destined for the new state of Israel. He was arrested for gold smuggling and prosecuted for infringing the laws on pharmaceutical products. His record required him to act with some circumspection. His bank, the Mercantile SA, had been adjudged fraudulently bankrupt in 1962 with liabilities of a million Swiss francs. He had then spent three years in Fresnes for false pretences and fraudulent misuse of funds.

While the Swiss and their Marseilles associate, Ange Simonpieri, were working out future plans, the confidences exchanged in the Federal gaol and picked up by the informer, bore immediate fruit. During a trip to the US at the end of April, Bille was apprehended at Kennedy Airport. Luckily for him, he had arrived without his usual consignment of heroin. The Narcotics Bureau released him for lack of evidence.

He decided that in the future he would devote himself entirely to the smuggling of currency; to replace him and to get the consignments of heroin to Grosby on arrival, he engaged someone called 'Victor', whose real name was Willy Wouters. The new recruit did not look very prepossessing, but in this instance his insignificance was a point in his favour: there was less danger of his being noticed. He was a Belgian, born in Antwerp fifty-four years before, and had spent the last few years in Bellegarde, where he had been a chef in a hotel. After the death of the girl-friend with whom he lived, he went to Switzerland where he became an interpreter – he spoke several languages – in a travel agency. His English was particularly good, having been refined at the American PX Store in Fontainebleau during the fifties.

The trouble in which Bille had been involved forced his associates to modify their programme and to put off the next consignment. 'During May,' Grosby said later, 'Bille and I had exchanged several letters. He asked me to wait, and said that arrangements had been made for another consignment. At last, in a final letter, he asked me to join him in Switzerland.'

So Grosby flew to Switzerland to meet Bille.

In the evening he went to a bar in the city with his host. Willy Wouters was waiting for them. Together they were to work out the details of their future collaboration.

'For business purposes,' the Belgian explained, 'I shall be Victor and you will be Kennedy. I'll take your address and phone number and I'll call you when I arrive.'

Grosby was to wait until the end of the month for news of his correspondent. On 26 June, as he was beginning to despair, the phone rang in his apartment on 72nd Street.

'Hallo, Kennedy? Victor here. I'm at the Belmont Plaza.'

'I'll be there in an hour.'

Grosby called Stepenberg, then Metnik. An appointment was made with Stepenberg for ten o'clock that evening. As soon as Metnik appeared, he and Grosby went by car to the Belmont. They stopped in front of the hotel entrance. Victor appeared and got into the car.

'The goods are at the Shelton,' he said. 'I couldn't get a room at the Belmont.'

A quarter of an hour later, in the hotel foyer, he handed them a suitcase.

'I'm expecting a new delivery in three or four days. Ask your client if that's all right with him. Give me the answer tomorrow, here, and bring the money.'

At ten in the evening, Grosby and Metnik were parked in front of a white-painted hamburger stand, at the corner of the car-park where Stepenberg's second-hand cars were on show. Jack went up to Luis' office, leaving Daniel at the wheel.

'I'm going to introduce you to my client,' said Luis. 'He'll be here any minute. I haven't time to deal with this matter, but

I've got some news for you. I'll pay you eleven thousand dollars a kilo instead of ten.'

Their visitor appeared at eleven. Stepenberg introduced him to Grosby as Bruno. He was a strapping, sinewy fellow, wearing casual trousers and a gaudy shirt, whose real name was Jimmy Christian.

'I wanted to see you,' he said to Jack, 'because I don't want anyone else involved. You deliver the goods direct to me and I'll give you the money. There are no cash problems. Luis will look after the book-keeping.'

Jack Grosby was soon to have every reason to congratulate himself on his patience. After a year of travelling in Brazil, the Argentine, France and Switzerland, the mirage of the gold-mine which several deliveries of white powder had already conjured up, began to assume solid form in the shape of an almost uninterrupted flow of dollars. At the end of June he received another telephone call from Willy Wouters:

'Hallo, Kennedy? Victor here. I'm back.'

Another rendezvous at the Belmont. This time, Victor delivered six kilos for which Stepenberg was paid seventy-two thousand dollars. For Grosby they represented a net profit of thirteen thousand dollars and for Daniel Metnik – who had transported the goods from the Belmont to Jimmy Christian's – a commission of eighteen hundred dollars.

Six more kilos arrived in the same way on 7 July, and six more on 11 July. On the 15th, Grosby gave Willy Wouters a hundred and two thousand dollars in his room at the Belmont Plaza. On the 18th, Wouters reappeared with ten more kilos, then with twelve on the 21st.

In fact delivery and payment did not always proceed so smoothly. The chief problem was still the negotiation of the numerous small notes that Christian handed over at each settlement. At first Grosby tried to mobilise all the available Argentinians, sending them from bank to bank, but the avalanche of banknotes was too great for so homespun a technique.

Grosby therefore set out to find a money changer. He had in

mind a friend of Bonsignour, known as Chino, but whose real name was Domingo Padrone. His headquarters was a bar on the corner of 71st Street and Columbus Avenue, Victor's Bar. Chino was aged about forty and wore thick spectacles. 'I asked him if he could negotiate small banknotes for large ones. He said he could. I offered him a two per cent commission and he accepted. He noted down on a Victor's menu a phone number where I could always reach him.

They met a dozen times, sometimes at Victor's, sometimes in the lobbies of the Franconia or Ruxeon. Each time, Chino went off with about twenty thousand dollars in wrapping paper and reappeared an hour later with wads of perfect dollar bills.

Naturally Chino had his suspicions about the type of trafficking his client was engaging in and, on 11 June, the subject was cautiously broached. Despite the considerable sums he had amassed without much effort, Grosby could not help feeling that Stepenberg was getting the lion's share, without even leaving his office. Like all traffickers, he told himself that he could find more generous clients.

'If you need any junk,' he finally said to Chino on 11 July, 'I can get the stuff at thirteen thousand five hundred dollars a kilo.'

The money changer did not say no. The next day, he said he was willing to take two kilos. On the 15th, the two men met in the bar of the Franconia, then joined Metnik who was waiting in the lobby with the two kilos taken from the last consignment. The next day, Chino handed over twenty-seven thousand dollars. Grosby had thus effortlessly earned eight thousand dollars unbeknown to his partners, and this was a vein he intended to exploit.

17

TWA Flight 709

Still, Grosby's activities were nothing compared to the very full timetable of his supplier Willy Wouters. Since his arrival on 25 June, the Belgian had spent most of his time flying over the United States, from New York to St Louis or Denver, from Washington to San Francisco or Chicago, on TWA planes arriving from Europe and continuing their flights inland.

The goods – packets of heroin packed side by side into stockings in a long string – were concealed shortly after take-off in the lavatories by a courier who joined the plane either at Geneva, Zurich or Frankfurt. Carefully concealed behind plastic panels, they went unobserved by stewards and hostesses. As soon as the plane landed on the runway of the first American airport, the courier would follow the crowd and undergo customs checks without the slightest danger. All he had to do, after getting his commission, was to return to Europe, sometimes with a consignment of dollars he had been given.

In New York, Wouters, whose job was to retrieve the goods, had only to board the plane as it continued its journey across country. During the flight he would go to the lavatory, retrieve the string of packets and hide it under his clothes before putting it away in his attaché case. At the following stop, he would change planes to go back to New York, where he would inform Grosby of the successful outcome of the operation.

It was an exhausting process, which he could not carry out alone for long. For this reason his Geneva employees sent him an assistant, a young Frenchman of about thirty, Jean-Marc Montoya. He had his own client, but when circumstances required it, the parcels of the one could be delivered to the client of the other.

Wouters was concerned above all with international flights 709 and 711, which meant two to four deliveries a week. Bearing in mind that retrieval often took him to the shores of the Pacific, it is easy to grasp that he rarely slept in his own bed. Sometimes, the two 'retrievers' made a trip together, pretending not to know one another. The one who had retrieved the goods discreetly handed the precious parcel over to his colleague.

It also happened that one or the other joined the TWA flight at one of its American ports of call, so that their presence would not be too obvious at Kennedy Airport in New York or Dulles in Washington. On 15 June, bad weather prevented them from getting their hands on a consignment of twelve kilos. At New York, at the moment of embarkation for St Louis – where they were intending to take flight 765, whose two lavatory cabins each contained six kilos of heroin – their plane's departure was delayed by an hour.

The TWA plane did not wait for them and continued its route. Its flight plan allowed it to go several times around the world with its clandestine cargo.

Daniel R had been an employee at Washington airport in the TWA cleaning department for ten years. He was a conscientious worker and never felt any desire for the blue yonder on entering the passenger cabins of the airliners arriving from Europe. He would go round them, brushing, wiping and rubbing upholstery, plastic panels and curtains. He emptied out the plastic pockets on the seat-backs which passengers always tended to use as ashtrays.

On the morning of 26 July he was told to give the Boeing, flight 709, which had just arrived from London, a quick going over, as it was to set off again for St Louis and San Francisco. Entering the lavatories, he noticed a piece of string sticking out of the paper towel disposal bin. When he pulled it, he discovered a series of plastic bags stuffed into a nylon stocking.

He showed his discovery to his colleagues, who informed the foreman. The Narcotics Bureau agent on duty at the airport was notified. A pinprick in a bag, and a pinch of powder on the tongue provided speedier information than a laboratory analysis. He was promptly joined by customs agent George Festa.

'One thing is for sure,' Festa said, 'and that is that they won't have given up on this junk. Someone is going to get on this plane and retrieve it. We mustn't arouse any suspicions.'

Hastily, and in the traditional fashion, they emptied all the bags except one and replaced the heroin by Epsom salts. They put the stocking back where Daniel R had found it and plunged the modest employee into a state of delighted confusion with hopes of a generous reward. Loud-speakers invited the passengers to board the plane. Festa decided to accompany the cargo while his colleague from the 'narcs' informed their respective bosses.

The customs man took a seat near the lavatories and a few moments later the plane took off. After half an hour the shuttling of passengers between seat and lavatories began. As soon as one came out, Festa leapt up to check if the packets were still in place, avoiding the hostess's increasingly embarrassed gaze.

At St Louis, the nylon chaplet was still in its hiding place. A few minutes before arrival at Denver a passenger entered the lavatory with a small travelling bag in his hand. As soon as he came out Festa checked that this was indeed his quarry and kept his eyes glued to him.

This passenger was Willy Wouters. Festa still did not realise his luck. The man he was watching was not alone. Montoya was on the trip too. Before San Francisco he was to retrieve another six kilos concealed in another hiding place. Wouters had only to hand over his parcel to him for Festa to return empty-handed.

At Denver Wouters left the plane with the customs man on his heels. He went straight to put his bag in a luggage locker. He pocketed the key and sauntered off around the airport hall, under the discreet surveillance of several police, customs and 'narcs' men notified by Washington. One of them was posted in front of the luggage lockers, in case the traveller should manage to slip the key into an accomplice's pocket.

Then Wouters went to the booking office and bought a ticket for United Airlines flight 178, back to New York. Festa and two of his colleagues boarded the plane behind him. On 27 July, at six in the morning, a positive delegation was waiting at the bottom of the gangway. Wouters was immediately swept into a car – like a VIP on an official visit – and taken to the customs offices. During the journey there he listened, shattered, to a litany of his remaining rights: he could refuse to talk; what he said could be taken down in evidence against him; and he could request the presence of a lawyer.

The small Belgian with the hazel eyes realised that his situation was extremely awkward. He had been caught red-handed and his only hope was to co-operate with the police.

'I don't know much,' he admitted. 'I only know the person who employed me at Geneva – he's called M Robert – the name of my buyer – Jack Grosby and the name of the fellow who works with me – Jean-Marc Montoya. He should be arriving from San Francisco with six kilos of heroin. He usually stays at the Lexington or the Roger Smith.'

Policemen and customs officers seemed satisfied with his initial information. They accompanied Wouters in a customs office car to the Belmont Plaza and settled into his room with him. A rapid search yielded, not drugs, but a wad of fourteen thousand dollar bills.

'That was to pay the couriers,' explained Wouters.

Two hours later, the telephone rang. It was Montoya, who had just arrived from San Francisco. The journey had been uneventful. This time he was staying at the Berkley.

Following his gaolers' instructions to the letter, Wouters replied, 'We'd better not wander around with the goods during the day. Call me this evening at eight and we'll arrange a meeting.'

In the afternoon the hapless Wouters was taken from the customs department to the law courts. He answered hundreds of questions; he signed statements and passively underwent all the formalities of legal identification: personal details, photographs, fingerprints, etc. At seven in the evening he was back in the street, alone but under surveillance from a distance. He went back to his hotel. Two customs men were in his room.

At eight the telephone rang again. Wouters asked Montoya to join him at the Belmont drugstore where several policemen were at the ready and watching the exits. Half an hour later, the Frenchman appeared, a leather money bag in his hand. He sat down opposite his companion; they exchanged a few words. Then Wouters stood up, picked up the money bag and went off. As soon as he had disappeared into the foyer, Montoya too went off, followed by the two policemen.

Wouters spent a restless night; he gazed enviously through the half-light at the two policemen, one sprawled on the couch, the other in an armchair, and deeply asleep. At eight the phone rang. It was a call from Switzerland.

'Hallo, Victor? Robert here . . . everything okay? When you get the money, don't give it to anyone. I'll call you back with instructions. Have you got a pencil?'

He listed the planes in whose lavatories further parcels of heroin would be concealed during the following weeks. The receiver pressed against his ear, one of the policemen took notes along with Wouters.

A little later, another call. Montoya, all unsuspecting, informed his colleague that he had tracked down the TWA plane that had been flying around the world for nearly a fortnight with the two parcels of six kilos which they had not managed to retrieve. It was to leave Kennedy Airport in two hours for San Francisco.

'I'll just be able to get it. I'll telephone you when I get back.'

Promptly informed, the airport customs men proceeded to a rapid search of the toilets on the plane and discovered the nylon stockings containing the plastic bags. With one exception, they were emptied of their contents and filled with flour, then put back into their hiding places.

The operation was completed by the time Montoya emerged from his taxi and went to buy a ticket for San Francisco. He then sat down amid the other waiting passengers.

But suddenly a voice announced that that plane was to go to Rome and that another aircraft would be made available to San

Francisco passengers: a plot concocted by the customs men with the co-operation of the TWA administration.

The policemen who were tailing Montoya saw him freeze, desperately gather his wits, then rush towards the relevant official.

'I've left my glasses on the plane,' he explained. 'I absolutely must get them. I'm lost without them.'

The employee nodded wisely and went along with him. In the cabin, Montoya pretended to search feverishly for his glasses, then gave up. He then asked for permission to use the lavatory and bolted the door behind him. Emerging a few minutes later, he uttered thanks, apologies and bounded off towards the exit.

In the bus taking him to Manhattan, two customs men sat down beside him and told him he was under arrest. A rapid search produced eleven and a half kilos of flour and five hundred grams of heroin, rolled around his torso.

While all this was going on, in the room at the Belmont Plaza the third act of the operation had already begun. Wouters dialled the number Grosby had given him. Grosby had returned from Switzerland the previous day. When Wouters told him that he had another parcel, he suggested meeting Metnik in front of the hotel half an hour later. As the faithful errand-boy stopped his car at the kerb, Wouters plunged into it with his suitcase, promptly followed by two customs men. Metnik defended himself spiritedly, claimed he was being tricked, that he had never set eyes on his passenger before in his life. But he could not explain away the fifteen thousand dollars which were later found in his room.

A raid on Grosby's apartment – whose address the police had obtained from the telephone company – presented them with an unexpected situation. The trafficker, abandoning sordid business affairs for a while, had preferred to go off to bed, where two charming young ladies awaited him. He surrendered gracefully.

18

Argentinians in New York

Eduardo Poeta was perfectly happy spending his days in the small confectioner's at 3379 Broadway. He had friendly relations with his clients and asked no more of life. Sometimes he would think a little regretfully of the wife and children he had left in Buenos Aires two years ago. The winding up of the various businesses in which he had been involved – a taxi company, second-hand cars, a carriers' firm – had left him only two thousand dollars.

He had arrived in New York at the beginning of 1967 and had worked as carpenter in the studios of a film company called Melbee Pictures. There he had met a certain Ricardo Fernandez, then running the confectioner's, and had helped him, out of working hours. One day, Stepenberg, the owner of the shop, sent a message asking him to come and see him.

'Fernandez has to go back to Argentina,' he had explained. 'Would you like to take over the shop? We'll be partners. No need to sign any papers, I'll look after the accounts.'

During the following months, Poeta had divided his time between the confectioner's and his small apartment on 137th Street, a few minutes' away.

Towards the end of July, a storm shattered his fragile universe. As he was making supper, Stepenberg appeared in the small apartment and flopped down on the sofa.

'I've come to live with you. I'll sleep on this sofa. Jacobo has problems and I don't want anyone coming to my place to ask questions.'

An hour later, leafing through the *New York Times*, Poeta learned the nature of Jack Grosby's problems and the activities he was involved in. 'I asked Luis if he was involved too, and he said yes. He added that if I wanted to get involved in drugs, he could help me. I asked him if it was dangerous. He said no, and anyhow he was going to see to it that Grosby got out of prison. I said I agreed.'

A few days later, a man came into the shop. Stepenberg, who had arrived a few minutes earlier, introduced him to Poeta as Bruno. It was Jimmy Christian.

'I have complete faith in Eduardo,' Stepenberg stated. 'From now on it will be he who delivers the parcels to you and brings me back the money. You'll see. It will all be fine.'

Stepenberg took a selfish interest in his friend's fate. Grosby did not seem to have mentioned his name to the investigators during the questioning which took place at the beginning of August. 'All I said at that point,' he admitted later, 'was purely to gain time, because I was counting on being released on bail.'

Bail was fixed at a hundred thousand dollars, a very considerable sum but not one that could break Jack's Swiss bank account. Stepenberg engaged Paul Rao, who had defended Bonsignour the previous year, to defend his friend and partner. The lawyer's first concern was to reduce the bail; gradually it was whittled down to fifty thousand.

For their part, the Swiss employers of Wouters and Montoya – Hirsch, Brique and Simonpieri – had decided not to pay out the bail demanded. After all, they were only minor figures. Still, they employed the lawyer Ralph Nigrone to advise them and sent him an advance of twenty thousand dollars as a retainer.

Meanwhile, the customs men at Kennedy Airport in New York and Dulles in Washington – following the details on the list telephoned by Mori to Wouters after the latter's arrest – retrieved half a dozen strings of six kilos of heroin from the lavatories of TWA flights from Europe.

Robert Mori was the one Swiss member of the organisation against whom the American authorities had enough evidence to be able to ask for extradition. Arrested by the Swiss police, Mori was to set off for prison in America the following month. (His associates paid out the requisite bail.)

The information assembled during the previous months enabled the agents of the Narcotics Bureau and the customs to pursue their enquiries with the help of their colleagues in Europe. Agents Edward Coyne and Albert Seeley, who had questioned Wouters, Grosby and Montoya, now started to follow a new trail, the route taken to Switzerland by the money paid in New York, so as to establish the links between Mori, Brique, Hirsch and Simonpieri. Several months of perseverence revealed the ramifications of an enterprise of Byzantine complexity which indicated that bankrupt ex-banker Hirsch had lost nothing of his financial touch.

On 25 August, Jack Grosby came out of prison and returned home. It was Stepenberg who had advanced the fifty thousand dollars the judge had asked for. The lawyer Rao had already succeeded in getting his mistress (Nelly A, who had been found in his bed the day of his arrest) released for lack of evidence.

A few days later, Grosby and Stepenberg met in Eduardo Poeta's apartment.

The used-car salesman had brought his friend a passport which would enable him to leave the US without problems. The Argentinian hesitated. He was ready to face justice and remained convinced that he could not be convicted on Wouter's statements alone.

'Be careful,' Luis warned him. 'You've been watched ever since you took up the cudgels for Bonsignour. They know everything about your comings and goings. For all you know, on the day they could come up with new evidence of which you know nothing.

They've also notified the Swiss police. If they get their hands on your friend Bille, you're done for.'

What Grosby did not know was that his partner's insistence was not merely friendly concern. Stepenberg was thinking of the future; he needed to keep in touch with his French and South American contacts.

At the beginning of September, therefore, Jack Grosby flew to Rio de Janeiro on an Aerolineas Argentinas plane. A week later, he went to Montevideo for two or three days. Then he went to Buenos Aires. On his arrival he got rid of his false passport and applied for another from the Argentinian police, a legal one this time in his real name, which he had dropped several years earlier: Jacob Grodnitzky. Then he went to El Sol where he received a hero's welcome. He now belonged to the bail-jumpers' élite and had become a fully fledged member of the South American network. Auguste Ricord embraced him warmly and poured him a pastis; Louis Bonsignour loooked on tenderly.

He went back during the next few days and saw Bonsignour again, together with Christian David and François Chiappe, both eager to launch new schemes. He managed to convince them that his absence from New York would not jeopardise future deliveries, as his friend Stepenberg was ready to take over when necessary. The used-car salesman was kept up to date with these daily negotiations. The post from the Argentine was addressed to him at Poeta's. Reassured by the silence of the police, he slept less and less frequently at his employee's and began to take up his business once again.

One evening he informed his host that the heroin deliveries were to begin again shortly. The parcels would be brought to him by a man wearing a wig and calling himself 'Peluquita'. All Poeta would have to do was to give the parcels to Jimmy Christian.

'When he arrives, Peluquita will telephone you. He'll tell you that he has just come back form Buenos Aires, where he had been to see his mother. He'll make an appointment to meet you and you will go with a carton of Pall Mall under your arm so he can recognise you. He'll have one too.'

But in the end the plan was put off. Geneva and Buenos Aires had decided that a 'summit meeting' was necessary before launching the new network. 'Several days later,' Poeta remembered, 'Luis telephoned me from abroad to tell me to send him his suitcases with his personal belongings to an address in Switzerland. I did so that same day.'

This address was the Hotel President in Geneva, where Jack Grosby was already staying. He had been able to meet the new organisation's boss on several occasions. These meetings had taken place in André Hirsch's apartment. After Robert Mori's arrest and extradition to the US, the ex-banker had taken over the running of the enterprise, with Bille and Brique as partners.

19

Paella Marinara

André Hirsch had considered several plans. One of them was particularly dear to him, and had been inspired by one of his favourite books, *The Adventures of Tintin*, by Hergé, and in particular the story called *The crab with the golden claws*.

His idea was to send large quantities of tinned food to the US, including several tins – which could easily be spotted by an expert – containing heroin. For this, he would need the unwitting assistance of a respectable manufacturer; he would also have to set up a legitimate import company in New York, to be managed by one of his associates.

Although it did not appear in the Trade Register and had no trade name, the new company had at its disposal a capital sum which might have been envied by many more established enterprises. Hirsch was asking fifteen hundred dollars per kilo of drugs delivered on the deals he had already taken part in, plus twenty per cent of the profits. The customs men's current enquiries revealed that six hundred thousand dollars sent from the US had been paid into Hirsch's Swiss account in the Wideman Bank in the previous months.

The board of directors of Hirsch, Brique and Co consisted of half a dozen French and Swiss members: Daniel Vuille, known as Bille, aged thirty-nine, Gilbert Grandi, forty-eight, Marcel Glarner, fifty-seven, and Brique, who held the purse strings, did the investing and recruited the necessary personnel. Brique had employed a young man, Christian Hysohion, who spoke English, was highly personable and might make an excellent managing director.

On his arrival in Geneva, Stepenberg met Bille, Brique and

Hirsch. They met again on several occasions, to work out the final details of the deliveries, both of the South American network and of the network to be created. Hysohion was present at one of these business meetings. Stepenberg helped him to complete the administrative formalities for the future company: Panamanian Chemist and Food Products.

Before leaving Switzerland, Stepenberg took Grosby to the racecourse at Divonne, across the frontier, where they met Mario Deniz and his two henchmen, René Santamaria and Joannes Muñoz, (alias 'Peluquita') who was to sort out the problem of future deliveries to Eduardo Poeta with Stepenberg.

During these negotiations, Louis Brique met a former co-prisoner of Hirsch's from Fresnes. He was called Eugène Castaldi and had earned a certain notoriety for his activities in the OAS. Louis introduced himself as Pierre Dujardin and asked him to meet him in Geneva, where he explained the general outline of his plan.

'I need you to build up an export company in Spain, specialising in tinned goods and olive oil. You will buy them from manufacturers and send them to a firm in New York. Find out about the best brands available. What we're doing is smuggling certain goods into the United States.'

Two days later, the different roles having been allotted, the group dispersed. Stepenberg flew off for Buenos Aires, Grosby for Rio, Hysohion for New York and Castaldi for Malaga.

Enquiries about André Hirsch's circle revealed the existence of Christian Hysohion and his plan to go to the US. Region 17 of the Narcotics Bureau tracked down his request for a visa made to the American consulate in Paris. With the collaboration of the French Office, agents of the BNDD and the American customs established a list of his possible ports of call in the US. The collaboration of the two Federal departments enabled them to locate the headquarters of Panamanian Chemist and Food Products, recently registered with the customs.

The firm operated from the garage of a private house in the suburbs of New York, at Whitestone. Its manager was called

Charles D and he knew nothing about the schemes hatched by André Hirsch and Christian Hysohion. He was inadvertently acting as a screen for Hysohion by giving the enterprise a genuine commercial façade.

As the weeks went by, new investigations produced new information about the organisation of the trafficking. The investigations carried out in the US, France and Switzerland also soon led the Federal agents to request the assistance of the Spanish police.

The Ribas y hijos company, a family firm in Vigo, had long specialised in the manufacture of tinned foods based on fish and shellfish. It sold quality produce and its *paella marinara* was very popular in Spain. Its factory employed about sixty workers.

At the beginning of October 1968, a dapper visitor appeared at the Madrid office on via Ampara Usera.

'I represent a Panamanian company marketing foodstuffs and pharmaceutical products,' he announced, producing his accreditation papers from his briefcase. 'We are interested in selling your tinned foods in the US. Before concluding anything definite, I would like to order fairly considerable quantities of certain lines, to see how they are received by our American clients.'

After examining the specialities the firm suggested, the client, Eugène Castaldi, settled for the *paella marinara* and promptly ordered two hundred crates of twelve tins each. He wrote out a cheque, drawn on a Madrid bank, which would undoubtedly be honoured.

'I'll let you know when to deliver them. I'll send them off myself with any further orders.'

The crates were to be sent to 13 Calle Merlo, Malaga. The client would pay for transport. The firm's chairman, Don Juan Ribas, was naturally a little surprised by these commercial methods. It seemed odd to dispatch two thousand four hundred tins across Spain when it would have been so simple to load them straight from Vigo on to a cargo boat bound for New York. But the customer is always right, particularly if he has paid cash.

Ribas would have been even more surprised if he had been able to see the destination reached by the Vigo truck driver after a thousand-kilometre Odyssey: it was a sumptuous abode on the outskirts of Malaga with a swimming pool, luxuriant flower-beds, statues and greenhouses. A fortnight later, Eugène Castaldi informed his supplier that the merchandise had arrived in New York and that his American clients had found it delectable. Indeed, they anticipated devoting a considerable sum of money to the launching of *paella marinara* on the American market.

The manufacturer immediately sent his client the posters, photos and publicity material asked for, adding a hundred and twenty-five tins labelled but empty, intended – Castaldi stressed – to show the customers the quality of the packing and tinware. At about the same time, the Swiss police informed the Narcotics Bureau in Washington that André Hirsch had ordered a gadget for sealing tin lids, which was to be sent to Spain.

But Brique's team were already putting their plan into action, without waiting for Ribas y hijos to conclude negotiations. During October, one of the couriers had gone from Geneva to Barcelona via Paris. In his luggage he had a parcel of ten kilos. He had handed it to Brique in a bar of the hotel on las Ramblas, where he had made the acquaintance of Eugène Castaldi. A few days later, he delivered a second parcel to Castaldi in Madrid.

At the beginning of November, it was Gilbert Grandi, an associate of Hirsch and Brique, who took delivery of two suitcases containing thirty kilos of heroin, and passed them on to Castaldi, also in Madrid.

When the former member of the OAS had told the Ribas company that he had sent the crates of *paella marinara* to New York, he had not been entirely lying. A first consignment contained not the slightest trace of heroin and had proceeded to the States on board a German cargo ship, the *Kallopee*. It was intended to test the reactions of the customs administration and sound out American administrative procedures.

As all had gone smoothly, a first consignment of ten kilos of heroin followed. As the sealing machinery had not yet arrived, the packets were concealed in the cans of olive oil. They reached the Panamanian Chemist and Food Products firm safely, joining the now superflous crates of *paella marinara*.

Also at the beginning of November, Castaldi and Bonsignour had met at the Hotel Imperatriz in Malaga, to put the finishing touches to their enterprise, which was now getting into its stride. This seems to have been the moment when Castaldi was informed of the real nature of the traffic in which he had agreed to take part.

Auguste Ricord's nephew was soon to go to Paris, to look into other projects. But the French and American police had been kept abreast of his movements and his relations with André Hirsch. One of his accomplices in New York, Armando Gagliani, had also been identified through a phone call, noted at the Hotel Imperatriz. Despite the code name used, 'Lunardi', the police tracked down the recipient in the register of the Americana in New York. He had already been convicted several times for infringement of gaming regulations; he was known in the New York underworld and, furthermore, he was the owner of the house where Panamanian Foods had its premises. On 17 November Bonsignour was arrested, by chance, at the Col du Perthus in the Pyrenees, while on his way to Paris, and charged for his part in the oscilloscopes affair.

Behind the high wrought-iron grilles of his villa and beneath the alert gaze of a couple of Alsatians, the former OAS man spent his evenings filling empty tins with packets of three hundred grams of heroin, adding lead chippings to make the containers up to the weight indicated on the label. A layer of rice, peas and sausage ensured that the merchandise would stand up to superficial examination. Then all that had to be done was to put on the lids and seal them.

These tins were then distributed among the crates of genuine *paella marinara* – bearing a discreet mark to enable Hysohion to distinguish them – and the exotic load, a hundred odd crates, was entrusted to the mercies of the Fresco Shipping Company, a Spanish firm. Twenty-eight kilos of drugs went to sea on board the cargo boat *Ragunda*, one of the company's four vessels.

But entering New York harbour the *Ragunda* and her cargo were immobilised on board because of a potentially long-drawn-out dockers strike.

This mishap also prevented the customs men from getting the tins delivered to the Panamanian Foods and from laying hands on the recipients and their clients in a single haul.

20

A Novelist Finds Inspiration in Heroin

During the years 1965–73, the group of petty crooks, procurers, gangsters, burglars, swindlers and down-and-outs who turned to the heroin trade were a mediocre crowd but they included a few really picturesque personalities. Some were particularly vicious, others daring and some stood out by virtue of the greed which finally led to their downfall. What they all had in common was a total lack of moral sense, an astounding indifference to the harm their activities could cause to tens of thousands of human beings.

It is tempting, therefore, to make certain allowances for Edouard Rimbaud. He possessed one quality which was in short supply in the circles in which he had moved since spring 1968: imagination. He was born in Marseilles in 1920, had gone into the French Air Force in 1939 and had done a cadet course at the Cazaux air-base in the Gironde.

He did a stint as a police inspector in Marseilles until the German invasion of the free zone in November 1942, when he opted for the Resistance. 'I belonged to the Fer and Marco Polo networks and I worked for the BCRA . . . My activities earned me two citations in divisional dispatches, the *croix de guerre* and a letter of congratulation from the government. After the Liberation, I was reinstated in the police force.'

He began to arouse comment about seven years later, by which time he was running a bookshop at Salon-de-Provence. By now he had married, had two children and been divorced. In November 1951, he went to law, claiming that a crook had sold him false gold ingots on payment of a sum of ten million francs, his savings.

The enquiry revealed that this crook was a pure figment of his imagination. He himself had had the false ingots made out of copper, and the ten million francs had been misappropriated by him. They represented the proceeds of the sale to local councils – at a loss – of school books he had not yet paid the publishers for. The purpose of his scheme was to dodge this payment and avoid fraudulent bankruptcy.

This plan had been worked out with the thoroughness which was to distinguish his later operations. The most remarkable of these was set in the spa of Vichy and the coup he so daringly but carefully pulled off there in the summer of 1956 is still talked of; it casts an interesting light on his personality.

He appeared in the Auvergne with a self-styled Count Foucou d'Inès, whom he had met in les Baumettes, and a considerable number of cheque books corresponding to fictitious deposits. Foucou was accompanied by his wife, a former saleswoman at the Dames de France in Marseilles, who was to declare after his arrest that Edouard Rimbaud was her husband's evil genius.

Rumour spread rapidly through the district that the trio had come as an advance guard for a Swiss company, the 'Swift, Wesland Trading Company', to buy a chateau and estate with a view to starting a factory making detergent products based on maize. On the eve of 15 August, Foucou went to a notary and signed the official documents making him owner of the property of La Rapine and its livestock for the sum of seventy-five million old francs, as well as the chateau of Teillat, whose former owners had agreed to leave by the following day.

The aim of this first operation above all was to gain the trust of the Vichy tradespeople, taking advantage of the fact that 15 August (the feast of the Assumption) fell on a Thursday and that the banks would not be open until Monday. That same day, the Countess Foucou d'Inès and her secretary Roucas – Rimbaud – began their rounds. Beforehand, as was sometimes the custom, the secretary had asked for a rebate on the total of subsequent purchases in each shop, 'in cash', as he specified.

In this way they purchased rare books, five paintings including a Corot and a Daubigny, two Chinese vases, silverware, dinner services, leather luggage, gold cigarette lighters, coats, household appliances, typewriters and calculators, cameras and cine cameras. For his part, the Count bought an Aston Martin and a Citroen van, a diamond collar, two bracelets and a ring.

For two days there was a positive stream of delivery vehicles in the *cour d'honneur* of the chateau of Teillat, and the Count signed cheque after cheque. He sold a horse-dealer the estate's livestock, for which he was paid an instalment of two million 'in banknotes, because of the holiday'. As soon as Rimbaud finished collecting his rebates, the trio took to the road with the booty. The three accomplices were arrested by chance, a fortnight later, in a luxury villa in Antibes.

So Edouard Rimbaud put the finishing touches to his schemes in prison. He always prepared a carefully elaborated plot, issuing dud cheques, purchasing real estate or valuables, which were to be delivered to sumptuous premises which inspired confidence but which he left the next day. As soon as he was released, he put his plan into action. Each time he found victims and each time he was arrested but was undaunted by his repeated ill-luck. Indeed, he concentrated on perfecting his methods by learning from his mistakes.

So one spell in prison followed another, and the circle of his acquaintances widened. It was in prison that he met Jacques Douheret and Ange Lucarotti, who were to become stars in the drug business, and Jean D – a young man of good social position who had gone astray and whose brother was a prosperous industrialist – the future protagonist of the 'ski sticks affair'.

At the beginning of 1967, Edouard Rimbaud was once again at large. During his latest session inside he had done some hard thinking and had decided to change his life-style. He intended to devote himself to a career which had long appealed to him and where his imagination could be put to more fruitful use: that of writer. At the beginning of that spring, he went back to stay with his mother at Salon-de-Provence and got down to work.

A few months later, Gallimard accepted his manuscript and signed him in for the '*Série Noire*' series. *Comme à Gravelotte*, by Louis Salinas, appeared on the shelves at the beginning of 1968.

Encouraged by this first success and the glimpse it gave him of a better future, Edouard set to work on a new novel.

One day, he was visited by Jean Mariolle, whom he had known in La Santé, where he had been imprisoned for political reasons. Mariolle too had submitted a manuscript to Gallimard but it had been rejected: 'The plot works but the syntax leaves something to be desired.' one of the readers had commented.

'Rewrite it in your style,' suggested Mariolle. 'We'll work something out about payment. I just want to put my name on it to prove I'm earning an honest living.'

Rimbaud buckled to and, a few weeks later, sent the final version to Gallimard. It was to appear as *Les Louchetracs*. Jean Mariolle scrupulously sent his rewriter half his royalties.

During this same period, Nonce Lucarotti renewed acquaintance with Rimbaud through accomplices from the Atlanta penitentiary. 'I have a client who is prepared to buy some heroin, to be delivered to Canada, at eight thousand dollars the kilo. Find a supplier and let me know his rates.'

Rimbaud decided to drop his second novel for a while and to use his free time to look for a possible supplier.

He decided to turn to a respectable retired man, Félix Olivié, who had a villa in Lambesc and whom he had met in a bar in Salon. He suspected him of shadier contacts than his well-groomed exterior might imply. 'At the time,' as Rimbaud described him, 'he must have been about sixty-seven, tallish, slim and always well dressed with a lively turn of phrase. He was well connected in the underworld and knew all the big names.'

Ensconced in a deep leather armchair. Félix Olivié heard him out, stroking his chin thoughtfully.

'In Marseilles you find junk as easily as peppers,' he said. 'You say how many kilos you need; then they weigh it out and put it in your shopping bag. The difficult part is to unearth a client; and you tell me you've got one . . .'

The prudent Rimbaud had not given him the name of his contact in Atlanta, and the story of the dollars awaiting him in Montreal left his interlocutor somewhat sceptical.

'It's the first time I've ever heard of a client advancing you money to set up your little business. You're sure your friend isn't in cahoots with the Narcotics Bureau?'

The name Lucarotti finally slipped out, and Olivié relaxed a little. When Rimbaud came back from Montreal with his dollars, Olivié would find him the goods 'at under twenty thousand a kilo, a very decent price'. He even suggested taking a share himself.

'You'll need a courier. I think I know the very person. Come round to my place this evening, I'll introduce you.'

Rimbaud knew this candidate well. He was called Gilbert Bordure, short and fortyish, with a shock of black hair and a big nose. His father was a local tradesman but he himself was more drawn to the local petty criminals.

Towards the end of July 1967, everything was ready. Edouard went to Paris, where Félix telephoned him to inform him of Gilbert's arrival. He had clinched the deal for eight and a half thousand francs the kilo. Their courier was to hide it under his raincoat to go through the customs.

The final arrangements were made during a meeting in Avenue de la Grande Armée. The following evening, Rimbaud landed in Montreal and booked into the Laurentien.

The next day he went to Dorval Airport. The place was thick with tourists, all of whom seemed to be sailing through the teeming customs barrier with ease. Edouard recognised Bordure, who was holding a suitcase to which a customs man glued a piece of green paper. He followed him to the bus stop and boarded the bus behind him. During the journey he leant forward:

'Have you got the stuff?'

'In a minute,' murmured the courier.

Edouard was puzzled. His companion's raincoat did not seem to be hiding any tell-tale bulge. Could he have kept it in the suitcase, despite instructions? At the terminus, on the pavement, his curiosity was satisfied.

'On landing, I had the feeling some guys were following me. So I lost my nerve. I put the junk under a bench in the airport. I think I had a lucky escape.'

'That's marvellous! No one searched you at the exit. If what you're saying has an ounce of truth in it, it will be all over the papers tomorrow.'

Bordure looked increasingly uneasy.

'I can't be sure,' he mumbled. 'Someone could have pinched it.'

Rimbaud was sure that the little tough was lying to him, but he felt obliged to contain himself, out of respect for Olivié's recommendations. There was only one thing to do; to pass the news on to his buyer, Antonio Florès, in New York.

The Greyhound Bus journey from Montreal to Manhattan takes a whole day, but Rimbaud felt that the moment had come for economies.

Antonio Florès was a small swarthy Puerto Rican, with a round face and quick, nervous movements despite his corpulence, and a suspicious, glowering expression. He expostulated loudly in both Spanish and English, which did not help communication. Trussed up in a loud check suit, he flicked feverishly through the Canadian newspapers he had bought.

'If there turns out to be no mention of five kilos of heroin found at Dorval airport . . .'

'Don't waste your time,' said Rimbaud firmly. 'That little crook has done us. It's as clear as the nose on your face.'

Florès then suggested sending a Puerto Rican friend of his to Bordure, someone very reliable and discreet, who would slit his throat from ear to ear before he could say Jack Robinson. But he admitted this would not solve the problem. His oft-repeated refrain was, 'You need money and I need money.'

At last he came round to Edouard's suggestion; Edouard undertook to obtain his associates' agreement, though he suspected that Félix would be rather hard to manage. 'I promised him I'd get hold of five kilos of heroin on credit. He would come to Paris to get it himself. When he had sold it, he would keep the sixteen thousand dollars I owe him. I would buy in a larger quantity of heroin with what was left, which he would take over, and so on. . . .'

They fixed the price of the drug, as delivered in Paris, at six thousand dollars a kilo. Florès would thus pay two thousand less than in Montreal. Rimbaud would make four thousand per kilo just by going from Salon to Paris.

The Puerto Rican seemed convinced of the other man's good faith. He even went so far as to tell him confidentially of a long-cherished scheme of his, to establish a laboratory on the outskirts of New York for transforming raw morphine into heroin.

'He's double-crossed us, the little bastard,' was how Félix greeted Rimbaud on his arrival in Salon. Bordure, the unscrupulous courier, had been back for several days, but his explanations had not dispelled the doubts of the ex-gaolbird, who had known craftier swindlers during his long career.

When Edouard informed him of the agreement he had had to conclude with Florès in order to contain the damage. Olivié was shattered. The prospect of advancing five million old francs so as to reimburse the Puerto Rican offended his moral sense and thoroughly sickened him. He did acknowledge his responsibility for the failure of the operation. It was he who had involved Bordure; but five million! However, he promised to consider the matter.

The days passed. Each time he met Edouard, he greeted him with the same words, 'I haven't forgotten you.' Pressed to be more precise, he hedged desperately. 'He put up a smokescreen, he floundered, he rationalised,' as Rimbaud said later. 'You would have thought there was no more heroin on the face of the earth. All the chemists had gone to earth, the laboratories were lying idle, hung with cobwebs. As soon as he had to find the money from his own pocket, the stuff was unobtainable. We would have to wait until the police lost interest and calmed down, so that the chemists could re-emerge and start work again.'

In New York, stung by the legitimate urge to get back his money and earn some more besides, Antonio sent telegram after telegram.

'I'll find your junk for you. Ask your client when he can come,' Félix at last said to Rimbaud.

Two days later, he received a message from Antonio, sent from the George V in Paris where he was staying with friends.

Félix, who was still playing for time, panicked. The Puerto Rican must be made to wait. Edouard took the train for the capital; before he left, he attempted to hearten Olivié, who looked drawn and feverish.

'In your place, I'd watch out! The guy is a tricky customer. He's got his heavies. Don't forget he wanted to cut Gilbert's throat.'

With these ruffians breathing down his neck, Félix Olivié, with a dreadful sense of foreboding, was forced to set to work seriously. A few days later, he picked up Edouard in his BMW, drove him to Callas and asked him to wait in a bar, opposite the chateau. Half an hour later he came back with two kilos of heroin. 'That's all they had. I'll probably get another kilo this evening.'

It was better than nothing; at least it would keep the Puerto Ricans quiet for a bit; they seemed already to have wearied of Avignon. Antonio was clearly a little disappointed. On the off-chance, he asked Edouard if he could not buy some stolen jewellery from a fence. Then, after having changed several travellers' cheques in a bank, he went into a ladies' lingerie shop to buy the corsets in which the packets of heroin were to be concealed. Edouard decided not to follow him into the shop.

That same evening, since Olivié had not obtained the extra kilo, the four tourists, now in fine spirits, took the train for Paris. A few days later, Rimbaud was to receive a card informing him that the return journey had gone off smoothly.

21

The Frank Sinatra of the Côte d'Azur

Each time he came back to Marseilles after a tour of the cabarets and night-clubs of the Riviera, Geneva, Brussels or Montreal, the singer Edmond Taillet would greet his wife and son and then immediately go for a turn around his own city. Here at least he did not have to grovel for admiration. The *Petit Méridional* and the *Provençal* had recounted his triumphs with all their customary lyricism.

At the Versailles or at Annabel's, he could proclaim himself as the French Frank Sinatra without arousing the slightest doubtful titter. His ego thus mildly boosted, he could await a somewhat tardy recognition with renewed confidence. But he was already thirty-nine, and fame and fortune were somewhat sluggish in responding.

That evening, he had been stopped only half a dozen times on the Canebière by some rather unenthusiastic autograph seekers. There were so many other idols to adore. He went into the Versailles, and looked round the room. Several diners looked up but then lost interest. The only person to approach him was the head waiter, with the professional smile reserved for good customers. Edmond followed him meekly to the back of the room, keeping a hawk's eye out for any sign of recognition. Suddenly an arm shot up and a hand flapped a beckoning gesture. At last!

Behind the bottle of Dom Pérignon lying in its ice-pail, Edmond recognised Jo. Monsieur Jo – as the young crooks who still had any sense of hierarchy called him – was a well-preserved fifty-year-old who affected a jaunty yet calculated elegance: he wore a polo-necked cashmere sweater and a Prince of Wales suit, a tasteful solid gold signet ring on his well-manicured hand; the eyes in his soft, pleasant face were gem-hard.

Edmond knew that the modest tradesman, who lived in Sauvagine Buildings in the 'Rose' district, was actually an underworld boss. Two years previously, in this same restaurant, he had been seated at a table with Antoine Guerini, an undisputed sovereign in his dubious field.

A lot had happened since then. Antoine had been shot eleven times, seated in his own Mercedes, under the eye of his eighteen-year-old son, in a service station in chemin St Julien. His brothers Barthélémy and Pascal were in prison awaiting trial for the murder of an insignificant burglar.

The young singer had been summoned to this table before. At that time, when he had no engagements in Europe, he had been in the habit of doing a stint in Montreal, in rue de la Montagne, where an expatriate Marseilles widow, Clairette Oderat, had a night-club. This detail had caught the diners' attention.

'Do you often go to Canada?' Jo had asked.

'Whenever I want. I telephone Clairette and tell her I'm on my way.'

Jo leant towards him.

'I'll have to see more of you. If you listen to me and do what I say, you and I will be able to make a lot of money.'

Matters stopped there. But when the moment came to go, Jo joined him in the cloakroom and asked him for his phone number, reiterating his promise for a bright future together.

A few months later, they met again on the stairs of the Ascenseur Club, on place Thiard. 'I haven't forgotten you, young man,' Jo said as they passed. Their paths had not crossed again until this evening in autumn 1968.

'Well, my lad,' said Jo, waving Edmond to a seat, 'how's the singing going?'

Edmond resisted the temptation to boast; he knew he would never be a Claude François or an Yves Montand. Indeed, at the moment, employment prospects were so dull that he was considering going to do another session at Clairette's. M. Jo nodded approval and asked him some questions. Was he taking a lot of equipment with him? Did he know any other singers going to Canada? Did the Canadian customs search baggage very thoroughly? He made enquiries about the bulky amplifiers used by the artists of the current generation.

That evening they went no further. But three days later, on the terrace of La Mer, appropriately overlooking the sea, the plan began to take shape. As Jo spoke – his official name was Joseph Marro – Edmond gazed at the last of the summer's pleasure boats dancing on the swell. He tried to convince himself that he could still refuse. He felt himself drawn towards an alarming future; he knew it was a question of drugs, and this was soon confirmed.

'In a year or two, you'll be able to make enough to live on quietly for the rest of your days. You're a singer, you have no police record, no one will suspect you. If they do search you and find anything, act dumbfounded; say you didn't know anything about it. Someone must have hidden it in your luggage. What can they do about it?'

The profits shimmered like a mirage: five hundred thousand old francs a kilo. Three million in a double-bottomed suitcase. Ten million per amplifier, all expenses paid. Later, a percentage on all operations carried out by others.

'Don't accept any engagement for a fortnight from now. This *loup au fenouil* is excellent, don't you think? And the *muscadet* is top class. First of all, find out about musical instruments that could be used to conceal the stuff. I think amplifiers are a good idea. Okay, then? Go to Paris. In about a week, you'll be hearing from me. Here, this will cover expenses.'

He put a thick wad of hundred-franc notes down on the table. A last scruple stayed Edmond's hand. If he took the money, he would have burned his boats. He clenched his fist and shook his head.

'No, I've got everything I need. We'll see about that later.'

22

Ups and Downs of a Novelist

Waiting for things to improve, Edouard Rimbaud had gone back to his typewriter. Novel writing might play a less important role in his budget, but it had become a vital cover. He continued to receive visits from old friends.

Jeannot D had just been released from a German prison. He passed through Salon, where Edouard agreed to take him back to his brother, who ran a ski factory in the Chamonix region. En route, he was struck by the idea of a network transporting heroin into the United States by concealing it inside skis. Jeannot soon scotched that dream. Skis, it seemed, were compressed, and nothing could be concealed inside them. Back in Salon, Rimbaud met Félix Olivié. Two of his friends, le Frisé and Bati, wanted to meet him and talk to him about a possible partnership.

Rimbaud was still unaware of the importance of the part the two men played in drug trafficking. He knew only that le Frisé ran a bar on the Vieux Port in Marseilles, the Gondolier.

'It's like this,' explained Félix. 'They'll supply the drugs and you'll supply the client. Knowing a buyer is worth a fortune.'

'I realise that. That's why I never told you his name. But how did they know that I had one?'

'I didn't tell them. It must have been Bordure. He goes to the Gondolier.'

'If they know Bordure, they must think we're suckers.'

A few days later, the four future associates met around a table in the villa at Lambesc. The two newcomers severely condemned Olivié for behaviour which had caused the precious buyer to hang around for weeks in order to be delivered a derisory quantity of heroin. But they smiled again when Rimbaud told them he undertook to re-establish the broken contact and that he agreed to go to the US to organise deliveries.

'I say, young fellow,' said Bati imprudently, 'don't you think you might do better to give us his address? If anything happened to you . . .'

Rimbaud had every intention of retaining his advantage. But he promised that in the case of trouble, he would get it to them immediately. The two visitors took no exception to this and even proved their trust by revealing how they proposed to carry out the first consignment. They knew a singer who had agreed to carry ten kilos in an amplifier for a thousand dollars a kilo. He, Edouard, would not have to pay out a penny. They would advance him his part in the deal. Bati showed his guest a leaflet announcing the imminent issue of a record by a local entertainer: Edmond Taillet. 'He's our courier,' he announced proudly.

On another occasion, Edouard enthralled them for a whole meal while he revealed a grandiose plan he was incubating, a scheme inspired by General de Gaulle's famous phrase during his visit to Canada: 'Long live free Quebec.'

'There you are! We create a France–Quebec committee. We appoint a front-rank personality as president – an honorary post, largely. But the secretary will be one of our men. There'd be a parallel committee in Montreal. Delegations from Poitou, Brittany and Gascony would solemnly hand over great earthenware jars filled with the earth from their provinces to the Canadian committee. There'd be the Marseillaise, tears, a lot of back-slapping. In the evening, while everyone was dancing, our secretary would remove the layer of earth from the top of the jars and retrieve the packets of heroin.'

His audience remained motionless for a few moments, forks poised. Then le Frisé collapsed, helpless with laughter, while Bati patted Rimbaud gently on the shoulder.

'Brilliant! We'll make a packet together,' he prognosticated.

Winter was approaching. Muffled up, shoulders hunched, the inhabitants of Salon went about their business in chilly isolation.

Seated at his typewriter, Edouard Rimbaud gazed through the window at the familiar spectacle. He heard his mother doing the housework or preparing the lunch. Inspiration was sluggish and vague plans loomed in his mind.

A Ford Mustang turned into the street and drew up in front of the house. Edouard recognised his friend Jean Mariolle at the wheel. At his side was a young man whose elegance was indefinably Madison Avenue. A few moments later, Rimbaud had learned that he was called Christian Hysohion, that he came from New York, that he was on holiday and that he had not been able to hire a car in Paris because of the holidays.

'I brought him to you,' said Mariolle, 'because he might be able to palm our books off on an American publisher.'

Christian nodded quietly. He knew someone called D'Acosta in New York who was a good friend of a publisher. They all three went to a restaurant at Lançon a few kilometres from Salon. Edouard and his new acquaintance were immediately drawn to one another. 'Twenty-three years old and well built,' Edouard described him, 'extremely pleasant and fond of good food. First of all we talked about books, then we talked about him. His firm in New York was called Panamanian Chemist and Food Products Inc. He imported tins of sardines from Spain and sold them in the US. But he seemed to me to be much too smart a customer to be selling just fish.'

On the return journey, Jean Mariolle revealed the true aim of his friend Hysohion's visit. He wanted to buy ten kilos of heroin 'for an Italian client'. He had other suppliers, but there were too many intermediaries taking their cut. Indeed, he did not want his Swiss associates to know of this new branch of unofficial activity.

During the conversation, Edouard caught the name Louis Brique, and guessed that he was one of the organisers of the Swiss network: useful piece of information.

All he had to do now was turn to Olivié, who was still available. He would levy a thousand francs a kilo in passing, which he would share with Edouard. Delivery was to take place on 2 January.

Meanwhile, the writer nipped up to Paris to ask his publisher to hang on for a few weeks and to see Jeannot D.

'I think I've got some interesting news for you,' Jeannot D informed him. 'You may not be able to put heroin in skis, but you can hide it in ski sticks. I've tried it with flour. You can get at least half a kilo in each stick.'

The future looked rosy for Edouard Rimbaud; particularly since, at the end of the year, he had at last heard from his buyer in the US, Antonio Florès: 'If we are to continue working together, you'll have to be a bit more reliable. The last time you upset a whole team, and we waited around for over a month in France, all for a mere two kilos. In the future, I want it delivered to me in New York.' Rimbaud was satisfied. He had not burned his boats.

For his part, Edmond Taillet, after a few weeks' equivocating, was ready to leave for Montreal with his amplifiers. He was to take ten kilos of heroin. Bati provided precise instructions: the address and phone number where he could be contacted, the Geneva bank where funds should be deposited on return ... he was relying on Rimbaud for all that. 'And give Taillet two thousand dollars and not a dollar more. If he gets all his commission he'll start acting big and draw attention to himself.'

Rimbaud arrived in New York on 12 January; a layer of snow lay over the city. As soon as he had booked in at the Commodore, he telephoned Hysohion. Two hours later, they were dining with the director of the Panamanian, Charles D, at the Petite Marmite. His new friend suggested that he might put him up during his stay; so it was in a house in Whitestone, in Queens, that Rimbaud learned all the details of the Swiss network, and the names of its organisers: Hirsch, Vuille and Louis Brique, whose name he had already heard.

'At last,' he said later, 'I had the whole organisation clear in my mind. My instinct had been correct. The heroin was sent from France to Spain. There, it was concealed in tins of preserved foods. Hundreds and hundreds of cartons were sent to New York by boat.' The next consignment was to contain a hundred and sixty kilos of drugs.

He then put forward the main outline of his plan.

'You're being had. I have a client who pays me ten thousand dollars a kilo as delivered in Montreal, which makes twelve thousand in New York, Since your Swiss are satisfied with eight thousand, you buy the consignment from them and we'll resell it. Four thousand dollars profit per kilo, that's three hundred and twenty thousand dollars each, enough to retire on. In this game, it's better to pull out after a big deal. You know what you could get if you were caught? Twenty years.'

Christian Hysohion, both panicked and dazzled, accepted the suggested partnership.

On 14 January, Rimbaud left New York for Montreal and booked in at the Laurentien. He wrote to Bati and le Frisè to let them know how his mission had gone. Certain that they would be satisfied on learning that he had got eight and a half thousand dollars per kilo, he then went to Clairette's where Alain, the barman, informed him that Taillet was arriving the following day.

On his arrival at the Dorchester, Taillet handed over the amplifier to the receptionist and went up to his room. He picked up the phone and asked for two numbers: over the line to Marseilles he told his listener that the car was in the garage. To Rimbaud in the Laurentien he simply said, as agreed, that he was coming to collect his car.

He had managed very well, for a beginner. His fears and scruples had faded away.

The following day, Rimbaud came to the rendezvous at the agreed time and found Taillet comfortably ensconced in an armchair in the hotel lounge. He asked him if he had the goods. The singer nodded in the direction of the suitcase and microphone standing near him on the floor.

'I don't want to mess around with suicases and amplifiers,' the writer exploded angrily. 'I want the junk.'

Crestfallen, Taillet explained that he had no tools to dismantle the device or remove the bottom of the suitcase. They decided to meet an hour later before going back to the Dorchester. Rimbaud was holding a leather bag into which he had slipped a few tools. Once in his hotel room, half an hour's fiddling sufficed to produce twenty-five packets of heroin from their hiding places. Taillet seemed surprised. Bati and le Frisé had spoken of only ten kilos. Rimbaud shrugged his shoulders.

'They're always trying to crook you. They just can't help it. But don't stand for it.'

Rimbaud immediately telephoned Florès in New York, to ask him to come to Montreal.

In due course Antonio Florès arrived at the Laurentien. He had not had time to collect enough money to buy all the twelve kilos but suggested that he should take the lot and come back to pay later.

'I've got a better suggestion,' said Rimbaud. 'Buy what you can, take it to New York, get paid and come back for the rest. Cash!'

Florès hesitated. Just as a matter of principle, because he knew quite well that he had no choice.

Towards the end of February, a summit conference on Félix Olivié's villa at Lambesc brought the members of the 'ski sticks group' together: an unregistered company, with no initial assets but with a promising future. Léon Panizzi, Louis the chemist, Félix and Rimbaud. Bati and le Frisé had not been asked to attend. Jeannot D had come from Paris to show them a ski stick – which was passed from hand to hand – and to explain the use to which it could be put.

He pointed out that the Americans were keen on French ski equipment. Jean's brother, who manufactured this equipment and knew nothing at all about their plans, had in fact just left for the US, hoping to set up a ski-hiring firm with depots in various winter sports centres. This development might be very convenient for the plans of the group, who instantly started to discuss the share-out of the future profits.

The quantities involved were several hundreds of kilos of

heroin, on which Edouard, Félix and Jean would jointly reap a thousand dollars per kilo in return for ensuring their dispatch. Apart from skis, the company – which we shall call 'France-skis' – also provided its clients with a number of accessories made by other firms – ski sticks, attachments, sundry equipment – but which it would order from various European makers. These orders were sent to a centre in the Paris suburbs, where France-skis had a depot. From there, skis and accessories were distributed to the various clients.

A single employee could carry out all the jobs that had to be done at the depot: van deliveries to shops in the Paris region; customs formalities, labelling and sending of parcels abroad. When Jeannot D had come out of prison the previous year, his brother, who wanted to give him an opportunity of going straight, had entrusted him with this position.

Jeannot had seemed to take his duties seriously, and his brother had every reason to be satisfied. His younger brother had even found a client in the US, a certain Georges Roupinian, a Frenchman of Armenian origin born at Gréoux-les-bains, and who had settled in New York a few years previously. Roupinian wanted to buy a number of sticks and skis and even suggested keeping some in store on behalf of France-skis on his own business premises, in Middlesex, New Jersey.

Roupinian, who had a hairdressing business on the east coast, and whose sudden interest in sporting equipment apparently had no connection with his usual line of business, seemed very much absorbed in his new activity. A few days after the meeting at Lambesc, Christian Hysohion announced that 'the publisher was waiting to sign the contract', which meant the end of the dockers' strike in the port of New York. The cargo ship *Ragunda* was about to be unloaded and the tins of *paella marinara* to be delivered to the Panamanian Chemist and Food Products. Rimbaud left for the US.

Passing through Paris, he saw Jeannot D again to ask him how the ski-stick business was going. D evinced a certain distrust for the southerners he had met in Félix Olivié's villa. 'Just try to get hold of junk without involving a Corsican or Marseilles man in the affair,' suggested Rimbaud ironically.

A new delivery of *paella marinara* was on its way. It had been loaded on to the cargo vessel *Grunsunda* – belonging to the same shipping company as the *Ragunda* – under the discreet surveillance of the Spanish police and customs men who immediately notified their American colleagues. The cases contained twenty-nine kilos of heroin, twelve kilos in tins with a red mark and eighteen in tins with a black one; they were destined for two different buyers. Four days after the end of the strike of New York dockers, a hauliers' truck arrived in Whitestone. The driver helped Hysohion to stack the cases in the storeroom under the circumspective eye of policemen disguised as street sweepers.

'One case is missing,' observed Hysohion.

But the delivery man was categorical. They were all there.

The truck driver's calm assurances did not convince Hysohion; he did his sums again. At this very moment he received a phone call from Edouard Rimbaud:

'I'm at the Commodore in New York, come and join me.'

An hour later the two friends were together in the hotel lounge.

'One case is missing,' said Hysohion without more ado. 'I don't know if it's been stolen, or if the customs men have kept it. It's one of the marked ones.'

'And you think they took just one, so that you'd get the message?' snapped back Rimbaud. 'The simplest thing is to check again.'

Together they returned to Whitestone and went down to the basement which served as a storeroom. The place was piled high with boxes. They had to be brought up a narrow ladder one by one to the apartment above.

The two men put gauze masks over their faces. Using a tin-opener, they removed the heroin from the wrapping paper and laid it on a table. They then had to extract the bits of lead chipping which had been put in to make up the weight.

The white powder was weighed, then poured into transparent

bags whose openings were sealed up with a machine. Then the empty tins had to be washed and thrown away together with the lead; the walls had to be rinsed down and so did the equipment in the kitchen, as it was impregnated.

The two men were exhausted. With the first glimmer of dawn the houses began to loom up from the shadows and the first furtive passers-by could just be made out. Christian shook Edouard. They had to load up the junk and hide it in a locker on Grand Central Station. They called a taxi.

The packages had hardly been piled into a zip bag when the taxi stopped in front of the door and hooted. Edouard opened the door and threw the bag onto the seat. Christian joined him and gave the address: Grand Central Station.

The taxi drove off. Edouard looked around him. The street seemed deserted and the cars lined up along the pavement, empty. They drove through the snow towards their destination.

Almost immediately, the lights of two other cars went on. They too drove off into the roadway, keeping a prudent distance. The BNDD agents inside were quite unworried. The telephone line from the Panamanian Chemist and Food Products was being monitored and a radio message informed its followers of the taxi's destination.

But the car they were following gathered speed. Edouard had asked the driver to make a sudden spurt.

The two cars turned into the parkway at about a hundred and twenty kilometres an hour. There was no point in any further concealment. Sirens began to whine, red lights blinked. Acceleration was accompanied by a long skidding motion in the snow. One of the police vehicles came alongside the taxi, swung into the right, straightened out, skidded and slewed round violently before coming to a halt. The taxi driver managed to avoid it by drawing up crosswise on the roadway.

Immediately, the BNDD agents pounced, revolvers in one hand, police identification in the other. In two seconds the four doors of the taxi were thrown open and its occupants dragged out. The driver protested but was silenced by the barrel of a revolver pressed to his ear. Docilely, the three men put their hands on the roof of the cab and underwent a summary search. A BNDD agent appeared, a plastic packet in each hand.

'This is it! We're in,' he shouted.

He was given a series of mighty pats on the back. The two Frenchmen and the astonished driver were handcuffed and driven off to the police station, on the way being given a recital of their rights and the uses they could put them to.

When the *Grunsunda* entered the port of New York at the beginning of March with twenty-nine kilos of heroin sent by Eugène Castaldi on board, the network set up by André Hirsch and company had been completely smashed. After the arrest of Edouard Rimbaud and Christian Hysohion, the evidence amassed enabled the Swiss police to proceed to a wide-ranging haul. One after the other, Hirsch, Brique, Vuille, Grandi and Glarner were arrested. The tapping and recording of telephone calls made by Hirsch during the last weeks revealed his links with Eugène Castaldi, who was arrested on 9 March.

Shortly after the arrest of Castaldi at his home in Madrid, 11 Calle General Goded, Charles Dauga, manager of the Panamanian Chemist and Food Products, returned to New York. Since his duties did not require his consistent presence, he had taken several weeks' holiday in Puerto Rico. He knew nothing about the events that had taken place in his absence. He had hardly entered his house on 22nd Avenue, when three Narcotics Bureau agents entered on his heels. They apprehended him and once again read out the legal rights afforded to those under arrest.

Dumbfounded, he went before a judge. He protested his innocence vehemently. Christian Hysohion, taken from his cell for the purpose, confirmed his statement. He was released two days later.

On 23 December of the same year, Hysohion was sentenced to thirty years imprisonment. In Switzerland, on 3 March and 29 April 1971, Brique, Vuille, Grandi and Hirsch were sentenced to five, four years, fifteen months and six and a half years respectively.

And Ange Simonpieri? When André Hirsch appeared in court, a very sick man but still superficially the prosperous 'chairman' in his dark double-breasted suit and horn-rimmed glasses, his lawyer Maitre Raymond Nicollet could not fail to mention Simonpieri and expressed surprise that he was still at large, in view of the fact that an order to appear had been issued against him eighteen months earlier. 'The powers of the French Home Office end at the gates of Marseilles.'

It was a clever phrase, but Simonpieri had not set foot in Marseilles for thirty years. He lived in Paris. He had heart trouble and a duodenal ulcer. At fifty-five, he looked like an old man. He spent long periods on his estate at Marsangy in the Yonne. His ostensible position as a traveller for a Champagne wine firm left him plenty of free time.

When the *paella marinara* network was broken up, he went back to the village where he had been living. His doctors said that he was too ill to be moved. He then went to ground with his brother-in-law in Ajaccio. At the time of the trial he was in the *centre hospitalier de la Miséricorde* in Monaco. He was finally arrested in Ajaccio on 13 September 1971.

The evidence against him was slight. His name figured in several deals. After his arrest in September 1967, Willy Lambert, the friend of Josette Bauer and Robert Mori, stated that he had taken delivery of the heroin, found in his false hump, at the chateau of Marsangy. Two other couriers admitted that Simonpieri was their supplier. Presented with a sheaf of photographs after his arrest, Brique put a finger on the photo of Simonpieri and said, 'That's him.'

During 1968 he had travelled a lot in Switzerland and Italy, 'to get money and clothing to former members of the OAS in exile', as he maintained. He appeared before the sixteenth Paris court of summary jurisdiction in July 1972. According to the charge, his involvement in trafficking dated back to 1964. He died shortly afterwards as a result of his illness.

Apparently indifferent to the eddies produced by the arrest of his Swiss partners, a sunburnt Jack Grosby landed at Geneva

Airport towards the end of April. In his hand was a tawny leather attaché case which had been handed to him in Rio de Janeiro by an unknown man. This same stranger was waiting for him in a car and reclaimed his briefcase which contained two hundred and fifty thousand dollars. He dropped Grosby in front of the branch of the Union Bank of Switzerland, where the Argentinian deposited the several dozens of thousands of dollars which his services during the previous weeks had earned him in his account, numbered 309–7906M.

Then he went to the President where he had an appointment with Stepenberg. Recent events had caused the two friends to modify their plans somewhat.

23

The New York Argentinians Fall into the Trap

During October 1969 Eduardo Poeta, summoned by Luis Stepenberg, once again left his confectionery business and took the plane for Buenos Aires. At about the same time another intermediary, Jimmy Cohen, returned to New York to await a delivery of ten kilos of heroin which Grosby was to send to him. He was re-establishing contact with his buyers.

But already one of his accomplices – Ruben Alonzo – was under surveillance, and drew the attention of the police to Grosby.

The Federal Customs and Narcotics Departments still did not know the extent and complexity of the network set up by the *grupo frances* in Latin America. But gradually information gleaned in Paris, Madrid and New York began to fit together and form the skeleton of a vast puzzle. The chance arrest of Bonsignour at Le Perthus on the French–Spanish frontier, as he was going from Madrid to Paris, made it possible to complete the dossier on the oscilloscopes affair.

Larrain Maestre, awaiting extradition in prison, was visited by a Narcotics Bureau agent and produced several names.

The role of Bonsignour's uncle emerged when a French prisoner in Atlanta revealed the position occupied by Auguste Ricord in the hierarchy of the South American network and his relations with one of his Marseilles suppliers, Joseph Orsini.

Things fell into some sort of shape only after December 1969. It was to be years before the identities of various members of the organisation, most of them being known to their accomplices only by their nicknames, were discovered.

Luis Stepenberg and Jack Grosby were mentioned several times in reports of hearings. Unconcerned by the curiosity they aroused, the two accomplices devoted themselves to their still prosperous business.

On his return to New York, Eduardo Poeta resumed his routine of assignations, comings and goings, deliveries, payments and updating of accounts with Joseph Stepenberg, the jeweller, Luis' brother.

Jack Grosby, who was still in Geneva, telephoned Jimmy Cohen and reproached him vehemently: 'My partner tells me that your orders aren't big enough. If we can't dispose of the whole lot within the time given, our suppliers may well look for other outlets. We simply must find new clients.'

As it turned out, James Cohen was never to have the opportunity of complying with this request. On the morning of 12 February, outside the Camelot Building on 45th Street, he informed Poeta of the telephone call and told him that he still had seventeen packets of five hundred grams each, for which he had been unable to find buyers.

Two hours later, the Narcotics Bureau agents and the New York police entered his apartment and seized seventeen packets. During this same operation, his buyers Frank Hughes and Félix Martinez were arrested; five hundred grams of cocaine were seized from Hughes. Martinez was released. Considerable quantities of glucose and sodium carbonate had been found in his possession – used for diluting heroin for retail sale – but their possession was not illegal.

Poeta immediately telephoned Stepenberg to tell him that 'the Turk was ill'.

After his stay in Switzerland Jack Grosby, who was following operations from a distance, went to Brazil where Christian David was waiting for him. Together they went to the Rio Carnival. Condemine had rented an apartment at Copacabana for the occasion. He was joined there by his henchmen, William Perrin and Michel Nicoli. Life was sweet.

Amid the hubbub, the kaleidoscope of colours and frenetic dances, the bright costumes and flowers, Christian David and Stepenberg, who had joined the group, found time to discuss the delivery of sixty kilos which had arrived in the US the previous month. The used-car salesman agreed to deal with them, but he asked for a certain amount of grace.

During this whole period, the New York police and the Narcotics Bureau agents continued watching the comings and goings of Luis Stepenberg, and tapping his telephone calls.

On 19 July, a charge for drug trafficking and associated crimes was issued by the American courts against Jack Grosby, Stepenberg and Poeta.

The extradition orders for Grosby and Stepenberg were drawn up at Region 17 of the BNDD in Paris, who notified the governments concerned. The Brazilian police were the first to respond. They reported Grosby's departure for Geneva.

Stepenberg joined him there. He had deteriorated visibly within a few weeks and was worried about his health; he told his friend that he intended to give up trafficking. He no longer had the necessary resilience to take the constant strain his illegal activities demanded.

On 18 August Jack Grosby was arrested by the Swiss police. On the 24th, Stepenberg was picked up by the French police at Nice Airport and questioned. On the 27th it was Poeta's turn to be arrested by the Spanish police, at Barajas Airport in Madrid, just as he was about to take the plane for New York.

During the following months, Grosby was to reveal all he knew about the various South American networks and the activities of the *grupo frances*. The investigators thus learned that almost a tonne of heroin had crossed the Mexican frontier to Texas in 1969. It was stored in an apartment in Houston and distributed to clients in various states. His revelations made a considerable contribution to the breaking up of the organisation and earned him a greatly diminished sentence.

Poeta, although he was only an intermediary, was to be sentenced to forty years in prison. Stepenberg died in the infirmary of the New York Federal prison on 11 March 1971, after a long illness.

24

Amplifiers, Ski Sticks and Noella's Comet

Back from Montreal, Edmond Taillet had gone to the Royaume du papier peint (Wallpaper Centre) in Marseilles; there in the back of the shop Joseph Marro had handed over a wad of four million old francs. Edmond had thrown it angrily down onto the desk, reminding him he had carried four more kilos than originally agreed.

'Come on now,' said Jo. 'We're good friends. I wouldn't like us to quarrel, I'll talk to my partners and see what can be done.'

The next day, in the restaurant La Mer, he offered him a million francs more, implying that this was his final figure.

A few days later Taillet learned that a well-known singer was to join his band on the Canadian trip. Jo declared himself delighted by the news. For forty-eight hours Edmond and Jo plodded from one music shop to another; at last they were stopped short by the sight of an impressive Vox amplifier.

'That's just what we need,' Jo said, pointing to it. 'It'll hold a good ten kilos. Let's buy two.'

'But they cost over two thousand francs each.'

'So? In our game, there's no penny-pinching. You concentrate on trying to find a way to get them on board with your star's equipment.'

Edmond then thought of Jacques Bec, a smooth and charming impresario who was a noted backstage hanger-on at Olympia and Bobino where he was on the lookout for up-and-coming talent, for whom he always felt he could do great things. At the moment he was trying to find employment for five somewhat louche entertainers who, despite the conservative outlook of wary night-club owners, did ultimately have a limited success: the Charlots. Ever optimistic, Bec added the phrase 'theatrical director' to his visiting card. But times were hard and money scarce. His hard-won capital had been sunk into a single unsuccessful venture. A telephone call from Taillet had him running. He was ready to do anything to earn some money.

'Even smuggle heroin?'

'Anything, except that.'

'I haven't anything else to offer. It's not risky. All you have to do is to get two amplifiers on board with J's equipment. Jean Pons, a friend of mine, is dealing with it. All you need to do is tell him that I have excess baggage. It will sound more natural, coming from you.'

The task seemed easy enough, and Jacques Bec forgot his scruples and went off to look for Pons. Meanwhile, Taillet sent the amplifiers off to the Royaume du papier peint where Jo had arranged to see him the following day.

Everything was ready at the agreed time. Jo boasted about the quality of the craftsmanship to his new recruit. The amplifiers' lights lit up when they were plugged in, despite the presence of forty packets of heroin. A few hours later, the warehouseman at the freight shed at Orly, after speaking to Pons, put them alongside J's impressive battery of equipment which was to precede the band on a cargo plane.

Taillet rewarded Bec's efficiency with an advance of five thousand dollars on the ten thousand promised; this was nothing to the singer who was to earn twenty thousand dollars from the operation. On his arrival in Montreal, Taillet booked into the La Salle. He spent the whole afternoon in his hotel room waiting for Jo's call, but the telephone remained obstinately silent. He turned on the television. After announcing a forthcoming session of the Etats Généraux of French Canada, Richard Nixon's visit to Paris and his discussions with General de Gaulle, the newsreader announced the break-up, in New York, of an important network of drug traffickers who had cunningly concealed heroin in tins of *paella*. Numerous arrests had been made. Edmond was distraught. In a blinding flash he understood the very real risks he was running. He was seized with an intense desire to run away; but he did not know where.

The noise of the telephone burst in on his panic, and the peaceful sing-song voice of Jo reassured him, 'There's been a small setback. "John" is seriously ill. He won't be coming. But I'll be sending you someone else. Tomorrow. He's called Ricard, that's easy to remember.'

The next morning Edmond was woken by a call from reception. His luggage had arrived. A few seconds later there was another call. It was Jo again, ringing from Marseilles:

'Listen carefully, kid. There's been a change of plan. You'll have to hire a car and take the parcels to Boston.'

'In the US? Out of the question. I'm sticking to our previous arrangement.'

'Don't be difficult. I'm asking you a favour. Listen, you're a good friend. If you agree, I'll double your share.'

But Edmond Taillet would not hear of it. After the previous evening's haul, the customs men would inevitably be on the alert. This was not the moment of an encounter with them. Jo did not press the point. He sensed Edmond's nervousness, and nervousness was bad news in his game. He would therefore have to wait until Ricard arrived, as agreed.

Ricard did not turn up until the following day. A meeting was arranged in a nearby bar, the St Tropez, with a key-ring as distinguishing token.

Ricard took the 'luggage' and met Taillet again an hour later at the La Salle.

Ricard – who was in fact Guido Rendel – gave Taillet a paper bag full of dollars.

'There were twenty-three kilos,' he stated; 'at six thousand a kilo, that makes a hundred and thirty-eight thousand dollars. Here are eighty. I'll give you the rest tomorrow in New York, in the Marsch Steak House, at seven o'clock.'

Counting the notes out in his room, Taillet discovered that a thousand dollars were missing from the agreed sum. The next day, in the Woodstoke Hotel in New York, Rendel handed them over protestingly, together with the balance of fifty-eight thousand dollars. The inexperienced trafficker was later to discover that, in his new profession, such mistakes were not unusual and that one had to be on the lookout all the time.

During twenty years spent inside French prisons or in illegal activities outside them, Edouard Rimbaud had accumulated a good deal of reliable information about the workings of the police and the law; he was now in the process of discovering a new and disconcerting prison world. The initial panic of his arrest had given way to stoical resignation, but he kept his wits about him and was already working on his defence and on plans which might enable him to escape the twenty-year sentence he saw stretching ahead of him. In fact, he was given a total of forty years by successive courts.

Edouard defended himself vehemently against the accusations levelled at him.

'I can't make head or tail of it,' he said, 'I came to New York to negotiate the publication of my books in English. In my hotel room you will find the correspondence with the publisher to whom Christian Hysohion introduced me. I've only known him a few weeks. I don't know anything about his activities.'

The reactions of his questioners and their exchanges with one another encouraged him to keep to this system of defence. Hysohion generally assumed full responsibility and exonerated Rimbaud. The interrogation was broken off.

Taken to the Federal House of Detention at 427 West Street, they were locked in an already overcrowded dormitory.

Rimbaud stretched out in the darkness and dozed off for a few hours, overcome by exhaustion and emotion.

When he woke up, it was light. The prisoners were wandering around and chatting. Suddenly, Rimbaud recognised a familiar face, that of Antonio Florès whose showy suit had attracted his attention. He pretended not to recognise him but sat down on a bed next to him and explained the circumstances of his arrest.

'They laid a trap for me at your hotel,' said the Puerto Rican. 'I said I didn't know you. If you keep quiet, I'll be released on bail in two days. I'll send my uncle to see you. He's a lawyer.'

Edouard agreed. Antonio, reassured, asked for the address and phone numbers of the Frenchman's suppliers. But Rimbaud remained evasive; he considered the initiative a little premature. Why not wait a few days? After all, American justice had nothing on him, except for having spent the night with a trafficker, and in any case Hysohion had cleared him.

The District Attorney notified him of the charge. A few days later, the judge fixed bail at a hundred thousand dollars. Rimbaud looked discouraged for a moment, then gave a ghost of a smile. He was thinking of how Bati, le Frisé and Florès would react when they heard of the figure. He was taken to the premises of the New York Customs for interrogation, and there he was introduced to a stout, swarthy sixty-year-old with thinning hair and bloated features, heavy-eyed but smart in a slightly vulgar way: Horacio Quinones, the lawyer, Florès' uncle.

'So you've engaged a lawyer?' customs agent Andrews asked in French.

'You don't have to answer his questions,' Quinones broke in decisively. I'll come back and see you in prison tomorrow.'

There was instant rapport between the two men. Quinones gave Rimbaud Florès' messages: Florès had been released on bail and was eager to get their business going again. The profits would make it possible for the Frenchman to be released in his turn. The lawyer offered to send off his client's post for him and to act as a letter box for replies. He told him to be sure to hide his messages very carefully in his clothes, because he might well be searched before each visit.

To prove his efficiency, Florès' uncle informed Rimbaud that he had obtained a considerable reduction in the bail, which was now down to seventy-five thousand dollars; indeed he thought it possible, by playing on the thinness of the documentary evidence, that he might achieve a further reduction.

* * *

During the following weeks, Edouard became friendly with another prisoner who was soon to be released, a coloured man called Willy Everett who would proudly produce an article in the *New York Times* which told how he had fired at FBI agents while being arrested. He had already approached Christian to ask him how he could get hold of heroin. He was prepared to pay thirty-five thousand dollars a kilo, which was the 'kilo-men's' current tariff; the 'kilo-men' were the small wholesalers on the New York distribution market.

'I can get you two kilos in a month,' said Rimbaud. 'They'll pay my bail. As soon as I'm released, I'll get you as much as you want at a much better price.'

'All right, but make it fast. When I'm out, it will be much harder to work out the details.'

Three weeks later the scenario was set up. Two kilos of heroin could easily be concealed in the clothing of a single courier who would do just one trip there and back. On his arrival, he would telephone Willy Everett with the simple message 'Hello . . . Mr Five ?' This would indicate that the seller would be in the Rocking Chair Coffee House in Manhattan the following day at two o'clock, with the goods. He would hand them over to Willy in exchange for the money. The sum would then go to Quinones who would pay the bail through the intermediary of a special agency.

A few days after the plan had been set up, Everett was freed. As soon as he was out of prison, he was taken by taxi to the 'narcs' building where Federal Agent Francis E. White awaited him.

'Everything is set,' he said. 'All I have to do now is to wait for a phone call from "Five Fingers", the courier. He has already accepted the work in Paris, but Rimbaud doesn't know his name. In the café, he'll be holding a copy of *Le Figaro* with the number five on the front page in red ink.'

'Did he have any other propositions for you ?'

'I've got to come to an arrangement with the courier in the coffee shop. He is supposed to be able to get me five kilos a month for fifty thousand dollars, ninety-two to ninety-six per cent pure heroin. I don't know how it's going to be arriving. The other prisoner, Hysohion, also offered me a kilo in the end. But it didn't seem genuine.'

The French 'stups' were informed of the developments of the situation by cable that same day.

Quinones, a model postman, Rimbaud informed of the progress of his varying projects. Jeannot D begged him to be cautious and not to write to him any more about the ski sticks. The Marseilles man had pulled out of the operation and he had made up his own team. He asked him to be patient about the two kilos.

At the beginning of June, two American tourists, Quinones and Florès, took a plane from Kennedy Airport for Orly. They had a letter of introduction and detailed instructions for Jeannot D.

At the beginning of July, several crates of ski sticks sent from Germany arrived at the Parisian depot of France-skis. Jeannot D took some home with him.

It was fiddly work, and meant making packets of the diameter and length of the sticks, filling them with heroin, sealing them up, putting them into the stick and putting the sticks back into their original wrapping.

The four crates, each containing fifty sticks, arrived in New York on 21 July on board an Air France cargo plane. Put in bond at Cargo Building 80 in Kennedy Airport, they went smoothly through the customs and were delivered to the France-skis agent on Park Avenue. All the formalities had been carried out by Georges Roupinian.

During the evening of the 25th, Willy Everett's telephone rang. It was 'Mr Five' confirming the time and place of the meeting for the following day. That same day at thirteen hundred hours, Robert C. Manning, who was directing operations, gathered together his forces at the Narcotics Bureau premises.

When Willy and Agent Ford went into the Rocking Chair Coffee Shop at 884 Second Avenue, four of their colleagues were already seated at various tables commanding both exits. 'I immediately noticed a man sitting at the counter reading the *Figaro*,' said agent Ford emphatically in his report. 'He had put a black briefcase down at the foot of his stool. He turned towards me lifting his paper and I could see a red five on the top left-hand corner of the page. I sat down on his right, with Willy Everett on his left and we ordered coffee.'

Roupinian then turned to Ford and asked him if he was Willy. The Federal agent shook his head and pointed to his companion, 'Willy is my partner. It's me who does the dealing. Have you got the junk?'

'Have you got the money?'

Ford tapped the briefcase he had put on the counter next to his coffee cup.

'When I've seen the stuff.'

Roupinian bent down, picked up the briefcase and opened it a little. Four transparent plastic packets lay inside. One of the agents, White, left his table and came up. He introduced himself, showing the metal tag hanging by a chain from his belt, and asked Roupinian and his companions to follow him.

A few minutes later, in Manning's office at 90 Church Street – the laboratory having confirmed the nature of the contents of the packets – Roupinian collapsed. He finally admitted that he had more heroin on his premises in New Jersey and agreed to take the agents there.

At six in the evening the group entered his apartment in Hamiltonian Gardens. On Roupinian's instructions, the agents discovered four packets similar to the ones they had already seized, in a chest of drawers and, in a cupboard in the bedroom, two hundred ski sticks, several of which contained long plastic tubes filled with heroin.

'Who were you going to deliver these to? Who was going to be the recipient of the money that Willy was supposed to give you?'

'I don't know. They're supposed to be telephoning me with instructions.'

The agents settled in for one of the long waits which are part of their professional routine, while Roupinian cooked himself a steak and opened a bottle of wine. After his meal, he played cards with his police escort. Still the telephone did not ring. He went into his bedroom, stretched out on the bed and went to sleep, leaving the light on.

The following day, at noon, he had just downed another steak and the remains of the wine, when BNDD agent Anthony Pohl arrived. He spoke fluent French. He began to question Roupinian who suddenly clasped his hands to his chest, his face drawn.

'It's a heart attack. Call a doctor.'

A few minutes later, an ambulance was taking him to the Rarity Valley Memorial Hospital. He was to leave it four days later to be charged, and claimed that he had been the victim of maltreatment by Anthony Pohl. But his efforts to stop the proceedings against him were vain.

The day after his arrest, in his prison in West Street, Edouard Rimbaud discovered the photograph and the identity of the courier sent him by Jeannot, on the front page of the *New York Times*. He read the article, in which his former cell-mate, Willy Everett, emerged as an undercover agent.

'Then,' Rimbaud was to say three years later, 'I had heard no more from Jeannot, Bati or le Frisé. I had to face facts, I would never get my five per cent. But I didn't co-operate with the American police out of revenge. All this happened in 1969 and I didn't talk until autumn 1972. I'm co-operating now because I want to come back into straight society and lead a decent life for the rest of my days. In St Exupéry's phrase, I want to be something other than a "superfluous brick".'

On 14 April 1970, Georges Roupinian, Edouard Rimbaud and Christian Hysohion were sentenced to ten years' imprisonment. The total of their sentences was forty years for Rimbaud and thirty for Hysohion. After his appeal, Rimbaud was to be transferred to the penitentiary in Atlanta.

He remained there until autumn 1972, a few months after the arrest and disclosures of Edmond Taillet. He was then brought back to New York and at last revealed everything he knew about the French heroin network.

* * *

When he was called to account by his partners after the delivery of the amplifiers, Edmond Taillet felt as though he were being practically court-martialled. In the slightly sinister setting of the Royaume du papier peint, with a lamp casting eerie shadows on the rolls of coloured paper, two hard-faced dark men, seated squarely behind the counter to whom Marro had not bothered to introduce him, stared at him unsmilingly. Provençal and Corsican accents mingled in a duet which singularly failed to charm the singer's sensitive ear. By refusing to go to Boston, he had forced his associates to sell the junk at a derisory price.

'We're all in the same boat. And when you're told to do something, you do it. It's in your interest, my friend. It's of no advantage to us if you get caught.'

To punish him for his lapse, four thousand dollars were docked from his share: plus another four thousand to assist the family of the unfortunate John who had been caught in New York.

'And the three extra kilos?'

'They were John's. Poor thing. You wouldn't want to finish him off completely, would you?'

Edmond resigned himself. As a consolation, the Corsican promised him a bonus of twenty thousand on the next deal. As a final blow, just when his two judges had disappeared into the night, and the two of them had slipped out under the metal blind, Jo took him by the shoulder and held out his hand. 'I say, you couldn't help me out to the tune of five thousand francs for a few days?'

Taillet was back in Paris the following day with thirty-five thousand francs in his pocket, when he had been hoping for a hundred and fifteen.

A few days later Jo phoned him. 'I'm coming to see you in Paris.'

At the agreed time it was not Marro who appeared at his door, but a small chunky forty-year-old giving a quite alarming impression of verve and energy. He introduced himself.

'Bati. Jo sent me. There's a hitch.' Taillet had already heard talk of Jean-Batiste Croce and of his skirmishes with the law over drug smuggling. He did not know that for a quarter of a century he had been known as Jean Bati. His visitor did not need references to make his authority felt.

So as to make up for lost opportunities, Bati had a 'nice, fat deal' to propose to the singer.

'Listen, my lad. You're not going to spend all your life messing about with amplifiers, pianos and trombones. You're a handsome boy; you know people in Montreal. I'm sure there must be a girl over there who would love to let herself be seduced by a fellow like you. So off you go. We'll look after the expenses. Get to know a girl and make sure she's got a car of her own, registered in the country. Invite her to France: "Darling, let's go to the Côte d'Azur for a couple of weeks. We'll put the car on the boat and do some sight-seeing. Don't worry, I'll take care of everything." You go to Marseilles and have a minor breakdown. You leave the car there for us for a night. Then you go back to Montreal. When the car arrives, you take it back to New York. If you don't want to drive, take the plane and arrange to meet her in New York. What do you think?'

A fortnight later, Edmond was going round the night-clubs of Montreal with Noella, a young barmaid from the old town. One of her several advantages was the possession of a white Comet convertible. Captivated by the smooth-talking young southerner, each night she slipped discreetly into his hotel room at La Salle.

She saw the trip (proposed to her between embraces) as an unmistakable proof of love and accepted gratefully. She sent her two children to stay with her parents. Edmond gave her seven hundred dollars for tickets for herself and her car. He went back to Paris and phoned Jo and Bati.

'It's in the bag. She's called Noella and her Comet will be arriving at Le Havre in ten days.'

A month later, at the end of June 1969, Taillet was seated on a bar stool at Clairette's, in Montreal.

'Have you seen Noella?' he asked the barman.

'She was in here an hour ago with Billy. They're inseparable.'

Edmond blinked. That was all he needed. She could be of no further use to him.

25

Just Like the Buccaneers of Old

In the bars on the Vieux Port in Marseilles, rumour had it that a new team had managed to deliver several dozen kilos of heroin to American clients of *Cosa Nostra* in the past few weeks. The two leading lights of the group spent only short periods of time in France. They frequently crossed the Atlantic and travelled throughout Europe. They were often to be seen in Italy, Austria, Germany and Belgium. They were called Jean-Claude Kella and Laurent Fiocconi, known as Charlot.

Jean-Claude was an athletic fellow with the dangerous allure of a hero in a Western. His previous activities had earned him an honourable place in the annals of violent crime. In 1966, aged twenty-five, he had broken open the safe of a film company on Boulevard des Batignolles. Someone tipped off the police, who soon arrived on the scene. Amid rifle-fire, the young thug had been wounded, apprehended and sent for trial. But some slip-up prevented the order from being renewed and Kella, to his surprise, found himself at liberty.

The following year Kella had joined up with Fiocconi, a handsome fellow with a high forehead and long side-whiskers, and the slightly affected elegance of a ladies' hairdresser.

Kella and Fiocconi's methods were still amateurish, but they were highly imaginative and extremely ambitious; and they were almost alone in realising the dream of most budding sailors: that of chartering a small, fast craft capable of crossing the Atlantic and delivering hundreds of kilos of heroin to their clients. It was through these two that Marcel Boucan and his boat, *Caprice des*

Temps, were to enjoy a limelight the owner might have preferred to do without.

On 20 August 1969, two policemen from the Bertincourt station in the Pas de Calais stopped a Ford Mustang registered 1815 K94 at Beugny and asked its occupants to show their papers.

Among the names of the passengers in the Mustang, that of Fiocconi might have caught the attention of the police had they been acquainted with the plans laid by Fiocconi and his New York buyer, the Mafia go-between Louis Cirillo (of whom, more later). The French Antilles played a part in their plans. The ever-increasing number of tourists arriving at Pointe-à–Pitre included several who were quite indifferent to sunbathing.

One of these was a former Marseilles procurer, Alexandre Orsatelli, known as 'Lizza'. He was still two years away from notoriety and the exposure in the press of his relations with Laurent Fiocconi.

He had been born in 1910 at Bastia, where he had lived in rue Garibaldi. But his chosen stamping ground was Marseilles, where he began his career as procurer; and like all old lags, he dreamed idly of the big deal which would allow him to retire.

Thus he listened with interest when his friend Laurent Fiocconi put forward his fabulous proposal: to charter boats to transport heroin from one side of the Atlantic to the other. 'There's no hurry,' said Laurent. 'If I don't want the partners to get the lion's share, I'll have to get a bit of capital together. You know all the guys who sail around here. There must be someone who will fill the bill.'

'Guys who will cross the Atlantic aren't exactly two a penny.'

'We only need one, to begin with. You know the ones who were involved in the cigarette smuggling before the Combinatie business. All I ask is that he should be straight and never have had any trouble with the police.'

Initially it looked as if this rare character would indeed be hard to find. But after mentally running through his personal file of petty crooks and toughs, Orsatelli came up with a name: Marcel

Boucan. He had all the prerequisites. When the cigarette smuggling had ended, at the beginning of the sixties, Boucan had tried his hand at an activity which would allow him to devote himself to his sole passion: the sea.

'Boucan by name and buccaneer by nature', he would say with relish. He thought wistfully of Mediterranean crossings on board powerful motorboats or small cargo vessels, midnight assignations at sea, with mysterious launches into whose holds he and his friends transferred cases of cigarettes, then the return to the free port of Tangier for another load.

Money did not interest him, provided he could charter a boat, like the *Angus II* belonging to Henri Helle. Despite his illicit activities – though the law of the land did not apply on the high seas – he had kept his distance from the underworld and retained a surprising naiveté.

In his book of memoirs, *Monsieur* —, Helle was to say of him, 'Marcel struck an odd note in the circles we frequented, as if he were there by accident, by an error of fate. But when the situation became serious, his men knew they were working for a real captain clear-headed, clear-spoken and unflustered. He was probably the bravest of us all.'

The two men had met in the Caribbean, which in the eyes of Boucan, who was also a knowledgeable historian, was hallowed by the glorious memory of piracy. They settled in Saint-Martin, a small island two hundred kilometres to the north of Pointe-à-Pitre, with twenty odd co-adventurers, some of whom were to become perfectly respectable industrialists or traders. On their arrival, they had all been employed by the Société des Hotels Caraibes which was hoping to attract tourists to the island's empty beaches, with their fringes of cocoanut palms. In ten years they built only one small restaurant, the Saint Tropez.

But it mattered little to Marcel Boucan. In St Nazaire, Henri Helle had come across one of the boats he had used for his cigarette traffic ten years earlier, an old English gunboat converted into a yacht, thirty-four metres long, equipped with two one-hundred and-forty-horsepower diesel engines. It had changed its name:

The Kenyan had become the *Oiseau des Iles*. With his partner, M. Malespine, a former shipowner turned restaurateur, with a weatherbeaten pirate's face and a halo of white hair, he bought it and put it into Boucan's hands. For two years Boucan plied the Caribbean and acquired a thorough knowledge of its secrets.

Then he left his employers.

For several years he pursued his preferred career, crossing the Atlantic in old tubs, entrusted to him by mysterious Liberian or Panamanian companies, or coasted from island to island on the sea of legends where he felt so curiously at home.

Yet he did not feel entirely fulfilled. He loved boats too much to be satisfied with sailing those of his employers. He too wanted to own his own vessel. This was the thought at the forefront of his mind when he received the message from Alexandre 'Lizza' Orsatelli.

On a voyage to the eastern coast of the Atlantic, he met Lizza face to face, in a hotel room in Tangier.

'I'm in no hurry for a decision,' Lizza said. 'The money is our problem. You choose your boat and we'll buy it for you. In your name. You do two or three crossings a year for us, no more. And you'll get at least fifty thousand francs a trip.'

'What would I be carrying?'

'Nothing bulky. Of course, there are risks. But not serious ones. We'll tell you more about it when the time comes. We'll work out the hiding places. You'll pick up the goods in Italy or on the coast and take them to Florida. We'll look after everything. All you have to do is to decide on the boat. When you've made up your mind, let me know.'

Alexandre sunk into the sofa cushions and gazed at the small, balding man; superficially he looked like any law-abiding Frenchman, his bright, guileless eye fixed on empty space. Alexandre could imagine his thoughts: the lure of the easy money that would enable him to realise his dreams, mixed with a fear of being caught up in something from which he might not be able to extricate himself. Everyone preparing to enter the twilight world beyond the law goes through this moment of silent reflection.

'You'll come round to it,' thought the procurer. 'As soon as you find a boat you want, you'll remember my proposition.'

He was right. A few months later, during the autumn of 1969, Boucan and Orsatelli met again in Guadaloupe.

'You want me to carry junk, don't you?' said Boucan without more ado.

'You suspected as much?'

Of course he had. But he had banished the idea from his mind, preferring to dream of some more honourable merchandise, precious stones perhaps: south African diamonds, Colombian emeralds. But now there was no longer any possibility of doubt. It was a bitter pill to swallow.

'Have you got a boat in mind?'

The sailor nodded. He had now made contact with several ship brokers. One of them, M. Lango, had replied to him from les Sables d'Olonne. He had a tunny boat to sell, or rather a shrimper, a solid nineteen-metre vessel which met Orsatelli's needs: it could carry provisions and fuel for several weeks, transport a considerable quantity of merchandise and weather Atlantic storms as well as Caribbean cyclones.

'He's asking thirteen thousand francs,' Boucan ventured. 'But it's already completely fitted out.'

Orsatelli did not flinch at the figure.

'If I get my partners' agreement, I'll give you the sum in cash! You will put it in your bank. We'll send you experts to carry out the various extra alterations.'

Boucan was dreaming of using his future plaything to do deep-sea fishing, underwater archaeology and locating wrecks of Spanish galleons. Alexandre reassured him: the boat would be his. Between deliveries, he could do what he liked with it.

'And with the money you'll earn, you'll be able to buy the best equipment. It suits us that you should have other activities. It's a good cover.'

This time Marcel Boucan was well and truly caught up in the works. He realised this, of course, but had no desire to escape. For now another passion had been aroused in him. Since his return from Guadaloupe, he had been sharing his life with a woman. While this conversation with Lizza was taking place, she was working as a nurse in the hospital at Pointe-à-Pitre.

It was not just a passing liaison but a long love story going back to 1943. The heroine of this romance was called Marie-Françoise de Passerio and she was fifty-five.

She had been twenty-nine when she met Marcel at Cros-de-Cagnes during the Occupation. He was twenty-eight, and secretary of the Fisherman's Union. They had married and had two children.

After the war, with the help of some friends, Marcel had bought some tunny boats to transport goods to and from Corsica. Then the opportunity of joining in the cigarette traffic arose and he went into it enthusiastically, out of a thirst for adventure.

'I always plied the same route, Ajaccio–Marseilles, Marseilles–Ajaccio; I began to feel that I was turning into a tram conductor.'

He tried to give up the sea for Marie-Françoise on several occasions. He worked for an estate agent and for the Nice harbour authority. But his passion was stronger than he was. His wife understood this all the more because she shared his taste for adventure. During the Spanish Civil War, still a very young woman, she had gone off to Catalonia with the Red Cross. She often dreamed of going to nurse in black Africa and working in a leper hospital in the tropics.

'I saw him less and less,' she was to say later. 'If it hadn't been for our two children, I would have gone with him. But separation became inevitable. I stood to one side; his mistress was the sea, and she was the stronger.'

They divorced, though knowing that they could not do without one another. Trafficking on the high seas was a hazardous undertaking; Boucan tried to concentrate on lobster fishing but finally went back to the woman he had been unable to forget.

'I'm going to Guadeloupe,' he said. 'Will you come with me?'

He knew what her answer would be. Without further ado she sold off the family furniture. The children were grown up now and posed no problems. A few days later, they went to sea in a very unsound thirty-three-metre boat.

'Everything is in order,' said the customs officer. 'I therefore have to authorise you to sail. But in my opinion it's suicide.' On a sunny spring morning in 1962 the boat sailed slowly out of Nice harbour, the small waves lapping at its sides. 'However, we did cross the Atlantic without mishap, except for a brief attempt at mutiny by the crew.'

In 1965 the couple separated again. Boucan sailed the seas, breathing in the sea breezes and plying between Guyana and Venezuela, Panama and Vigo. Marie-Françoise had resumed her job as a nurse at Pointe-à-Pitre. Friends informed her that her ex-husband was in France with new projects. Then he reappeared, determined upon remarriage.

26

A Quiet Citizen

At the beginning of October 1969 Jean-Claude Kella, Fiocconi's associate, arrived in New York and immediately telephoned an American girl-friend, Kathy, a dance hostess at the Metropole, a 'go-go' girl.

It was not clear whether the Frenchman was really in love with Kathy, who was charming but completely moulded by her background, or was just using her. He probably believed the latter.

But the way the relationship developed was to prove that his feelings went deeper than might be expected in a hardened criminal.

In the evening he went to collect her from her hotel to go out with some friends: an Italo-American, Louis Martino, and his wife Maria.

This man's real name was Louis Cirillo and he was Fiocconi's buyer. He was supposedly a bakery worker, but had not been working as such for some time. According to the American police, he had committed over forty murders in about thirty years. The first of these, just before the war, had earned him a certain notoriety. Barely sixteen, he had fired at one of the bosses of *Cosa Nostra*, Trigger Mike Coppola, seriously wounding him. The next day he in his turn entered hospital with three bullets in the thorax.

Despite two charges of drug trafficking, two others for theft and one for armed assault, he spent less than eight years in prison. When Kathy met him, he occupied a privileged position in the New York underworld. As a result of an agreement, four of the main Mafia families, Bonanno, Tramunti, Genovese and Colombo, had granted him a monopoly of the heroin supply for their respective rings.

His turnover figure would have aroused the envy of the most prosperous company chairman. None of the clients of the European traffickers had anything like his output. A positive fleet of little plastic bags filled with white powder – coming to him from France, Italy, Latin America, concealed in the couriers' clothing, in suitcases with false bottoms, in the hulls of boats, behind panels in aircraft cabins or in car upholstery – ensured his prosperity. They represented a sixth of all American consumption.

To all appearances, he led the quiet life of a wealthy citizen in his house in the Bronx, in the New York suburbs. He rented the first floor to his daughter and son-in-law and occupied the ground floor with his wife Antoinette, when he was in town. His bank account revealed only modest transactions. His real bank was *Cosa Nostra*, which made it possible for him to carry out large-scale operations without written accounts.

For his suppliers, he was the ideal buyer. Never the slightest delay in payment; never the slightest quibble, except sometimes in connection with the quality of the goods delivered. But then he would prove that his criticisms were justified. Whatever the size of the deal, he seemed to have an inexhaustible stock of hundred-dollar bills available. He had been known to pay out almost three million dollars in a single day, in ready cash in a series of beach bags, for a single delivery. After his arrest, a New York customs officer calculated that in two years he had handed over twelve million dollars to his suppliers.

Diluted with lactose and quinine and distributed in packets on the streets of New York, this heroin had brought in two hundred and ninety-three million dollars, unequally distributed among various members of the Mafia and their retailers.

More than eighteen months went by before his name appeared in the puzzle that was being pieced together with the collaboration of the European police. It emerged that this 'quiet man', together with his son Louis Junior, led a double life, and that he spent most of his time in a stylish apartment in Miami with his mistress Maria – the one whom Kathy had just met.

After the arrest of her lover, Maria disappeared along with

John Astuto, Louis' henchman. Despite extensive investigations, they were never found. The Narcotics Bureau has concluded that Louis Cirillo issued orders, from prison, that they should be silenced for ever; dead men tell no tales.

Louis's problems of conscience were restricted to respect for the law of the underworld and *Omertà*, dear to *Cosa Nostra*. One might therefore have thought that all his ambitions had been fulfilled. But he cherished a last grandiose dream, that of becoming the Onassis of drug trafficking, of commanding a fleet which would safeguard his supremacy in the market. Thanks to several annual cargos, he would avoid the risk of seeing his couriers fall victim to random customs snares.

He was not thinking of giant tankers, but of a small flotilla of pleasure craft, motorboats or sailing boats, capable of doing an Atlantic crossing to land discreetly on the coast of Florida after putting in to port in the Caribbean, on islands where law enforcement was the duty of a rural policeman or lowly constable. In short, he wanted to recreate the 'rum boulevard' travelled for so long by the motorboats of Al Capone's bootleggers and their fellow criminals.

Naturally, the craft making up this clandestine commercial fleet would not belong to him. He would simply be the concealed sleeping partner. He would subsidise perfectly decent members of yacht clubs, underwater fishermen, lone sailors or frogmen specialising in the refloating of wrecks. The recent upsurge in these maritime activities made their supervision difficult.

Louis Cirillo had confided his plan to Laurent Fiocconi.

27

The Drugs Syndicate and the Caprice des Temps

While Orsatelli was pursuing his negotiations with Boucan, and Kella was going through a series of stormy affairs with Kathy in New York or sunny Florida – still keeping in contact with Cirillo to whom he handed over the few kilos of heroin which continued to come his way – Fiocconi was attempting to make good the damage done to his network by a series of unfortunate seizures.

However, he remained prosperous, for he had the ideal client, Louis Cirillo, who meant a fortune on the market. After his second arrest Fiocconi himself was to reveal to the American police – and it was the only time he turned informer before lapsing into total and stubborn silence – that he knew all the Marseilles suppliers, including Joseph Mari, known as Zé-le-frisé, and his cousin Jean Batiste Croce. They ran their own network, but were not above supplying the goods to serious clients. They were in league with several clandestine laboratories, which enabled them, despite various setbacks, to keep a permanent stock of the commodity to hand.

These laboratories were supplied by Tony Pasqualini. Pasqualini had at his disposal a boat which enabled him to retrieve from the sea the watertight bales of raw morphine which Turkish sailors threw overboard with an anchor buoy before their cargo vessels entered the port of Marseilles.

Paul Pajanacci supplied the South American network of Auguste Ricord and Christian David, as well as the various groups based in Spain and whose members met in the Versailles and Vendôme cafés in Madrid.

Despite his widespread and numerous contacts, Fiocconi preferred to restrict his activities and devote himself to the organisation of the fleet whose finest ornament was to be Marcel Boucan's boat. Thus during the summer of 1969, he was very receptive to the propositions made to him by Joseph Signoli.

Signoli was thirty-five and had no police record. In his view the heroin traffic between France and the US was ripe for re-shaping and should be organised along new lines. He was strong-willed and energetic, hirsute and cheery, very secretive though silver tongued; his cordiality concealed a hardness and endurance that were positively steely.

To get ahead in this particular trade, it was necessary to sell the maximum amount of drugs in the shortest possible time. The smuggling of several dozen kilos on each trip entailed several problems. It implied the tying up of considerable sums to buy the goods. A single seizure was enough to ruin a network in a few hours. Signoli thought he had found the solution by creating a positive 'drugs syndicate', a clandestine 'trust' conceived on the American pattern and of which any experienced businessman would thoroughly approve.

His idea was all the more remarkable in that he himself admitted that he was totally uneducated: 'I left school at ten. I can read and count but I have difficulty in writing correctly.' In the Panier district, his tenacious qualities and ready wit attracted the attention of the discreetly elegant Joseph Orsini, big wig and 'quiet man' of the trade, whom Signoli called 'Tonton Orsini'.

At fifteen, Joseph Signoli had been a cabin boy for the Compagnie des Transports Maritimes, then a sailor with Compagnie Paquet. He was well acquainted with all the ports in the south Atlantic. He was drafted into the Fusiliers Marins in 1957 and fought with them in Algeria, though with no special distinction. There he acquired some rudimentary knowledge of mechanics, pastry-making and joinery.

Thanks to the position his father obtained for him in the port of Marseilles, he did not fall into the category of Marseilles ne'er-do-wells, procurers or burglars with their sporadic and shady sources of income. However, he did continue to consort with them, meanwhile preserving a façade of respectability with the help of a short-lived marriage.

After his arrest in 1971 he admitted 'confidentially' – without the knowledge of the examining magistrate – that within a few years he had saved over three hundred kilos of gold, in ingots, which he had buried in a remote corner of the Corsican *maquis*.

'The only thing that worries me is that they might make a motorway through the site of my hiding place. They could easily unearth the ingots with their mechanical shovels.'

When Fiocconi met him in August 1969, together with another Marseilles crook, Alexandre Salles, Signoli had just worked out a plan for a 'drug syndicate'. All that was needed to make it operational was an American buyer. They had naturally thought of Louis Cirillo, but they could not approach him without the agreement and recommendation of Fiocconi and Kella. Signoli, Salles and Fiocconi met in a hotel on the Tuscan coast, a no-man's-land safe from the investigations of the French police.

'Of course,' stated Signoli, 'there's no question of double-crossing you or jeopardising your men. We'll keep you informed of what we're doing. Tell us your price . . .'

'Listen,' broke in Fiocconi, who saw this plan as a source of safe and regular income, 'I've got something better to suggest. I'll put our network at your disposal. I'll talk to Jean-Claude Kella about it. As far as money's concerned, you'll give us a commission on every kilo you run. Have you got a supplier?'

'Tonton (Orsini) is going to introduce me to one.'

A long bargaining process now began and continued during the meetings that followed. Fiocconi was a tough businessman. He finally obtained an allowance of a thousand dollars per kilo delivered to Cirillo for his partner and himself. This portion would be remitted to him as long as the network remained active. Taking into account the boundless ambition of Signoli and Salles, the two crooks would be effortlessly raking in a positive fortune which would swell the profits from their other enterprises.

For another year, their numbered Swiss bank account grew accordingly. Fiocconi was then owner of two flats on rue Lafayette in Paris, a house in Goussainville and a pizzeria in Barbès. During his stays in Paris he lived quietly with his eighty-year-old grandmother in Montmartre.

All Salles and Signoli now had to do was launch their great plan.

While waiting for the 'drug syndicate' to take off, Fiocconi's whole team was extremely active. The dream conceived of by Louis Cirillo was about to become a reality.

The whole winter had been devoted to preparing the *Caprice des Temps* – as Marcel Boucan had rechristened the boat – for the mission it was to carry out: the transportation of large quantities of heroin from Europe to Miami. Orsatelli had handed over thirteen million old francs in five-hundred-franc notes to Boucan, and these he deposited in the Société Générale des Sables d'Olonne at the beginning of the winter. In exchange, he received a cheque drawn on the bank of France with which he paid for the boat.

A few days later, he went to a restaurant on Boulevard Magenta in Nice, where he met a thirty-three-year-old joiner-cum-cabinet-maker, José Peraldi, who had been recommended by Orsatelli. J Peraldi had a good reputation as a conscientious craftsman, although his lifestyle did not always seem to be in accordance with his earnings. Another of his advantages was that he was Fiocconi's cousin, since Fiocconi – a foundling – had been adopted by one of his close relations.

It seems that the two men did not immediately reach an agreement but during January the cabinet-maker received an urgent call from Boucan. The boatyards of Sables d'Olonne were on strike and the work was becoming pressing.

The cabinet-maker got down to some serious work and the fitting out of the boat went ahead. It is not clear what these alterations consisted of: whether cupboards or other hiding places for the drugs. The legal proceedings which took place two years later never managed to establish this clearly. On several occasions, during its two years of navigation, the *Caprice des Temps* was fitted out in Miami, in Pointe-à-Pitre and at Villefranche-sur-mer. This first session was to take a month and a half. Marcel Boucan helped and advised the cabinet-maker.

On 13 March, work stopped. Suitcases were concealed on board in the forepeak, inside a special locker. The peak itself was to be almost always padlocked, which surprised the crew engaged for the crossing to Pointe-à-Pitre.

On 17 March a slender traveller with fine, almost delicate features, very elegantly dressed, arrived in a Maserati at the luxurious hotel, la Lande Saint-Martin, at Haute-Goulaine, near Nantes. He was accompanied by a charming chestnut-haired young woman, taller than he was. On the hotel register the traveller informed the authorities that his name was Dominique Biaggi and that he was a teacher. This was Laurent Fiocconi, alias Charlot, who had come to check on the final work on board the boat which was due to weigh anchor shortly.

The last week in May 1970, the *Caprice des Temps* left the harbour of Pointe-à-Pitre and sailed towards Miami where various further alterations were carried out. Apart from Richard Lacascade, thirty-eight, the crew consisted of three sailors from Guadeloupe. Boucan was no longer on board. He took the plane the following day so as to be at their destination to greet them.

On the first day of June, under a blazing sun, the boat chartered by Fiocconi, Kella, Orsini and Co. entered the harbour. After going through the customs checks without difficulties, it moored in front of the Jones Boatyard where it was hoisted on to the bank for the work to be carried out. The first part of the plan had succeeded. The unloading process could begin.

Marcel Boucan had asked that a cabin should be designed on the afterdeck to house a kitchen and living-room. The walls of the hold were to be insulated so that it could serve as a cold-room. The compressor and the rest of the equipment would be housed in the engine-room.

The cost of the work on board the *Caprice des Temps*, at first estimated at twenty-five thousand dollars, soon rose to forty thousand because of the additional fittings requested by Boucan. These lasted three weeks altogether and were to be paid for in three instalments.

One thing remains unclear: how Boucan and his partners

managed to unload the heroin, all hundred kilos of it according to the figures produced at the Marseilles hearings, or over three hundred if the word of a drug trafficker is to be believed. None of the workmen who were employed on the refitting ever discovered any trace of a hiding place when the work was being carried out.

'I never saw them unload anything,' one of them declared to the BNDD investigators. 'There were no goods visible on board. They could have done it at night, but we didn't notice anything. Marcel Boucan never carried anything bulkier than a briefcase.'

Marcel told the builder that the boat was to be used to collect fish and shellfish from the Guadeloupe boats. Once frozen, the fish would be sent to France. A week before the work was concluded, the sailors (whose US permits had expired) were sent back to the Antilles by air. They came back by the same route on 17 July, to crew the *Caprice des Temps* as soon as she was seaworthy.

At his trial, in October 1972, Marcel Boucan was to claim the entire responsibility for the trafficking and did not implicate any of his accomplices. He admitted having received sixty thousand dollars for the first trip, all of which he had spent.

'I was the only person concerned with unloading,' he said. 'No one else on board knew of its existence. It took me several days. I put the stuff in the boot of the car I'd hired, and I left the car wherever I was told to on the phone. When I collected it again, the packets of heroin had gone.'

About 10 June, delivery was completed.

28

Moonlight Raid in Italy

During the night of 6 August 1970, the clouds slowly rolled back from the Riviera sky. A pale moon lit up the rocky outline of the coast.

Near the village of Andonesia a row of expensive cars – Bentleys, Ferraris, Lamborghinis – stood in front of a sumptuous villa ablaze with light. These were now joined by several more modest cars, from which a number of men emerged and scattered in the darkness. From the open sea came a distant sound of engines. Several boats, in complete darkness, approached silently and moored several dozen metres from the shore.

By the light of the dashboard of a Fiat that had stopped a few metres from the entrance of the villa, a man checked the time by his watch and then joined a group which was waiting for him, hidden by a clump of spindle-trees.

'Let's go,' he said.

The inspector's order seemed to have travelled over several hundred metres; police emerged from a variety of hiding places, went through the hedge surrounding the garden and approached the villa, keeping an eye on possible exits. The inspector and his assistants went up the flight of steps at the front and drew their guns. Slowly, one of them turned the carved wooden door handle, opening the door just a crack, so that a narrow rectangle of light fell onto the marble floor beyond.

The policemen now heard a buzz of voices, laughter, clinking glasses. At a sign from the inspector, the door was thrown open and his team rushed into the spacious living-room which occupied almost the whole of the ground floor. Men and women reclining in the tawny leather armchairs and sofas had no time to move.

They sat petrified in front of ice buckets, champagne or whisky glasses frozen in their hands.

They had been celebrating their first million dollars earned in the heroin trade. The luxury villa had been hired for the occasion.

'Don't move. This is it.'

A few minutes later the tenants, their guests and their luggage were piled into cars. A systematic search produced nothing. By daybreak, all the members of the group had been identified. Among them were Laurent Fiocconi, Jean-Claude Kella and Joseph Signoli. The former two, whose capture had been the main object of the excercise, tried briefly to take refuge behind false identities. Signoli, who had no police record and whose papers were in order, was released the next day.

'I'd love to know who the bastard was who informed on us,' growled Kella.

'Don't worry,' an inspector replied. 'We've had our eye on you ever since you landed in Europe. You have been observed by the French, Belgian, German and Swiss police one after the other. We took over from them this morning at the frontier.'

'What are we accused of, apart from false papers?'

'Nothing, for the moment. We certainly won't hold you for more than three months. But this morning the American embassy lodged an extradition order. The French will be doing the same tomorrow. The Narcotics Bureau has priority, which is inconvenient for you.'

Extradition to the United States, with the various penalties they might incur there, meant half a century of prison for each of the two criminals; they would have to give up hope of ever recovering their freedom. On the other hand, if they were dealt with by the French police they might get away with a few years' detention.

29

How the Syndicate Worked

The 'drug syndicate' conceived by Joseph Signoli was to be devoted entirely to the transport of heroin to the east coast of the United States. This was to be done with cars whose coachwork had been adapted for the purpose in a garage either in the Porte Champerret district or in Biarritz. The drugs were always put on board in one of these two workshops.

The cars, which came from various sources and were bought either in France or Canada, were dispatched to Boston or New York, sometimes via Montreal; sometimes they were unloaded at Montreal itself. They were sent by boat from Le Havre or Antwerp. On some occasions the car owners did not know the use to which their cars were being put.

The technique was not new, but it enjoyed a certain vogue at that time, when demand in the US was particularly great.

The quantity of heroin dispatched on each trip could be as much as a hundred kilos. The risk was obviously great because, if it was seized, the loss could mean up to fifty million old francs. The aim of the syndicate was precisely to minimise the effects of such a catastrophe, not only on the financial level, but also as far as the personal safety of each of the members of the syndicate was concerned.

When a deal was clinched and the quantity to be transported had been agreed, a budget was established and divided into a certain number of 'shares'. The members of the syndicate were then invited to take one or more of these 'shares', that is, to invest a sum corresponding to the purchase of a certain number of kilos of heroin, usually between five and ten, in the deal. To the purchase of the heroin were added transport costs, estimated overall at five thousand francs a kilo, as well as the purchase price of the car, which was negligible in comparison with the value of the cargo.

The shareholders were kept informed of the progress of preparations and were asked to pay their contributions only when the consignment was actually being sent off. When circumstances demanded it, 'Chairman' Signoli advanced the necessary sum, and sometimes even made do with a letter of credit from one or other of his partners – the sum specified being simply kept back when the share-out took place.

When the car arrived in New York, it was unloaded by the agents of the syndicate and the goods were handed over to the buyer. Then the vehicle was destroyed or abandoned. The sum remitted by the American recipient – Cirillo in this case – was sent to France during the month following the delivery on board another car or, if necessary, in suitcases with false bottoms.

On the money made, Signoli deducted a further twelve thousand francs a kilo to pay Kella's and Fiocconi's 'royalties' and to provide for payment of the organisers. Then the shareholders met again and each of them received a sum proportionate to his investment. The price of heroin being five or six times higher in the US than in Marseilles, the shareholders made several times their original stakes, despite the various deductions.

Part of the profits could immediately be reinvested in a new deal using the same procedures. The courier and receiver who had contributed to a successful delivery could also join the group of investors by ploughing back a portion of their fees. It might also happen that members of the syndicate would leave it to start up an independent organisation, adopting the rules of the original association. It was in this way that a second, then a third network came into existence, with varying degrees of success or failure.

The advantages of this method were obvious. First, each associate was personally concerned about the success of the enterprise, and felt a degree of responsibility for it. Secondly, since every member of the syndicate was aware of the role of every other member in a deal, he could not inform on them without laying himself open to the same proceedings. Obviously, only those participating in a deal would know the actual details, such as date of departure and delivery, names of couriers and receivers, type of car, the boat used and so on.

Within fifteen months, eight cars leaving from Le Havre, Hamburg and Antwerp arrived at their destinations with their cargo. Six hundred and fifty-one kilos of pure heroin were distributed on the clandestine American market. During this period Signoli and his associates pocketed almost three and a half billion old francs. This fantastic and profitable adventure was to end like a traditional detective story, with the arrest of most of the organisers and about thirty of their accomplices.

30

The Gentleman Burglar and the Distinguished Citizen

One morning at the beginning of March 1970, the gates of Fresnes prison opened to release a man of about thirty, of medium height and dressed in a smart suit which had been folded up for longer than suits usually are. He was called Richard Berdin, and he had just served a one-year sentence. He had the face of a spoiled but virile cherub and had already melted many female hearts, only to break them. He appealed to the maternal instinct.

The few passers-by hunched their shoulders in the teeth of an icy wind. Richard turned up his coat collar and hurried towards the metro.

His family background was the reverse of shady. He had been born in Angers, of a well-to-do family, which was given a touch of exoticism by a mother of Russian descent. One of his brothers was a bank manager. His sister was working quietly for an airline. After giving up higher education, he had gradually become one of the most gifted of a new generation of crooks and gangsters, elegant as James Bond dressed by Ted Lapidus or Cardin, and who, between 'jobs', frequented St Germain des Près or the Champs Elysées, scorning Pigalle or the Bastille.

Proceeding down the Avenue du Dr Tenine, Richard Berdin arrived at Croix-de-Berny station on the ligne de Sceaux, from where he telephoned Isabelle C, the call-girl who had been his faithful, patient and forgiving companion for several years, and who had bailed him out of more than one fix. He knew that he had three or four immaculate suits hanging in their plastic bags in a corner of her wardrobe, and that she would have put aside enough money to enable him to hold out until he could resume contact with various helpful parties.

'Is that you, Richard?' asked the familiar voice. 'I didn't come to meet you. You didn't tell me what time you'd be coming out. But I'm waiting for you, come right round.'

An hour later, Richard slipped into a warm bed; he responded to Isabelle's passion with an ardour increased by long privation, but his heart was not in it. He was not an emotional man; in his game, to lose his self-control, even for a few seconds, might be the beginning of the end.

His sensual needs satisfied, he picked up the telephone and dialled several numbers. Isabelle went into the kitchenette to prepare the champagne and caviar and smoked salmon toast intended to help him forget the last months of prison diet. At Richard's third attempt, a man's voice answered. But it was not that of Roger Preiss (also known as 'Eric'), whose Boulogne-Billancourt apartment corresponded to the number he had just dialled.

'Roger? He's not here. Shall I give him a message? Who's calling?'

Something in the tone of the slightly suspicious voice was familiar to Berdin. Suddenly a face came into his mind: François Scapula, known as 'Francis', a fellow who seemed to know all the princes of the Marseilles underworld, and to whom Roger Preiss had introduced him on the terrace of the Pam-Pam on the Champs Elysées during the summer of 1968. The two men had met in the prison at Pau, where Preiss was doing three years and Francis one year.

Berdin gave his name and explained the situation. Scapula replied that Roger had lent him his apartment but he did not know where he was. Learning that Berdin was at a loose end, Scapula arranged to meet him the next day at the Orphéon. He had a suggestion that might interest him.

'Big money? Risky?'

'No risk. And the millions will flood in so fast you won't be able to count them.'

* * *

'Francis' Scapula, an habitué of the Club des Corses on the rue Picpus, was one of the recruiting agents of the drug syndicate which Alexandre Salles and Joseph Signoli were in the process of setting up. Though he did not reveal the carefully worked-out plan of the future enterprise in detail to Berdin, he did inform him of the nature of the traffic in which he was proposing that Berdin should take part. He painted a glowing picture of the profits realised for every kilo which arrived at its American destination; the ever-growing demand; the Marseilles laboratories working flat out.

Richard held back. Like all loners, he was unwilling to enter an organisation in which he could be at the mercy of someone else's treachery. The problems of the society on whose fringes he lived, did not concern him. The jungle law he had chosen left scant room for pity; and the motivations of the people from his own original milieu were utterly alien to him.

'Roger talked to me about this before the cops got me. I'm sure he wouldn't have had anything to do with your scheme. It's too dangerous.'

'He will, when he grasps that you can make ten million francs with the danger of only two or three years inside. You'd get more than ten for armed assault and you have no way of knowing in advance whether you stand to make anything at all. Didn't you read *Le Monde*, in Fresnes? You should have. It said that the American customs don't seize a tenth of the junk taken into the US. You have a one in ten chance of getting caught. It's as easy as falling off a log. The people who do get caught, when they do,' he continued helpfully, 'are the runners, either with the stuff on them, or else concealed in the coachwork of their cars.' But that was not the kind of work he was proposing to a boy like Richard. All he would be asked to do would be to recruit couriers, voluntary or otherwise – both kinds had their advantages – and ultimately to take delivery of the goods on arrival in the US.

'There you will hand them over to our agent and he will deliver them to the American client. Actually, you don't even have to touch it. No one will be able to catch you in the act. And in this business, if they don't catch you red-handed, they have nothing on you at all.'

'What type of couriers do you want?'

'People you can vouch for: small men going off on holiday, big businessmen who are about to sign contracts, artists on tour . . . If they haven't got cars, we can get them for them. If, for some reason, they don't want to travel under their own names, we give them other papers . . .'

He then explained to the surprised Berdin that a hairdresser from the Marais did the rounds in his district and could always find guys ready to ask for a passport and unload it for a thousand or fifteen hundred francs, only to make declaration of loss once it had been used.

Despite all these arguments the aspiring gangster, whose memories of his stay in prison were still all too fresh, was not entirely convinced. He promised Francis he would call him a few days later at Eric's place (Eric being Roger Preiss).

Berdin went over everything that Scapula had told him. On several occasions he had met a character who handled large sums of money but was always short of the odd million, who dined with former (and future) ministers in smart restaurants and enjoyed the reputation of being in close contact with secret service agents. The man in question was called André Labay. He was an occasional film producer, owned a clothes factory in Haiti and was constantly launching new business projects.

A plan began to grow in the ex-prisoner's mind. If he managed to involve Labay in the plans of Francis and his friends, Labay would always be able to bail him out in case of need. He had met Labay on several occasions over the years. He had been introduced to him by one of his friends, Gerard Hotte, who already had several convictions. If the industrialist was not choosy about his associates, he was probably not finicky about methods for earning a lot of money in a short time.

Two days later, Richard Berdin went to Avenue Gabriel, where André Labay gave him a hearty if patronising welcome in a lavishly furnished drawing-room. He asked for news of Hotte, currently in prison in Hagueneau, poured two glasses of whisky and settled down in an armchair, oozing charm. He propped his head, with its halo of almost white hair, enquiringly on his hand, as though he had nothing more pressing to do than listen to his visitor's suggestions. Berdin remained impervious to these attempts at seduction. He was an expert in these matters. While bringing the conversation round to the proposals Scapula had just put to him, he noted the rings round Labay's eyes, the tic which sometimes distorted the corners of his mouth, the slight trembling of the hands. He guessed that the businessman was going through a bad patch; he was ripe to lend an attentive ear to his proposals.

'Labay was receptive,' he was later to reveal. 'He asked for a few days to think about it and for fuller information about the possible profits. I contacted Scapula and the Salles–Signoli team whom I'd met with him on several occasions since 1968. They told me that the courier would get a thousand dollars per kilo of heroin delivered to New York, payable in cash on delivery there.'

At the following meeting, the size of the figure finally swayed Labay. He needed something to get himself out of trouble. The opportunity was golden. Ever since Berdin had painted such a rosy picture for him, his active imagination, now directed towards a precise goal, had come up with multitudes of possibilities. He told Berdin about the plan he had worked out.

'Transporting, even at that price, doesn't interest me. This is what I'm putting to your associates. I've got a pearl-grey Bentley with a T registration plate, in a garage near the porte Champerret. If they want to see it, it's on the right when you come from the Porte Maillot, in a small cul-de-sac just before a service station. I have to go to Haiti on business. It's quite normal for this car to leave France; it's got a temporary registration plate.'

His insistence – and his nervousness – did not escape Berdin. The fish was well and truly hooked. Labay wanted the plan to be carried out as soon as possible because, he claimed, he had to leave for the Caribbean in the next few days and the problems to be sorted out there could not wait indefinitely.

He suggested that he should set off as soon as the goods had been concealed in the doors and under the seats of the Bentley. He would deliver it to Miami, to the Fontainebleau. He thought that the car could hold fifty or so kilos without arousing attention. His position as international businessman would expedite formalities.

A few hours later, Richard Berdin went back to the Orphéon where he met Salles, Signoli and Scapula. He told the team of Labay's suggestion and finally told them who he was. Salles knew of him vaguely, but did not seem enthusiastic. Members of the underworld always hesitate before associating with the middle classes. But Berdin persisted.

'He's desperate. He'll eat out of our hands, in fact on bended knee. Furthermore, it won't be he who gets the car out of customs. He's getting a chauffeur to do that, a bloke he did a favour for in the Congo and who doesn't have any idea what's going on.'

'You must understand,' interrupted Signoli, 'it's not that we don't trust you. We're not doing this first trip for ourselves, but for the fellow who got us the buyer, in New York. It wouldn't be too good if things went wrong straight away.'

A quarter of an hour later, they had reached an agreement. As soon as Signoli had contacted Fiocconi, Scapula would go to Marseilles to get the junk from the supplier. He would hand it over to Berdin who would deliver it to Labay himself.

'As soon as you get it, you'll be responsible for it,' stated the ever-cautious Salles before the group separated. 'I advise you to keep a sharp eye on your businessman. He's always struck me as an unreliable type. According to my information, he's been mixed up in quite a number of crooked deals.'

Salles' misgivings in connection with Labay were justified, as were Berdin's observations. After impressing the business world with his dazzling achievements, the producer of a successful film, *Le Deuxième Soufflé*, had difficulty in getting back on his feet again. A series of setbacks and a period of bad luck had shaken him badly. Always more of an adventurer than a businessman, he was particularly vulnerable to failure. He counted on lady luck: she might have abandoned him temporarily, but soon she would be back at his side.

Of all the figures who were tempted by the prodigious profits of the heroin trade, Labay was one of the most unlikely. Hypnotised like so many others, he set out along the road that led to his downfall without a single backward glance. It is just possible that if either his conscience or his humanity had led him to resist Berdin's tempting proposition, he might have succeeded, if not in amassing another fortune, at least in regaining some of the ground he had lost. He had already succeeded at least a dozen times during twenty years of tightrope walking without a safety net.

'With his snowy hair, his clear blue eyes, his reassuring smile and smooth, pink cheeks, his tasteful and sophisticated *chic*, he looked as innocent as a newborn babe,' journalist Jean Noli wrote in *Paris-Match* when Labay was arrested.

Like Berdin, Labay came of a respected and wealthy family. Before the war his father had founded and directed the Institut Gay-Lussac, where many important figures had done their classical studies. Under his firm guidance, André had passed both parts of his *baccalauréat* at the age of fifteen. While waiting to be old enough to go to the Faculté de Médecine – he wanted to become a surgeon – he became interested in mathematics and wrote a treatise on algebra.

He had just passed his preliminary medical examination when war broke out, promptly followed by the occupation of France. While continuing his medical studies in Paris, Rennes and Dijon, Labay worked for an English intelligence unit. He carried out his missions with remarkable coolness and composure. His imperturbability and effrontery came to his rescue in the most desperate situations. Arrested by the Gestapo in Dijon, he managed to make use of an administrative error to get himself released. About this time he married and had two children.

The war ended. For many underground fighters, this meant the end of adventure. André Labay could not resign himself to that. He gave up the idea of finishing his studies and got divorced. Thanks to the contacts he had made in the Resistance, he obtained a licence to set up an airline, Air Senegal, despite the protests of important businessmen who had asked for the same authorisation.

He sold the airline a few months later and again thanks to his connections obtained permission from the Treasury to repatriate a considerable quantity of piastres from Indo-China for a friend. His intervention enabled this friend to double his capital on the unofficial Hong Kong market. In gratitude, he remitted a sum of a hundred million francs to the obliging intermediary.

André Labay then settled in Tunis and promptly launched into real estate. He spent his life in aeroplanes, at receptions, always accompanied by an attractive Cuban woman. He bubbled over with ideas and drive; he was popular and much sought after. Fate smiled on him and his affairs prospered.

He decided to buy a private plane, went to Paris, then Brussels. In the train, he found himself seated opposite an astonishingly beautiful young woman. They started at one another. It was love at first sight. She was called Danielle and had been a dancer with the Ballets des Champs Elysées. For a month now she had been a cabaret star at the Nouvelle Eve in Paris.

Within a few weeks, Labay had liquidated his interests in various Tunisian companies and offered his Cuban friend the luxury apartment where they lived, as well as his four cars. He went back to Paris and plunged into new deals. He was seen in ministers' ante-rooms and in the company of notorious members of the French secret services. Each night at three he waited for Danielle in the bar or at the artists' entrance of the Nouvelle Eve.

Then suddenly, for reasons unknown, fortune stopped smiling on him, though his state of bliss continued. He stopped being a tycoon and became a commercial traveller. He scoured the roads of provincial France at the wheel of a 2 CV, going from farm to manor house, offering household linen on credit. He and Danielle could not bear to be separated, even for two or three days. She gave up her career and followed him on his rounds. Together, their turnover equalled that of ten ordinary commercial travellers. But at week-ends they exchanged their 2 CV for the Buick André still owned and frequented luxury hotels and casinos, drinking in an ambiance which helped them bear the long gruelling weeks on the road.

Then fortune smiled once more. Once again Labay was seen with big names from the worlds of finance and politics. Danielle was dressed by the best couturiers. The couple popped up in London, Brussels and Rome. The businessman moved in Pious XII's circles and had a private audience with him on several occasions. The Vatican granted him a world monopoly on the distribution and sale of the medal commemorating the centenary of the appearance of the Virgin at Lourdes.

New projects took him to Morocco. At the wheel of the Buick Danielle had a head-on collision with a taxi in the Bois de Boulogne. When her shattered body was extricated from the crumpled metal, her face was a bloody mass. The house physician immediately signed a death certificate at the emergency unit of the hospital. But a breath of life persisted. When Labay returned a fortnight later, she was just coming out of a coma. He spent six months at her bedside. She was saved, but disfigured for life.

So as to get his business on its feet again, André set off for the Belgian Congo to buy coffee. The Prime Minister of the young Republic, Cyrille Adoula, knew of his activities in the secret services and asked him to organise a world-wide intelligence net. Labay accepted, with the blessing of the French SDECE and the American CIA, who were delighted to have one of their men on the spot. He had unlimited credit at his disposal and spent freely, making appearances in every capital in the world.

He was suspected of having tried to kidnap the king of Kasai, Kalondji, whose country was rich in diamonds. He followed a Belgian international lawyer to the Antilles; he seduced another Prime Minister, this time the leader of the new federation of the islands of St Kitts–Nevis–Anguilla. He obtained the sole licence to set up a bank there. He bought a thousand hectares of land in Nevis and sold off part of it a few days later for eight hundred thousand dollars. He chartered a Boeing to go to meet Queen Elizabeth and Prince Philip, who were on an official visit, and presented the sovereign with plans for a millionaires' leisure and holiday resort. He appeared at her side on television screens.

Then he sold off his bank to the Bank of America and his project to some American promoters.

Back in Paris with Danielle, who now led a hermit's existence, Labay launched into further enterprises. With three associates he bought a hotel on rue Pierre Ier de Serbie, which they intended to turn into a club for international businessmen, the *sine qua non* being proof of an annual turnover of a million francs. Several incautious company chairman paid out contributions in advance.

But Labay's partners, if perhaps less talented than he was, were none the less rasher and bolder. After handing over a dud cheque for seven million francs as an advance on the purchase of the hotel (which was valued at sixteen million) to a credulous notary, one of them, Michel Leroy, proceeded to sell off the carpets, furniture and china. In October he used it as a refuge for Colonel Dmili, head of the Moroccan *Sureté* and deputy to General Oufkir, who was accused of having been involved in the kidnapping of the Moroccan politician Medhi Ben Barka. Other mysterious tenants lodged there: the mercenaries recruited by a third associate, Thierry de Bonnay, who trained them on an abandoned farm in the Ardèche.

Thierry, a Resistance fighter at seventeen, ex-US army volunteer, and former Congo mercenary, was in the process, with assistance from certain mysterious sources, of attempting to organise the cadres of an African revolution which would bring to power men likely to serve the very considerable western financial interests in the newly independent states. At the beginning of 1968, a commando in Algiers was awaiting orders to free Moise Tschombe, who had been imprisoned by Boumedienne in June 1967. The fourth associate was a Swiss banker, Schwarm, for whom the adventure was to end in a Geneva prison.

Labay and his two companions belonged to the clique, particularly prosperous during the sixties, which straddled the worlds of politics, finance and intelligence. They were like the bubbles which come to the surface of a pool when the muddy bottom is stirred up. And there was a lot of stirring going on during that period throughout the world. Labay appeared alone when the bankruptcy proceedings for rue Pierre Ier de Serbie took place. His two friends had died, both in car crashes, after having been arrested and then released for equally mysterious reasons.

Belgian justice awaited Labay in Brussels. Here he was director of an insurance company, the Belfort, which was in the process of collapsing, caught up in a real estate crash of eighty million francs in the south of France. The managing director who had chosen him for the post was called Rives-Henrys de Lavaysse. He was to enjoy a doubtful sort of fame with the collapse of the Garantie Foncière.

These few incidents, by the way, did not prevent Labay from investing several tens of millions in the production of the film *Le Deuxième Soufflé*, which had an immense success two months later. He then rushed into another production, *Anastasia*, sinking a fortune into it, but it came to nothing. His overdraft in a Geneva bank rose to seven million Swiss francs. He invited the self-styled sole survivor of the Russian imperial family massacred by the Bolsheviks to France, a publicity stunt which won him further notoriety.

Then he turned up in Switzerland once more, again in partnership with Schwarm, with whom he planned to coin and distribute gold coins and medallions bearing the heads of the black kings of Africa, Papa Doc of Haiti and even General de Gaulle. Several political figures were involved with this last project, which never came to anything. It was then that Schwarm was arrested. The people who had begun to back these various enterprises never saw their money again.

In Rome Labay met the widow of an industrialist. Love at first sight again. Danielle, still a recluse, had sadly resigned herself to his long absences. Each of Labay's lady friends was kept in ignorance of the other. He and his new conquest set up a company specialising in the issuing of gold postage stamps. He went to Haiti, charmed Papa Doc, obtained an advance of a hundred thousand dollars, became both *chevalier servente* of Marie-Denise (one of his two daughters) and the dictator's *eminence grise*. He started up a clothing factory which was to give work to four hundred Haitians, and entertained visiting Americans, some of whom belonged to the 'special services'.

He became the black dictator's adviser, dividing his time between Port-au-Prince, Washington and the European capitals. Then he invested his own remaining funds, his mistress's fortune and all the money he could lay hands on in a real estate deal. But the persuasive businessman to whom he had entrusted it used this money to silence his own creditors. Bankruptcy followed.

It was then that Richard Berdin visited him. Despite his misgivings, he dared not reject the proposition.

31

Cadillac, Bentley, Lancia . . . Smart Cars

Berdin resumed his apparently idle life, once more returning to his old haunts le Bistingo, l'Orphèon and the Club des Corses. He was unobtrusive but friendly and attentive. Each snatch of conversation was noted and pigeon-holed. This helped him to pick up the threads of relationships in a scene to which he had been a stranger for a year.

He took up with old friends, such as Roger Preiss, alias Eric, who, thanks to a profitable but mysterious deal, was going on holiday to Italy. Berdin and Preiss were birds of a feather: slightly shady, attractive, Priess was a tall, well-built man, fair-haired and blue-eyed, at ease in all walks of life. His temporary prosperity allowed him to turn down Scapula's offers. Drugs were not his thing.

Scapula, who was to go to Marseilles, introduced Berdin to several of his friends. This was how the newcomer met Francis-le-Belge (Francis Vanverberghe) and learned of his association with Fiocconi. Francis was a regular at the Pub Renault. Presentable, amiable and smiling though he always was, members of the underworld knew that he was merciless.

Berdin saw him again a few days later in Preiss's apartment, with Pierre Lastroyoli and other members of the syndicate: André Lajoux and Antoine Grisoni, alias Tony-le-Corse.

After Scapula's departure for Marseilles where the goods were waiting for him, Berdin continued to frequent l'Orphéon. There he met an elegant little pimp whom he had known before his period in prison, Dominique M. Dominique had seen him with Signoli and Salles and, like most of the regulars, he had a vague idea of his new activities. 'At the beginning of our relationship'

Berdin was later to reveal, 'he'd told me confidentially that he had a fairly close friend in the SDECE. This meant that there was a possibility of obtaining good quality false identity papers.'

This relative was called Roger Delouette. At the time – it was the beginning of 1968 – Dominique had several women working for him on the streets of Marseilles and Paris. His side-line was the disposal of counterfeit Algerian banknotes. Now he, too, was taking an interest in the drug scene, and was to invest a fairly considerable sum of money in an imminent consignment.

'If you ever have any difficulties with your new associates, come and see me.'

One rainy morning at the end of April, Berdin was waiting for the *Mistral* at the Gare de Lyon. At last he saw Scapula appear, preceded by a porter wheeling two heavy suitcases. He took them to the car he had hired for the purpose.

'I've brought you thirty kilos. Fifteen in each case, in packets of five hundred grams.'

Half-an-hour later, Berdin was parking his car behind André Labay's in a quiet cul-de-sac near rue Guersant, about a hundred metres from the garage where the heroin was to be concealed in the Bentley.

'Everything is already organised,' announced Labay. 'I've got someone to take the car to Le Havre and put it on the *France*. He will take it out of customs in New York. I have to go to Haiti on business. I'll let you know when everything is ready. We can meet in Miami. Come to the Fontainebleau.'

The 'someone' was called Raymond Moulin, and Labay had met him in the Congo. According to Berdin, the carrier in question had acted as Labay's bodyguard when he was running the young republic's secret services. Officially, Moulin ran a snack bar in Leopoldville called the Pam. On his return, after working for several months in a drugstore near the Champs Elysées, he had asked Labay to help him out.

The following week Moulin drove to Avenue Gabriel. Labay got into the Renault beside him. They drove off towards the racecourse at Auteuil. The Bentley was parked in front of the entrance, its glittering metallic coachwork providing quite a spectacle. Labay went up to his companion and handed him the keys and papers of the car.

'Among the papers there's the address of an agency which will deal with the registration and embarkation at Le Havre. You'll take a plane a week after the *France* has left, and stay at the Waldorf Astoria, where I'll call you. Oh yes – here are your travelling expenses.'

He produced a wad of notes from his pocket, handed it nonchalantly to his unsuspecting courier and sat down at the wheel of the Renault.

'You'll find the Renault in the car-park at the Georges V. I'll leave the slip at the service station.'

Two days later, Raymond Moulin was driving towards Le Havre and André Labay was preparing to go to Port-au-Prince. The evening before, he had told Richard Berdin, 'Have a good rest in Miami. Don't worry about anything. The goods will already be in New York. But one never knows. In case of trouble, I'd prefer them not to know where to find them.'

Armed with a fistful of dollars – the equivalent of seven thousand francs – and a light suitcase, he took the train for Luxembourg. An Icelandic Airlines plane deposited him in the Bahamas a few days later; that same evening, he slept in the room he had reserved in the Fontainebleau, in Miami.

The following morning, he received a phone call from Labay telling him that the goods were awaiting him at the Waldorf Astoria on Park Avenue, Manhattan.

In New York, Raymond Moulin – who had just arrived at the Plaza – joined Labay in the almost empty street-level car-park; he was at the wheel of the Bentley which had gone through the customs without any problems.

'He told me he had to dismantle the doors,' Moulin said, 'and of course that was where the stuff was. Three doors had been successfully dismantled, and from these we extracted the packets of white powder. The handle of the fourth door was broken and we couldn't dismantle it so the packets were removed by pulling the lining out from above.'

It took Labay four trips to get the whole load up to his room. When Richard Berdin arrived, the goods were waiting for him in two suitcases, which he took away with him. The next day, he met the man who was to hand them over to the American buyer and then to remit the various payments. He was called Jean Dumerain. Berdin had already met him in Fresnes; his was not the kind of appearance you forgot. He was a squat man with a weaselly face of astonishing ugliness. Whatever the provenance of his clothes, he looked as if he had just emerged from a second-hand clothes shop. His procurer friends had several girls working for him, to help him survive. The suitcases were transported from car to taxi. Berdin's part in the deal was over.

Dumerain gave him another appointment for that evening in the bar of the Hilton on the Avenue of the Americas. Arriving a few minutes late, he sat down on the bench beside the delivery man and discreetly handed him an envelope.

'Business is picking up,' he said with a wink. 'Here are thirty-seven thousand dollars, that's your share and Labay's. You can see it's a good scheme. If your mate brings another carload next month, as arranged, you'll get the same again, or possibly more.'

A few moments later, at the Waldorf, Labay pocketed twenty-seven thousand dollars, his profits, and announced that he was going back to France.

A new consignment was planned. Several times Labay urged Berdin to find a house with a garage on the outskirts of New York, but the gentleman burglar had no desire to go from agency to agency traipsing through the suburbs. Thinking that his collaboration in the first deal would safeguard him from betrayal, he introduced Labay to Signoli, who described himself as a businessman called Lambert. Agreement was soon reached on a second consignment.

In June 1970, Labay had been patronising a garage called the Spega, near Porte Champerret, for several months. 'He was a regular client,' said one of the employees, 'because he had several personal cars and seemed to be involved in a lot of accidents.'

One of the mechanics, Claude, who did the repairs, owned a car which caught Labay's attention. It was a Lancia Flaminia, and Claude was prepared to sell it for four thousand francs. Labay did not hesitate. He bought it cash down.

Various alterations were carried out to this vehicle, in particular to the back part of the wings and in a space between the back of the back seat and the boot. Raymond Moulin, the 'chaffeur' had no idea how much heroin had been concealed in these hiding places: a hundred and forty plastic bags, representing seventy kilos of heroin which Louis Cirillo was to buy at ten thousand dollars a kilo.

At the same time, in New York, Berdin received an unexpected phone call, from Joseph Signoli. 'I've just arrived. Meet me tomorrow at the Hilton bar at the corner of Fifth Avenue. Delivery will take place in a week.'

André Labay had taken up residence at the Waldorf Astoria. Berdin was still in the Hyde Park, where he had intended to stay for just a few days.

His part in the affair meant spending long hours with Signoli, who had no liking for him at all. His failure to find a house with a garage for the unloading of the Lancia, the breeziness with which he received criticism and his lack of enthusiasm for the enterprise in which he was involved, were all irritants. It looked as though Berdin's heart was not in the venture.

For the moment, the gentleman-burglar's energies were devoted mainly to the pursuit of a small, plump, snub-nosed girl with innocent wide eyes as blue as a mountain lake and a permanent grin: pretty Nancy G.

In short, Labay and his Lancia arrived at a bad moment. Richard wanted to have done with the transfer of the merchandise as soon as possible. His accomplices found him more negligent than ever.

Finally, Labay and Moulin in the Lancia, followed by Berdin

in a hired Mustang, set out for Brooklyn. They stopped in an almost empty car-park. While Berdin kept watch, Moulin slid under the car, unscrewed the panels beneath the front wings and passed the packets one by one to Labay, who put them in a Samsonite case which Berdin then placed in the boot of the Mustang.

Then the group broke up. Berdin returned to Ocean Avenue alone; there Signoli was waiting for him in front of the building where Kathy and Jean-Claude Kella had pursued their love affair. The men from Marseilles, Richard Berdin and Guido Rendel (alias Ricard), took the cases up to the apartment. Signoli opened them to count the packets. Grim-faced, he turned to Berdin who had stretched out on the sofa.

'One kilo is missing,' he announced.

'I didn't put the stuff in the cases. I just transported them.'

'You're the receiver. It's part of your job to check the consignment.'

'Bah, you'll find your kilo somewhere. It's probably still in the Lancia.'

The next day, when the two men met again, Signoli made no reference to the missing kilo. He handed seventy thousand dollars over to Berdin, who kept ten thousand and gave the rest to Labay that evening: Labay was leaving New York the following day.

The Lancia abandoned by Moulin in a car-park was not in a fit state to drive. Labay therefore needed another vehicle for the next trip, as soon as Scapula and Salles had brought the agreed quantity of heroin, seventy kilos, from Marseilles.

The wife of the owner of the garage on rue Guersant had a Mercedes big enough to conceal a considerable cargo. It had been in the garage for several months and could quickly be adapted for the purpose. All that was needed was a courier to play the part of the car owner. One of Labay's contacts worked in a photographic laboratory; he was called Jean-Claude Demeester, and he cherished a dream of a holiday in America; but currency laws caused problems, limiting the sum he could take to a thousand francs.

'I think I've found a solution for you,' Labay said to him one evening in July 1970, on the terrace at Fouquet's. 'I've got a friend who has a Mercedes for sale. You buy it and take it to America by sea. I've got a client over there who's interested in it. The price of the car will pay for your trip. If necessary, I can advance you the money and I'll take care of all the formalities.'

Everything went smoothly and the following month, the Mercedes was safely in the hold of the *France* among the other vehicles doing the crossing.

When Berdin asked for his instructions for this third delivery, Signoli seemed embarrassed. 'I think it would be better if you kept out of it; Kella didn't trust you. He didn't like the way you went about it. He's asked me for a report on you.'

Berdin burst out laughing. 'A report! Who does he think he is? The chairman of a multi-national company? He's forgetting that it was me who brought in Labay and that I get my share of the deal!'

Jo reassured him. There was no question of doing him out of his share. But, as Fiocconi and Kella were involved in the deal, it would be as well not to cross them, even though they were in prison in Italy at this time. They were arrested in a castle near Milan.

On 12 August 1970 the *France* entered New York harbour. Moulin, who had arrived the day before by plane, had met Labay at the Waldorf. When the immigration formalities began, he went into the street that sloped up from the exits of the port. The cars came through the grille one behind the other. At last the Mercedes appeared, with Demeester at the wheel. Moulin gestured to him, opened the door and flopped down into the seat.

'We'll park the car at the Waldorf. It's murder driving around New York by car. Any problems with the customs?'

'None at all! They hardly looked inside. There were hundreds of cars on the boat.'

The next morning, Demeester and Moulin met in a cafeteria,

went to the car-park and got into the Mercedes. 'We were to go to the corner of 20th Street and Third Avenue, draw up at the pavement and wait for three men in a car to signal to us to follow them.' All went according to plan. The three men were Signoli, Rendel and Andreani.

One after the other, the two vehicles crossed the bridge out of Manhattan and drove through endless suburbs. At last they arrived in front of a garage with an open door. Signoli signalled Demeester to drive in. He himself parked a little further down the street, got out and came up to the Mercedes.

'Your businessman has told you where the goods were hidden,' he said to Moulin. Unload them, leave them here and go off with the car. We'll stay outside to keep watch.'

'What "goods"?' asked Demeester, flabbergasted.

'Never you mind,' replied Moulin. 'I'll explain later. Powdered diamonds.'

Together they dismantled the doors and the back seat and piled a hundred and forty packets against the wall. The unloading over, they got back into they car, reversed and drove off; the other car took their place. An hour later, they were back in the Waldorf. The following morning Signoli brought Berdin seventy thousand dollars, his share and Labay's.

'Sorry about that business,' he said to him. 'It might be better for you not to hang around in New York. I'll be in touch.'

Labay took back the Bentley documents, which were still with the agents. He had found a buyer, a young dancer on tour, a friend of his mistress Elizabeth. He took advantage of the respite to try and put a little order into his many and confused affairs.

Back in France, Berdin went to take a few days' holiday on the Côte d'Azur. He was driving along the coast road at the wheel of a hired car in the direction of St Tropez, when his car hit a pylon at a turning. In a state of semi-consciousness he heard the sound of police sirens and an ambulance.

Then he remembered that he had a small amount of marijuana in the glove box, and imagined himself appearing before a court for being found carrying twenty grams of grass. His eyes glazed over and he lost consciousness. When he came to, he was in a hospital bed.

Two days later, an unexpected visit caused his stock to soar in the estimation of the hospital staff. A Rolls-Royce stopped in front of the flight of entrance steps; a suntanned fifty-year-old, quirkily elegant, with a halo of white hair, emerged from it. Taken to his friend's bedside, he drew up a chair, saying cheerily, 'Look after yourself, get some rest. There's no hurry. I'll take care of everything till you're back on your feet.'

He leant over and murmured, 'I've found a stunning car for the next trip. A pre-war Cadillac. Been used in several films. Big as a bus, and could hold two hundred kilos of junk. A real museum piece. No customs man would dare dismantle it.'

The 1939 Cadillac, registration number 49 DK 75, had arrived in the Spega garage, near the Porte Champerret, towed there by a breakdown van. A number of repairs had to be carried out before it could move under its own steam, as it had deteriorated as it lay among cinema studio accessories and, before that, had been banged about during film sequences.

It was parked in a corner of the garage and as the months went by, and as the various parts became available, Claude the mechanic gradually reassembled it.

Georges Leakovic, the garage owner, did not really know what he was going to do with it when it was ready. But the successive purchase of several second-hand cars by André Labay – for himself and his friends – gave Leakovic the idea of offering it to him. The industrialist had let slip remarks which implied that the cars he bought had been used in smuggling operations.

André Labay asked the garage-owner to carry out various alterations which would elude the most meticulous customs' searches. He decided to entrust this task to a Spanish coachwork builder employed by his company and known as Franco.

Together, Leakovic and Franco examined the possibilities afforded by the Cadillac. Under the floor of the boot, above the petrol tank, a container could be placed so that to the naked eye it would be indistinguishable from the tank itself. Furthermore, the streamlined outline of the front wings, behind the wheels, provided two spaces which could be closed in with a sheet of metal following the exact sweep of the wings.

Lastly, and most important, there was the chassis: a cross-shaped metal frame, thirty-five centimetres thick. On the sides were triangular metal plates, punched with openings for a number of cables, wires and ducts for ventilation etc. The chassis itself included various openings, with the exhaust pipe coming in on one side and the petrol intake on the other.

Franco's work thus consisted in replacing these lateral triangular plates with triangular containers measuring one metre twenty at the base, forty centimetres in height and thirty-five in depth, with access given by trap doors let into the upper part. Once the coachwork had been reassembled, the two trap doors were invisible under the floor of the car.

The work took several weeks. Labay went to the garage almost every day. He would look on for several minutes in silence while the Spaniard worked on. One Sunday Demeester came too, with Moulin.

That Monday morning, for the first time, the garage office was locked. On Tuesday, during the course of various comings and goings, the Spaniard noticed a small brown leather case and a large blue metal suitcase standing in a corner of the room. The Cadillac was due to leave the following day, Wednesday.

'That morning,' Franco was later to recount, 'I lay under the car and put my finger in the air hole of one of the containers. I came across a lining of plastic which gave under the pressure. I looked through this hole and through the plastic I could see a sort of white powder. I said nothing, but I realised that it was drugs.'

At the beginning of November 1970, Berdin was well enough to return to Paris, putting in appearances at his old haunts the Bistingo and the Orphéon on rue Picpus.

Salles and Signoli had not been in touch since his return.

At last they resurfaced and began to express impatience at Labay's dilatoriness. He was never there when he was needed. They asked Richard to use all his influence on the businessman.

'But I thought you didn't trust me any more, that I made too much of a spectacle of myself driving around in flash cars, throwing money around and dressed to kill – behaving like a Marseilles gangster!'

'Forget it! That was Fiocconi and Kella. Now they're inside doing a hundred years!'

The mission they had come to entrust to Richard was not very demanding. Two days later, André Labay appeared, edgy and complaining in his turn of the slowness and casual behaviour of his Marseilles associates. The reason for his impatience was because he had discovered that his affairs, which tottered on only thanks to the frenzied use of accommodation bills, were on the edge of collapse. He needed to find several tens of millions of francs as soon as possible to refloat them. Hence his new-found eagerness for the operation.

The Cadillac, its chrome gleaming as if it had just come off the assembly line, left the garage once and for all, driven off by Demeester and Moulin, towards Germany, on its way to Hamburg where it would be put on board the *Hermann Russ*, destination Montreal.

During the first week of December 1970, the cargo boat, flying the East German flag, sailed slowly up the St Laurence river and docked at a quay in Montreal. On deck, a passenger watched the banks of the mighty Canadian river move past. He was experience-ing the anguish felt by all smugglers as they are about to face the customs, but he had one advantage over other drug smugglers, namely, that he did not know the precise nature of the goods that had been put into his care.

The passenger was Jean-Claude Demeester. Men in uniform – police, customs officials, quarantine and immigration personnel – soon poured onto the boat and proceeded to carry out routine checks. Two hours later, the Frenchman had been through the various ordeals which lay between him and Canadian soil. Only one remained – the examination of the Cadillac itself. A crane lifted it out of the bowels of the *Hermann Russ* and placed it neatly in front of a transit shed.

Customs men crowded round it, pushed it to one side. Some climbed in, lifting up the seats and carpets, looking behind the dashboard; then they jacked it up; slid underneath on low trolleys and examined the chassis and the wings.

Demeester looked on. A man in uniform asked him to accompany him to an office, where two men were waiting for him. The questioning began. A mere formality at first, it gradually became treacherous, insistent.

'Were you carrying drugs? Before replying you should know that if you admit as much before we've discovered anything, this will be taken into account.'

Demeester expressed indignation and trotted out the explanations supplied by André Labay, which were received with polite scepticism. Two hours later, an employee in blue overalls came in, leant over to one of the customs men and murmured a few words. Then he went off again. The customs man turned to Demeester.

'The car is an old model our men are unfamiliar with: we'll have to call in an expert and this formality may delay you a little. But in the meantime we will take you to a hotel.'

At the wheel of a hired car, André Labay, who had arrived the previous evening by plane, had been waiting at the port entrance for his 'carrier' for several hours. Suddenly he saw a customs car and recognised the hapless Demeester in the back between two uniformed men. He felt a surge of panic, sat still for a few seconds and then set off to follow the vehicle to see where his accomplice was being taken.

This tailing led him to the *Laurentien* which the customs men had suggested to Demeester, since rooms were a modest fifteen dollars. Getting out of the official car, the courier recognised André Labay. He smiled and signalled, but the businessman had already driven off and disappeared into the flow of traffic.

It was all too clear. The presence of the customs man meant that his accomplice had been caught. If he was being taken to a hotel, it was merely to lay a trap for those who were coming to take delivery of the heroin, a trap his vigilance had foiled. He drove rapidly to his hotel, packed his bags, asked for the bill, drove to the airport, returned his hired car and rushed to the ticket office: 'What is the next plane for Europe?'

'Swissair for Zurich, in half an hour.'

He bought a ticket, boarded the plane and did not relax until after take-off. He now began to sketch out plans to extricate himself from his predicament unscathed.

Not knowing what reactions he had just provoked, Demeester had gone to his room in the *Laurentien* and, after a brief wash and brush-up, emerged to join the customs men who had accompanied him. But he was informed at the reception desk that they had gone off again. This behaviour slightly reassured the apprentice trafficker. He took a taxi and went back to the port. He was made to wait over two hours at the customs. At last he was handed a paper – after a further interrogation about the purposes of his journey – authorising him to take out the 1939 Cadillac. One hour later, he at last arrived at the *Laurentien*, put his car in the carpark and settled into his room to wait for the call from André Labay, in accordance with his instructions.

'Labay didn't seem to be making a move; Demeester was to reveal later. 'and all I had was twenty dollars. So I decided to go back to Paris. I changed my return boat ticket for a Montreal–Paris ticket on Air France. I had to pay a twelve-dollar supplement.

Two days later, Demeester was already back in Montreal with two thousand dollars which Labay had handed over to him after a series of embarrassed explanations.

He set off again at the wheel of his imposing vehicle; it was drizzling gloomily when he reached the American frontier. The customs men on duty received the arrival of this forgotten species as a welcome distraction. They sat the driver down, offered him a coffee, examined his papers, nodded quietly at his explanations and proceeded to carry out the same meticulous examination that their Canadian colleagues at the port of Montreal had engaged in.

After removing the seats, searching the boot and examining the chassis, they explained to Demeester with embarassed smiles that they would have to take the car to a local garage for a more thorough examination. 'They put it on an inspection pit,' Demeester stated, 'and examined the underneath, the engine, everything, including the interior. They even dismantled the front right-hand fan which was underneath the front seat. They found nothing and let me go on my way.'

In New York, he stayed at the Waldorf Astoria and put the Cadillac in the nearby garage, where it stayed until the evening. At ten o'clock Demeester and Moulin, who was staying in the *Ashbury*, got into the mammoth vehicle and drove into the street. At a signal from the lights of a blue Buick driven by Berdin, they slid into its wake. One behind the other, the two cars drove round town for a bit to check for possible tailing, then set off for Long Island. The building used as a garage by Louis Cirillo's associates was between Farmingdale and Amityville, on Picone Boulevard.

The two vehicles left the freeway at Farmingdale. It was pouring with rain and the headlights made little impression on the darkness. Suddenly Berdin made out the silhouette of 'Gros Dédé' Andreani on a hard shoulder, his open umbrella in his hand. He climbed in immediately. After several manoeuvres aimed at shaking off possible pursuers, the two vehicles drove into the Picone Boulevard garage; its sliding door was closed behind them by two attendants.

There were a few dozen cars parked there; the attendants shifted several of them so that their lights would shine on the Cadillac. Moulin, who knew where the caches were hidden, directed operations; his accomplices were armed with screwdrivers and monkey wrenches. One by one, the transparent plastic packets of white powder appeared and were piled into the Samsonite bags which Berdin had produced from the boot of the Buick.

Demeester now understood what kind of activity he was involved in. Moulin confirmed his suspicions. He had a retrospective shudder of horror remembering the scrutiny the Cadillac had been subjected to. And his horror deepened when he discovered that there was an opening beneath the fan placed under the left-hand front seat: the customs mechanic at the frontier had satisfied himself with unscrewing the front right-hand fan.

Suddenly Andreani looked worried. Soon all the packets would have been unloaded from the car, yet the number of those now lying in the suitcase did not correspond to the number given him. Inspection lamps were brought up to search the remotest corners, the cases were emptied and the packets recounted. There was no mistaking the facts: there were only a hundred and two kilos of heroin instead of the one hundred and sixty-nine announced. Sixty-seven kilos were missing.

Consternation all round. It is not easy to lose sixty-seven kilos of anything by mistake. The question was, therefore, when had they gone astray. It was unlikely that it would have been during loading, during the journey or during the Canadian or American customs.

'It's very simple,' said Berdin, 'let's put all the packets back in the hiding places. We'll soon see if there's enough space for sixty-seven kilos.'

Despite their exhaustion, the four men set to work. The experiment was conclusive. There was absolutely no space to stuff another packet. The missing kilos must have disappeared during loading.

The following morning, there was furious telephonic activities across the Atlantic. Andreani, the official representative of the syndicate, called his 'chairmen' Salles and Signoli. Their initial reaction was foreseeable: 'No one gets paid until we find the sixty-seven kilos.' Thus the loss would be limited, whatever happened.

Berdin and Moulin arrived to join Labay on Avenue Gabriel. Labay protested indignantly, claiming that the packets could only have been stolen during the crossing or at delivery. He refused to admit that the car could not contain a hundred and sixty-nine kilos. 'I was there when they put them in; everything fitted.' 'Did you count the packets?' 'No, but . . .' The mystery remained unsolved, and relations were strained.

Dissatisfied and penniless, Moulin and Demeester would have liked to go back to France without further ado. But there was the problem of the return fare and their hotel bills. 'We asked Berdin for money,' admitted Moulin. 'He didn't like the idea of lending us anything but at last he gave us enough for us to get our return tickets.'

In New York another problem remained: the incriminating Cadillac had to be made to disappear. 'Gros Dédé' strenuously refused to be involved. 'What if the police have got an eye on it? You've got the parking slip, it's your problem.' For two or three days, Richard drove it aimlessly from car-park to car-park, in search of some solution.

At last, one rainy evening, he set off for Harlem. After some reconnoitring, he drove up a small street ending in a deserted lot surrounded by apparently empty sheds and buildings. Patiently, by torchlight, ears pricked, he searched the vehicle, destroying everything that might lead to his identification. He opened the windows so that the vehicle would deteriorate more quickly. Soaked to the skin, he returned to midtown Manhattan.

32

A Miraculous Draught

Henri Hairabedian, twenty-seven, was a petrol pump attendant at the garage St Maurice on rue Paradis in Marseilles. In the late afternoon of Sunday 21 February 1971, he received a visit from someone who had become what he called his 'friend from the stade Vélodrome', because they often went to football matches there together. His friend was Edouard Toudayan. He was living at Rouquefort-la-Bedoule, where he had built a luxurious villa, legally owned by his wife. Though his official job was that of water-softener salesman, many people in Marseilles realised that he was primarily a 'quiet man', an important figure in drug trafficking. However, he had never been caught in the act. Although people who worked for him, like the gifted young chemist, Pierre R, had been arrested and imprisoned. Toudayan himself had been discharged. (See chapter 6 for an account of his activities.)

When Toudayan went to see his young garage friend on that Sunday in February it was to ask him if he could rent him a van to 'do a job'.

'I've got an appointment for the morning of the 24th at Port Carro with two Turkish sailors who are bringing in some goods for me,' he told Hairabedian. 'Come on,' he added, 'you won't regret it.' The financial implications were clear.

Since the breaking up of the organisation of the Lebanese Samiy Khoury in November 1965, the Turks had gradually begun to deal directly with the French over the delivery of opium or raw morphine.

Since the majority of the Turks did not speak French, they utilised as interpreters their old enemies the Armenians who lived around Marseilles.

There was no longer any question of going via Aleppo in Syria or Beirut in the Lebanon where smugglers specialised in this trade bought the goods from them. Now the Turks delivered directly and tripled or quadrupled their profits. There were a dozen of them, perfectly organised, including Huseyin Eminoglu, Hagi Kiver, Ibrahim Sen, Muhtar Berk, and Ali Kambur.

Ali Kambur, alias Ali Rizili, lived in Istanbul. He was one of the leading members of the traffickers' organisation. He was in direct contact with Toudayan, himself of Armenian origin though born in Marseilles.

They made use of sailors, on Turkish vessels, cargo boats or mixed cargo and passenger vessels, calling at Marseilles: when the merchandise was not directly unloaded at this port, it went to Genoa or Naples and returned to Marseilles by devious routes by land or sea.

In Istanbul in January 1971, two old friends had arranged to meet one Sunday morning in a café on Taksim Square, in the heart of Istanbul.

Hardly had Mehmet Faruk Savas, a sailor who had been temporarily laid off by his company in April 1970, parked his car (an Opel Rekord) than his mate Kahraman Sebas Rusen arrived at the wheel of his Ford Mustang. He too was an experienced sailor, also laid-off by his company, which was a state enterprise.

They had three expensive tastes in common: drink, gambling and women. Ali Kambur offered the two sailors the opportunity of earning enough to indulge in these activities to their hearts' content All they had to do was carry a little over three hundred and sixty kilos of raw morphine to Marseilles, preferably on a cargo boat.

Sebas Rusen, who had graduated from the Ecole des Hautes Etudes Maritimes Turques in 1954, had numerous contacts among the sailors and needed only two days to place the cargo on a suitable boat: the coaster *Divanbakirli* commanded by one Uludag, was to leave Istanbul for Port-de-Bouc. Rusen knew that the *Divanbakirli* would not have a mate when she sailed from Istanbul on 7 February.

A few days before departure, Faruk Savas and Sebas Rusen

met and agreed to meet again on 23 February, at about eleven, in a bar in Marseilles, at the foot of the steps leading down from the Gare St Charles.

Savas was to take the plane from Istanbul to Paris, then on to Marseilles–Marignane. On 7 February, at seven in the morning, the coaster *Divanbakirli*, 995 tons, with a crew of nine under their captain Uludag, weighed anchor. She left the port of Orkatoj, in Istanbul, went through the Bosphorus into the Sea of Marmara to Bandirma to load up nine hundred tins of boracite ore destined for the French port of Caronte, between the gulf of Fos and the Etang de Berre.

Because of a religious holiday, loading could not take place until two days later. On 10 February, after loading the *Divanbakirli* weighed anchor and proceeded to Derince to stock up with fuel.

Since the cargo boat had a capacity of less than a thousand tons, any captain or sailor with the necessary papers could be taken on as a mate.

It was in Derince, in agreement with the captain of the *Divanbakirli*, that his friend Rusen came aboard, presumably with the precious clandestine merchandise which was loaded under cover of dark. On the 11th, at thirteen hundred hours, the boat weighed anchor. On the 12th, at eight am, it went through the Dardanelles.

Uludag informed one of the two owners of the boat, Muzaffer Divan, of the state of affairs. Divan pointed out in a return telegram that he had no mate on board and the captain radioed back: 'Don't worry, I can manage.'

He did not mention that Rusen had come on board at Derince and was in fact fulfilling that position.

From the Aegean, the cargo boat entered the Mediterranean where she ran into bad weather, which, during the course of the 18th, forced her to put into port somewhere along the coast of Corsica, where she remained for two days. Rusen took advantage of this to ask the captain of the cargo boat not to put him on the crew list, on the pretext that being a naval officer of a state company, he could not sail on a merchant vessel. Rusen stated that he was going to France on holiday and also to see his friend Faruk Savas.

On 20 February, the storm abated and the *Divanbakirli* resumed her course.

On the 21st, at four thirty in the morning, Captain Uludag left the vessel in the hands of his mate Rusen and went back to bed until nine-thirty. Between seven and nine, the boat's course vacillated between 250 and 270, then veered progressively from 280 to 340.

Rusen then ordered the second engineer to set the engines running at 250 revolutions, then to raise it to 350, the maximum. Then he gave the order to stop the engines and cast anchor. The *Divanbakirli* dropped anchor and hoisted her flag at the entrance of the Caronte canal, about five hundred metres from the coast.

A few minutes later Rusen, claiming stomach and kidney pains, asked for permission to go ashore to see a doctor. At first the captain refused, then finally gave in. About thirteen hundred hours, Rusen was taken ashore by two sailors on a small boat belonging to the *Divanbakirli*, which dropped him at the outer jetty, at the entrance to Port-de-Bouc. Rusen hurried to a café to phone his friend Savas, who had been in Marseilles since the 14th, and Edouard Toudayan, to let them know of his arrival.

That evening, after his visit to Hairabedian, Toudayan went to see Gabriel Caillol, the superintendent of the port of Carro, to ask him to retrieve some merchandise from the open sea with the help of a harbour motorboat, the *Rieuse*.

'I'll come the day after tomorrow with two Turks who will go aboard with you. They will show you where to go.'

On the agreed day, 21 February 1971, at about eleven, the two Turkish sailors Savas and Rusen met in Marseilles, in the bar at the foot of the St Charles steps.

Pausing barely long enough to greet one another and gulp down a pastis, Savas and Rusen left the bar and walked a little way down the packed street; Rusen grabbed Savas by the hand, pulled him towards a car parked at the kerb and bundled him inside it. Toudayan, who was at the wheel, greeted them cordially in Turkish.

'We're going to Le Carro,' said Toudayan. After a good hour's drive, the car stopped at the harbour of Le Carro.

'Coco?' called out Toudayan to Gabriel Caillol who was in his motorboat anchored in the harbour. 'Here are two friends. You can go ahead.' But Caillol refused. It was too rough and the bilge pump wasn't working properly.

'Tomorrow morning at seven, okay?'

The next day, the 24th, as agreed, Caillol set out in his motorboat under the guidance of Rusen. The Beauduic lighthouse acted as landmark. Savas and Rusen anchored near a float made from a plastic jerrycan; they cast out a grapnel which soon picked up something heavy.

Caillol expressed concern about the nature of this load. Savas said something in Turkish and Rusen translated: 'Opium.'

Caillol became angry, cut the lines and started up the boat. The two Turks exhausted, went aft to the small cabin to recover.

It was at this point that skipper Rosaire Avit, on his trawler *Yves-Julien*, heard a string of profanities on his radio; they were coming from other trawlers who were complaining about a pleasure craft which was weaving around among them, getting in their way.

Avit then saw a small white boat with an aft cabin bobbing among the trawlers.

'Whoever it is must be mad to go in such a rough sea and such a small boat,' he thought.

Continuing his route towards the fishing ground, Rosaire Avit set his nets, then followed the ground line of ten metres to a point where the boat's rev counter indicated a considerable weight in the nets. At that point he thought he had made a good catch. He did not stop the boat or even turn the engine off, he was so convinced that he had struck a shoal of fish and was anxious to catch as many as possible.

He ordered his two employees to haul in the net. It contained some fish but also five jute sacks of which two were torn. They were linked together by a rope around their middle. They were also weighted by a twenty-kilo kentledge. The string of bags was about ten metres long.

In the torn ones, Avit and his men noticed a number of canvas packets tied up with string. Carefully Avit opened one of them, only to find that it contained another bag, plastic this time, tied up in the same manner and containing a brownish substance similar to gunpowder.

Not knowing what it was he had discovered, he decided to go straight back to Port St Louis du Rhône, since his net was broken. It was then 10.45.

Rosaire Avit got his men to carry the whole load to his home, then telephoned the police inspector at Port St Louis. While awaiting his arrival, he weighed the five bags on his scales and found that they weighed three hundred and fifty-eight kilos. For its part the Customs Department, immediately notified, sent out a motorboat to intercept the boat suspected of 'fishing' for the sacks, the *Rieuse*, to the west of the mouth of the Rhône.

The customs men accosted it and went on board. They discovered the two Turks in a rudimentary enclosed alcove astern, stretched out on bunks. They also discovered a four-fluked grapnel, a walkie-talkie and a reel with a rope.

The police went to Caillol's house, found a walkie-talkie identical to the one found on board the *Rieuse* and a 7·65 automatic pistol.

While making out a report of this operation, one of the policemen heard a man's voice asking Mme Caillol, 'Is Coco there?'

The police recognised the voice of someone who was well known to them: Edouard Toudayan.

When questioned, Toudayan took them to his car parked on the square opening onto Carro harbour, five hundred metres from Caillol's house.

Beside Toudayan's car there was a Renault van. The man at the wheel was clearly trying to avoid being seen, crouching down in his seat. This was Henri Hairabedian; he too was questioned.

The merchandise retrieved from the sea bed turned out to be two hundred and five packets, each containing a nylon bag of brownish powder, raw morphine.

It was now twenty-one hundred hours. It had been a long day for Rusen and his accomplice.

33

The Arrest of Edmond Taillet

At the beginning of 1971, which was to see the decline and in some cases the break-up of the more highly organised networks, the one run by Jean-Batiste Croce, known as 'Bati', Joseph Mari, known as 'Zé-le-frise', and Jo Marro was the most prosperous.

In the course of a brief but highly successful career, this team supplied the US with more than a tonne of heroin. They used the method which had replaced that of concealment on the person, with its insufficient yield, some time before. Instead, the packets were concealed in cars driven by so-called tourists on pleasure trips to Latin America, the Caribbean or the US.

They controlled almost all the clandestine laboratories and were their chief clients. They themselves supplied the laboratories with raw morphine, which they obtained from two suppliers: Ishan Ferat, who was to be arrested a few months later, and Toto Pasqualini, who had a boat, which he used for rendezvous with the Turkish sailors.

They sold a portion of their product to the 'syndicate' of Salles and Signoli, which made them far and away the most important suppliers of the American market. Croce did not hesitate therefore to charter a plane to take his friends from Bastia to dine in Marseilles or Nice, and could well afford to lose up to a million francs in a casino on the Côte d'Azur without batting an eyelid.

Most of the raw morphine dispatched from Turkey or the Lebanon was delivered to a villa in Roquefort-la-Bédoule, the house which Edouard Toudayan, former associate of the chemist Joseph Cesari, had had built in 1964. Other consignments were left in an isolated villa near the *autoroutes* A-7 and D-9, where they were picked up by someone called Fernand. Sometimes, too, illegal goods changed hands on a hill above Grasse: at the restaurant La Guérine where the various protagonist of this profitable trade sometimes met. In short, Croce known as Bati, Jo Marro and Zé Mari excercised almost absolute control over the clandestine heroin market in Marseilles. Only two other groups had sufficient turnover to warrant mention in the same breath. One was run by Paul Pajanacci and his managing director, 'Dédé' Andreani, who continued to feed the South American network, thanks to their Spanish branches in Barcelona and Madrid. The other group, whose leader has never been charged, had as clients le-Petit-Maurice, M Tête-cassée and a few old-timers from the 'Trois Canards', a part of the Lyon group, and several disaffected characters from among the former 'bad lads' of Buenos Aires. There were also several mavericks worthy of note, much talked about in the newspapers but never brought to trial because of lack of evidence.

Good relations were maintained between the competitors – old scores were settled only later, at the time of the *débâcle* – and the three associates had every reason to be satisfied with the way their business worked. There was only one snag in the otherwise smooth texture of their operation, but it was one which would have to be remedied quickly: the recruitment of receivers in New York. Some of them had been arrested and might well talk. Some, borrowed from the 'syndicate' or other teams, could not be wholly trusted, particularly since the sums passing through their hands might easily be as much as a million dollars. For this reason Bati and his friends decided once again to turn Edmond Taillet for the deliveries to be carried out this year. They were sure he would accept. They still owed him thirty thousand dollars.

The singer had already fallen into this snare twice already, and he was no wiser on this third occasion. Since the previous summer when he had somehow obtained a contract at La Napoule and sung every evening for two months, he had done nothing except one record and taken part in a television show.

Contact was made again at the beginning of February. Returning from a harassing day of rehearsal in a studio at the Etoile,

Edmond heard the almost forgotten voice of Jo Marro over the telephone, asking him to come and see him in Marseilles. The singer hesitated, then accepted. He always needed money. Clairette in Montreal seemed to have some serious problems, and once his record was made he would have nothing to do until the summer.

The following evening, he got off the plane at Marignane, to be driven by Jo to a country house at Carry-le-Rouet, where Zé-le-frisé was waiting for them. Edmond immediately came to the point, 'If it's about transporting junk, I'm not your man.'

Zé reassured him. 'You leave empty-handed. In New York, a Frenchman gives you an envelope. You give it to Tony Segura. The next day, Tony gives you back the envelope with the money. You give the lot back to the Frenchman, come back to Paris and pick up eight thousand dollars.'

A week later, Taillet was back in Marseilles. He met Jo at the Cintra. Together they went to the car where Bati and Zé were waiting for them, with a man of about forty with a distinctive mole, whom Edmond recognised from his nocturnal ramblings. This was Etienne Mosca; his employer introduced him as 'Pierrot'.

Etienne Mosca was well known in the Marseilles underworld. The son of a Corsican docker, he had done a spell in prison, and also in a psychiatric hospital. Outwardly his profession was that of hotel-based procurer. His former wife Georgette ran a hotel-bar for him in Bordeaux. Another woman of the world with the poetic name of 'Nightingale' did the same for him in Lyon. His brothers and brothers-in-law ran bars or hotels, when they were not engaged in brushes with the law. In reality, they were looking after Etienne's investments; for Etienne had added a highly profitable involvement in the heroin trade to his other activities.

'Look at him carefully,' said Bati. 'He's the one you'll be meeting in New York at the beginning of April, in a bar in Madison Square Garden. You'll be holding a key-ring. You'll meet Tony that same evening in the bar of the Hilton. Be careful, won't you? The next day, he'll give you a million dollars.'

Edmond, dazzled, took the key-ring and repeated the instructions.

Mosca and Jo were dropped off at the Vieux Port. On the way to the airport, Bati added that it would be a load of ninety-three kilos, in a Citroen. He slipped a wad of sixteen five-hundred-franc notes into the singer's pocket, for expenses. 'That'll be enough,' said Bati. 'You'll be away five or six days at most.'

At the end of March, Jo telephoned him to tell him that the trip was to take place on 5 April. He would see him at Fouquet's before he left. In the cloistered atmosphere of the well-known restaurant, the wallpaper king handed him another dozen five-hundred-franc notes above the plate of sea-food.

Turning his glass of Pouilly Fuissé between his fingers, the singer thought of the painfully wrested contracts, the hard-won fees. The plush setting and the hum of conversation blunted his anxiety. He did not know that the Champs Elysées, the indifferent or well-disposed colleagues, the swooning, eager girls, might now be things of the past.

A few hours later the plane taking him to Montreal took off from Orly. His gloom had lifted and he concentrated on the hostess's smile as she pushed the drinks trolley towards him.

In Montreal he learned that Clairette had gone bankrupt.

The immense circular building of Madison Square Garden in the centre of New York was a positive temple of travel and sport, with the faithful padding across it in all directions. The constant rumble of the trains in Pennsylvania Station rose from its depths. A host of lifts and moving staircases linked the various levels. Queues snaked away from the various ticket offices, especially for the big hall, site of the world's great boxing matches and able to hold tens of thousand of spectators.

Edmond Taillet wandered around the labyrinth, mingling with the crowd and fingering the key-ring Bati had given him. He scrutinised the faces, looking for Mosca's mole. After pacing around for an hour, he went to drown his sorrows in the Under the Stairs restaurant run by a French friend, between 93rd and 94th Streets, on Columbus Avenue.

The next day he called Jo Marro in Marseille. Jo, too, was displeased. After several hours, the rendezvous point was fixed: it was to be the bar at the top of the stairs leading to the Bowling Alley. The next evening, Taillet did indeed meet Mosca. Contact had been re-established. Together the two men went to a restaurant and during the meal, Edmond asked for news of their Marseilles friends. 'I haven't seen them since we last met.'

At the end of the meal, Etienne handed the singer the envelope containing the Citroen's papers and the car-park slips. But Edmond refused to take it before meeting Tony Segura, who was to join him at the Hilton bar.

He went back there twice a day, at midday and in the evening, for four days, but the Cuban did not appear; and each day he went to report to Mosca in the Under the Stairs. Mosca was becoming impatient. He needed the nine hundred and eighty-one thousand dollars, the proceeds of the deal, before returning to Europe.

On the 12th, Tony Segura appeared. He drove his royal blue Mercedes round the block until Taillet had retrieved the envelope. Another meeting was arranged for the following evening.

At the arranged time, the Mercedes left Manhattan. After a three-hour drive, it stopped in front of a sumptuous house in a residential district. Its passengers were received by a man whom Edmond could not actually name, but whose face was vaguely familiar to him. This man was delighted at his confusion: it was Antonio Florès, who had undergone plastic surgery, apparently highly successfully. His wife Sylvia, with a baby in her arms and a small girl clinging to her skirts, hugged him. It was a positive family reunion, with Taillet playing the part of the prodigal son.

During the meal his hosts spoke Spanish, only occasionally reverting to English. Then, sprawled over the armchairs of the vast living-room, the guests smoked a joint or two. Drowsy and slightly befuddled, the Frenchman got back into the Mercedes to drive back to New York. He barely reacted when he heard the voice of his companion informing him that twenty-one kilos of the load were missing.

'You haven't looked properly,' he murmured thickly.

They parked the Mercedes in a car-park. Reeling, supported by Tony, Edmond flopped onto the seat of the Citroen, which was parked a few yards further on. This time he was driving through familiar territory. He recognised the route he had followed the preceding year . . . he could not remember exactly how long ago it had all been . . . the car in the yard, the uncle driving the van blocking the entrance, the seats removed . . .

'There, under the back seat. There's a plate fixed with four bolts.'

A few minutes later forty-two carefully concealed packets were pulled out of the coachwork and put away in paper bags by the uncle. The effects of the marijuana began to wear off.

'One packet is torn,' said Segura. 'Be careful there aren't any signs of it left when you get rid of the car.'

Edmond at last found himself in his room at the Squire Motor Inn, with an attaché case which Tony had given him on leaving. He opened it on the bed, scattered the bundles of hundred-dollar bills and, before going to bed, counted them: three hundred thousand. He was to get twice that sum tomorrow, not to mention the residue for his last trip of the year before.

Inside the International Building at Kennedy Airport, a bland voice stood out above the other loud-speakers. It invited the Swissair passengers to board the Boeing 707 which was to take them to Geneva. A smart but slightly flustered young woman who was waiting alone in the concourse, picked up her case and set off towards the turnstiles barring the entrance corridors to the aircraft.

She proffered her passport and boarding card, then set off in the direction the hostess indicated. She then saw that the entrance was blocked by a group of travellers; they were being summarily searched by four customs men, two men and two women, who were frisking torsos, hips and legs and casting a rapid glance at hand luggage.

The young woman hesitated, put her hand to her forehead and collapsed on the floor, apparently in a half-faint. A hostess and a steward rushed forward and helped her up. She clung to them, regaining her balance with difficulty.

'I think I'll be all right,' she murmured. 'But I don't feel well enough to take the plane. Could I put off my flight?'

A hostess took her to the airline desk.

Two hours later, Etienne Mosca joined Taillet in his room and threw a woman's corset onto the bed. Inside it were seven or eight special pockets, filled with banknotes.

'It's all misfired,' said Mosca, more edgy than ever. 'I don't know what happened, but the customs men were searching everyone. You're going to have to keep this for me for a bit. My wife is going off again this evening, but just with a hundred thousand dollars in a briefcase.'

In fact, the check that has so alarmed the young woman had been just a routine operation checking the travellers for bombs, firearms or other dangerous metal objects.

After a fruitless discussion, the two men decided to phone Marseilles. Jo Marro's reply was to act for the best. Mosca then decided that he would use double-bottomed suitcases for the rest of the money. 'I've seen a fellow doing it. It can't be all that difficult.'

The next day, Friday 16 April, Mosca appeared again, rubbing his hands. He had managed to get rid of the car. He had sold it to a second-hand dealer for a few hundred dollars. Taillet was horrified, he remembered Segura's warning about the torn packet of heroin. 'You're mad! There was heroin in it. I warned you.'

'You're panicking about nothing. What does a car dealer know about drugs?'

'You really are a fool. To sell a car bought in France, your garage man has to get customs clearance. A car registered in Marseilles attracts attention. The customs men look inside. They discover that the carpets have been pulled up and the metal cut through with a blow lamp. They find a few grains of white powder, put it in a plastic bag and take them to the laboratory. Then the computers get clicking and lead straight to us.'

But Etienne refused to listen. If they hurried, the police would not find them. Tony must be told to get a move on and warn Jo. He picked up the telephone and asked for Marseilles.

'Hallo, bar César? Pierrot here . . . We've sent three hundred and eight photos. We'll probably have to find another method of sending the other.'

Taillet lept into a taxi. During his last trip, Segura had stopped in 83rd Street to take the attaché case to his sister. His memory was somewhat hazy, but he did manage to recognise the building, found the young woman's letter-box and left a message for the Cuban.

His companion had not wasted his time. On his return to his hotel, he noticed two new cases open on the bed, an array of tools, the contents of a pot of powdered glue emptied out onto a newspaper. Water was boiling on a primus stove. A pair of pliers in his hand, Etienne was cutting out rectangles of cardboard. Both set to work with such a will that the switch-board operator called to say that their next-door neighbour was complaining about the noise.

Tony had received the message transmitted through his sister. He made a further payment of a little over three hundred thousand dollars and guaranteed to get the balance to France by the middle of May. Bati and Jo were waiting for this money impatiently. They had admitted on the phone to Mosca that they had just gambled away nearly two and a half million francs. A further meeting was arranged between the singer and the Cuban for 28 April. Mosca was to take the plane for Geneva on the 25th.

While waiting for this meeting, Edmond decided to go to Montreal. One disaster seemed to be following another; Mosca's blundering worried him. He felt vulnerable.

What he and his companions did not know, was that the police had been watching Segura for several days and that their meetings had been observed. The police in question were Treasury Agents, concerned primarily with the financial doings of their buyer, which gave the heroin traffickers a brief respite.

On the 28th, Edmond was back in New York. He wanted to return to the room he had reserved, so that Tony would be able to find him easily. But the electricity was not working and he was put in another room, with lengthy apologies. Luckily, Tony met him in the foyer and confirmed the agreed dates.

The next morning, Edmond put the tools he had used to make the double-bottomed suitcase in a bag and deposited them in a luggage locker in Grand Central Station. Just as he was about to close the locker door, he was surrounded by customs men and arrested.

That was the end of the unofficial career of the singer who billed himself as the 'Frank Sinatra of the Côte d'Azur'.

'A few days ago, in a bar near the Place de la Monnaie, I met a fellow I had known vaguely for some years. He was a Belgian who was doing business in Spain. He was about forty and was called Donald Maenhout. He proposed that I should go to America with a car containing contraband goods. I wanted to hear more about it so I said I was interested.'

In an office in the American embassy in Brussels, special agent Guy, of the BNDD, listened carefully to the young man opposite him. If he accepted the proposition, he was to buy a car, register it in his name and drive it to the south of France where it would be fitted out and loaded up. He was then to go to New York by boat and wait to be contacted.

The young man was called Eric d'Hont. He was a Brussels trader and had never had any troubles with the police. Donald Maenhout was an acquaintance of someone called Mario Deniz whose name had cropped up several times in connection with drug trafficking, though no hard evidence had been brought against him. The pattern was only too familiar to the 'narcs' agents, they immediately contacted their Paris branch, the Washington headquarters and the French Office, since the operation was to be mounted in France.

The voluntary agent was advised to proceed with the utmost caution, and in as conciliatory a manner as probability allowed.

Almost the same day Georgette Gunther, former wife of Etienne Mosca and still his accomplice – since she ran an assignation hotel for him in Bordeaux – received a call from her ex-husband, asking her whether she knew anyone who would agree to lend him a French passport for a week or so. He was willing to pay five thousand francs for this service: 'Why don't you ask your brother? I don't think he's exactly rolling.'

Etienne Gunther, Georgette's brother, was not at all the kind of person with whom Mosca normally had dealings. He lived on the eleventh floor of a tower block in the Paris suburbs, in an unpretentious apartment with his wife Raymonde and their daughter Valerie, aged eleven. He ran a company concerned with building maintenance. Despite his official status as Sales Manager, he drew a modest salary. His wife was a secretary in the Caisse des Dépôts et Consignations.

Gunther knew all about his brother-in-law's shady activities – with the exception of the drug-trafficking – and of his sister's giddy existence. In the past, he had met the numerous Mosca tribe during holidays at Niolon, between Marseilles and Carry-le-Rouet, and had got to know some of his brother-in-law's close friends. Most relevantly he had played *pétanque* with a couple of charming fellows who had been passing through, Laurent Fiocconi and Jean-Claude Kella; there had been a lot about them in the papers a few months later.

When Georgette informed him of his brother-in-law's proposition, Gunther refused outright. He did not want any problems with the law. He remembered an occasion when his over-eager attentions to some young ladies outside a suburban dance-hall had earned him a minor conviction at the age of twenty; the memory was sufficiently painful for him to wish never to repeat it.

A few days later, Georgette broached the matter again. She asked her brother to get some American papers from the previous week, where Etienne Mosca hoped to find some information about one of his friends. In fact, what interested him was the account which his buyer Tony Segura had been charged. The part played by Edmond Taillet was also mentioned. He was somewhat reassured having read it. It seemed to imply that the singer had not denounced his accomplices.

But in fact Taillet had no hesitation in taking advantage of any leniency his judges might show, he did indeed 'grass' and, thanks to his co-operation, the last networks were broken up.

Two years later, the picturesque Jo Signoli, arrested in his turn, was to say, 'The singer? Talked under duress? It would be more accurate to say that the Yankee cops had to wallop him to make him shut up.'

During the first week in July, Eric d'Hont received a call in Brussels from Donald Maenhout; he had at last agreed to take a car to the US. The Belgian businessman arranged to meet him the following week in Paris. At last their meeting, twice postponed, took place on the afternoon of 27 July in a hotel on rue de Lille. Several agents from the 'narcs' and 'stups' had the district under discreet surveillance, but no microphone had been installed, to avoid arousing the trafficker's suspicions.

'Here are ten thousand dollars,' announced Donald, putting a bundle of notes in front of him. 'Now you can go to England and buy a Jaguar in Wembley. Have it registered in your name in London.' When he had done all this, Eric was to take his purchase to France and book a passage for the car and himself on board the *Queen Elizabeth* for either 27 August or 10 September.

The various formalities took the young dealer a week; these developments led to a flood of correspondence between Brussels, Paris, New York and Washington. On 8 August, Eric was once again at the wheel of a splendid ochre Jaguar saloon, registration number HMC 578K. He spent a peaceful week-end waiting for the phone call that was expected the following Monday. When he received it, he in his turn phoned special agent Guy of the BNDD. 'I have to go to Bayonne tomorrow and leave the car in the station car-park at midday, then go to Brussels to await further orders.'

The journey was uneventful. After hiding the key under the front seat of the Jaguar, d'Hont left the car-park and a long wait began for the watching policemen. It was nightfall when a man approached the vehicle, sat down at the wheel and drove off. As soon as he left the carpark he was followed by a Mercedes registered in the Pyrénées-Orientales. They drove towards Anglet, where the police gave up their pursuit so as not to be spotted in the almost deserted streets.

While Eric d'Hont was in Brussels waiting for a word from his mysterious partners, the Gunther family joined Georgette at Niolon where she was spending her holidays with her ex-husband. Etienne Mosca found them rough and ready lodging with neighbours, and the couple shared the amusements of the various Pierrots, Toulés, Loules and Jojos, and their assorted social activities which always seemed to entail a lot of heedless spending. After *boules*, they would drink champagne. Raymonde observed that her brother-in-law spent a lot of time making or receiving calls in the nearby café, the Pergola.

During a bathing session, Georgette approached her brother. 'Have you got any friends in America?'

'I know some Canadians. Why?' She shrugged, but did not reply.

A few days after their return to Paris, the Gunthers received a phone call from Georgette, offering her brother a trip to the US, all expenses paid. Gunther hesitated, interested despite himself. Then he heard Mosca's voice, 'Listen, could you come down to Marseilles to talk about it? I'll pay the fare.'

Four days later, Gunther was back in Niolon. Mosca explained to him that the problem was to smuggle dollars back into France, on behalf of an American industrialist. There was a thirty thousand franc commission to be made. For Gunther, it would be an opportunity to travel free of charge, as well as to settle several urgent but constantly postponed debts.

When he took the plane the following day to go back to his wife and child, he had already agreed. Mosca had told him that he himself had smuggled in considerable sums without any repercussions. He advised his brother-in-law to apply for his visa and be ready to leave at a moment's notice.

Informed of the plan, Raymonde felt nervous about accompanying her husband, despite her desire to see New York. She phoned

Georgette for reassurance. The former Mme Mosca was categorical: there was no risk. 'Listen, if you've really got the jitters, I'll gladly go in your place.' That did the trick.

At the end of August, Donald called d'Hont and arranged to meet him at Bordeaux airport the following day at 5.30. Before setting off in his own car, the young Belgian notified the BNDD agent in Brussels. Surveillance measures were immediately taken, in particular around the station car-park in Bayonne.

While Eric and Donald were driving through Les Landes, the Jaguar, followed by a DS 21 belonging to a bar owner in Marseilles, parked in front of Bayonne station. Its driver got out without locking the door, and walked off. The following morning Eric and Donald, who had spent the night in a local hotel, continued their journey, with Donald driving his companion's car. After a stop in Montbason they reached Paris, parked the Jaguar in the car-park at the Sofitel and booked a room there. Two days went by before Eric could communicate with the policemen who were watching them.

'Tomorrow I'm flying to Brussels to get my things,' he told them while Maenhout was out of earshot. 'On the 6th we'll be off for Le Havre, but we'll probably take the car ferry to England. Maenhout isn't coming to the States with me.'

When Eric took the plane to Brussels, Gunther once again set off for Marignane. He met Mosca in his sister Josette's flat in Marseilles. It was then that he learned that the money he was to bring back would be concealed in the false bottoms of suitcases. His brother-in-law showed him several that he had brought back from a previous trip. He explained how to make the false bottoms.

'On 16 September, you go to Bowling Alley 8, Madison Square Garden. A fair-haired man will give you a parking slip and some car keys. And at six o'clock, near the tobacconist's kiosk at the Abbey Victoria hotel, you'll meet a man with a folded newspaper under his arm . . .'

He described each of the gestures and movements he was to perform, how he was to retrieve the keys and give them back to the fair young man, anticipating possible hitches and possible remedies. He gave him ten thousand francs for the plane tickets and expenses during his stay. He insisted that he should not stay in the same hotel as his wife.

Despite the wad of notes he had in his pocket and the promises his brother-in-law had made him, Gunther felt unenthusiastic when he returned to Paris the following day; and his wife was even more worried than he was. Like so many others before them, they felt that they were hurtling to their downfall. They scented the dangers threatening their modest happiness but could not summon up the necessary courage to pull out.

Eric d'Hont had returned to Brussels and met Maenhout, who meanwhile had booked in at the Hilton with the Jaguar. On 7 September they set out for Boulogne, where they spent the night. The following day, independently, they embarked on the ferry. At Dover, they met again and went to Brighton and then Southampton in the Jaguar, which was then put on board the *Queen Elizabeth.*

Two BNDD agents were also making the trip. In New York a vast operation was being mounted, including BNDD agents, customs men and two French representatives of the 'stups' posted in the US.

Anthony Pohl, as Associate Regional Director, had set up the operation. He had selected the team, distributed the roles and given code names for radio exchanges.

The Jaguar was to be called the 'stagecoach'. Hotel Pierre, where the organisation had told Eric d'Hont to stay, was to be 'Dodge House'. Its garage where the Jaguar would spend at least one night would be the 'barn'. Madison Square Garden, where courier and receiver were to meet, was to be 'the long branch'. The garage in Madison Square Garden was 'the long barn'. Bowling Alley 8 was the 'long branch alley'. The American customs men, 'Wells Fargo', a Paris BNDD agent 'Delta Paris', the French agents in New York, Lafayette I and Lafayette II. The radio technician, the 'doctor' and the Jaguar mechanic, the 'blacksmith'. The call signal for all groups was to be 'Dodge City'.

Lastly, Eric d'Hont was to be Louis or SX110007. Surveillance points in the Hotel Pierre were in rooms 1234 and 1236. Anthony Pohl had asked for eleven vehicles with two-way radio, seven taxis, a truck, a stall selling ice creams and a helicopter, code-named 'the horse'.

On the morning of 14 September, Etienne Gunther woke up in his room in the Penn Garden Hotel, somewhat disorientated. He was alone. Following Mosca's instructions, he had booked Raymonde in at Taft's. They had even travelled in different planes, from Orly to Montreal first of all – where they had intended to see friends who had not been there – and from Montreal to New York. Etienne was still suffering from jet-lag and was unsure of how to go about getting his breakfast sent up to his room.

At last he went to get Raymonde. They decided to go and see an old friend of his who lived on Long Island. Once again they found no one at home and returned to Manhattan after having paid thirty-five dollars for a taxi. 'For two days nothing happened. As the Taft was so far from Penn Garden, my wife had moved to the Statler Hilton. We were together during the day but separated at night.'

On the 15th, while they were strolling along Broadway, the *Queen Elizabeth* entered New York harbour. Passengers, luggage and vehicles went through the customs. As soon as the Jaguar was given the green light, it was taken into a transit shed where BNDD specialists began to dismantle it. Meanwhile, Eric was in an office making his report to the officials who had taken over from their European colleagues.

'Tomorrow I'm to meet someone called Jacques,' he told them. 'He's going to take the car. Apparently he was the person who did the work on it at Bayonne. They're going to be sending another car soon.'

According to Eric, Donald had gone to Switzerland and was going to send him some money from there. All he had to do was to retrieve the car and leave it in a car-park at the Hotel Pierre, where he was staying before meeting his unknown colleague in Madison Square Garden.

In the shed where the Jaguar technicians, who had been specially employed for the occasion, were reassembling the car, one hundred and eighty-eight bags of heroin were piled on the concrete floor. One of them was put back in one of the hiding places in the front wings to act as evidence when the moment came, along with other packets filled with lactose. The whole process had taken nearly seven hours. One hour later, the car was in the car-park.

On the 16th, Gunther went to Madison Square Garden and stood around in the bowling alley at midday and again in the evening without meeting any tall, slim blond young man with a paper and key-ring as Mosca had described. He went back the following day and met him at last. Eric handed him the green parking slip and arranged their next meeting, for the following Sunday, same place, at fifteen hundred hours.

Gunther immediately leapt into a taxi and had himself driven to the Abbey Victoria where another unknown quantity was supposed to be waiting for him. He was left standing in front of the tobacconist's kiosk for half-an-hour. Discouraged, he went to join his wife and took her off for a meal. 'In the afternoon we went for a walk in Central Park. That evening at six I left my wife in her hotel. Then I went back to the Abbey Victoria, but found no one.'

The next day at midday, as he was leaving the Abbey Victoria after an hour's fruitless wait, he was approached by an unknown man who said, 'I know you, but you don't know me,' and handed him the slip. Gunther asked for the money that he was to take back to Paris the following day.

'The thing is, I've got to go back to work on Monday morning.' This argument did not seem to impress his Corsican contact, who was called Jean Orsini and who said he could not do anything before Monday night. They would meet at the Café des Sports on 51st Street.

Noticing Gunther's glum expression on hearing this, Orsini proposed a drink. They went into the nearest bar, the Canton Village.

Some ten minutes later, about 13.15, they separated. Gunther returned gloomily to his hotel; to kill time before going to fetch Raymonde, he started work on the false bottoms of two suitcases with some materials he had bought en route. He had intended to finish the task the following day but at dawn, when he finally dozed off, the BNDD agents burst into his room.

Orsini, who was also caught by the BNDD men, had taken a taxi to room 61 in the Alrae Hotel. Arrangements were immediately made for a policeman to move into suite 6J, adjacent to Orsini's room. The handle of the inter-connecting door was removed, thus affording a partial view of the goings-on in the room.

At 17.30 Orsini left his room and went out to look for a taxi. He found one driven by special agent John Pavlick, and asked to go to 1021 Kennedy Boulevard, in New Jersey.

During the journey, Orsini engaged the 'taxi driver' in conversation. He told him he was a Spanish citizen and that it was his second trip to the United States. At about eight o'clock, Orsini returned to his hotel. The special agent in suite 6J heard a conversation in a foreign language and, through the hole provided by the absent door handle, he saw a giant dressed in a beige suit, one of the two buyers, later to be identified as Luis Gomez Ortega, known as 'El Pavo', born in Havana in 1933.

During the night the two men went to join another client (also a Cuban, and well known to the BNDD) on Madison Avenue. Together they got into a light brown Chevrolet and drove to the car-park where the Jaguar was. Ortega went to get it, but the battery was flat and the attendant had to help them start it. One behind the other, the two cars drove into 31st Street. A further breakdown by the Jaguar again forced them to stop at 8th Avenue. Orsini lifted the bonnet, and while he was leaning over the engine in perplexity, the BNDD agents pounced and handcuffed the three accomplices.

The Jaguar affair was over. The sum total of the bail required for the captives' provisional liberty was almost two million dollars. Six months later, the hapless and imprudent Gunther was to be sentenced to five years, Orsini and Ortega to twenty-five each. Mosca was to be arrested at a prostitute's flat in April 1972.

Gunther's testimony proved crushing, as did that of Edmond Taillet who, seeing himself abandoned by his former accomplices, had decided to come clean. Jean-Batiste Croce and Zé-le-frisé met most of the network in prison. Zé was to die in August 1973. In all, thirty-six accused appeared before the County Court at Marseilles in May 1974. Jo Marro was arrested four months later. Jean-Baptiste Croce was to be sentenced to eighteen years.

Etienne Mosca did not appear. After trying to kill himself with barbiturates, he managed to remove the transfusion tube fixed to his arm on the eve of the trial. By the time the nurse noticed, it was already too late.

34

The Man from the Secret Service

In April 1971 John Ingesoll, who was running the anti-trafficking campaign in Washington, went to Paris to see the Director of the *Police Criminelle* (CID). Together they reviewed the results achieved so far: the arrest of Fiocconi and Kella and a large number of their assistants, the identification of Salles, Signoli and Tonton Orsini, the surveillance of Lajoux, of certain members of the Club des Corses on Picpus and certain members of the 'Trois Canards'.

Attempts to immobilise the network had been jeopardised by the premature capture of Signoli, which had threatened to make his accomplices disperse. Possibly it was his privileged position in the trade which allowed the young man from Marseilles to be treated leniently and released after a few months.

'From that moment,' Anthony Pohl stated in his report to the Senate Committee, 'all information on the affair was carefully assembled, but the moment for large-scale action had not yet arrived. The accomplice charged with receiving the goods in New York (Berdin) had not yet been identified and, without him, it was impossible to proceed to a seizure or discover the American client.'

Meanwhile Berdin, waiting the return of André Labay, who was still in Switzerland, set off in search of the sixty-seven kilos missing from the Cadillac (see chapter 30) and finally discovered that they were in the hands of Moulin and Demeester, who were dissatisfied with their derisory share in the deal. They would not return them to the off-hand businessman except in exchange for several millions they felt they deserved.

'What you don't realise,' Berdin explained patiently, 'is that if the Marseilles men learn that it's you who've got them, they'll have their hands on you within a couple of days.'

The argument went home and the load was returned to its rightful owners, which improved relations between Berdin and his associates. He none the less decided to keep his distance from the members of the Syndicate and to operate alone.

Richard Berdin was a valuable connection. He knew suppliers who trusted him, and in the United States he was in contact with buyers.

One day, in the Club des Corses on the rue Picpus, he met Dominique M, a small-time crook of his acquaintance whom he had not seen for some time. Dominique talked to Berdin of a friend of his cousin's who worked for the SDECE. He had serious money worries and might agree to transport a considerable quantity of drugs.

Berdin appeared interested. A few days later, Dominique phoned him and told him that the friend accepted the proposition. A meeting was arranged for the following day at eleven am in Fouquet's.

Berdin sat down at a table. The place was virtually empty at that time of day. He saw a man of about forty arriving: tall, dark and smartly dressed, in a well-cut navy blue suit. The unknown man sat down at a nearby table. Their eyes met, but neither made any move to start a conversation. Dominique was to act as intermediary; but by midday he had still not appeared.

After waiting more than an hour, the stranger paid for his drink and went off. Berdin followed suit. That evening Dominique M. telephoned him to apologise. He had spent the night at a club and had not woken up till two in the afternoon.

Things went no further, but some time later Berdin saw the photo and name of the stranger on the front page of one of the dailies: he was Roger Delouette.

Roger Xavier Leon Delouette was born in Paris on 10 May 1923 in a well-to-do middle-class family. After an undistinguished school career he went to an agricultural college, where he failed to get his diploma as an agricultural expert. In 1946 he was in the army, posted as an NCO to the French military mission within the framework of the United Nations to supervise the elections in the land forces. At this point he made the acquaintance of Colonel Barberot, who was commanding the naval detachment; the colonel's secretary was a pretty girl called Christiane Remusat, the daughter of a naval officer. Delouette, tall, dark and handsome, had urbanity and allure. The young secretary fell in love with him, and some time later, they married.

Delouette, who was intelligent and astute, worked occasionally for the DGER, the French espionage service. In 1956 when he was in Algeria with civilian status, he once again had the opportunity of giving information to an officer of the DGER, which by then, had become the SDECE. From 1963 to 1968, Roger Delouette was employed by Baron Guy de Rothschild to supervise his estate at Ferriere-en-Brie. In August 1968 Delouette got a job at the BDPA (Bureau de developpement de la production agricole), where he renewed his acquaintance with Colonel Barberot, its boss.

This office sent him to Cuba to study rice-growing using mechanical processes. In October 1968, when the boss of the BDPA was visiting Cuba, Delouette was contacted by a chief from the SDECE. The Cuba agent of the SDECE having been absent for a year, Delouette was asked if he would replace him. Delouette agreed.

Until June 1969, Delouette performed only minor missions. On 1 July 1969 he went back to France to attend some specialised courses. As he was about to leave again for Cuba, on 20 August, his trip was cancelled. He then went back to the BDPA, and in September the same year he was told, without further explanation that his mission to Cuba was adjourned indefinitely.

Rumours abounded: Delouette was said to have been seen several times in the company of a CIA agent.

Within the BDPA itself, opposition against him was mounting. He was given no more foreign missions. Now working for the

BDPA was a paying proposition only if one was sent abroad. In Cuba, for instance, his basic salary was 3,600 francs a month, plus a bonus of 3,400. Delouette, the father of six children and divorced, had to give his wife an alimony of 3,000 francs. When he was working in the Paris office all he had left was 600 francs a month to live on. Delouette liked good living, and had a demanding young mistress. He was in desperate straits. The SDECE promised to help him. In November, one of the directors of BDPA got him sent on a brief mission to the Ivory Coast. In February 1970, having concluded this mission, Delouette returned to France. In May, a SDECE official suggested he should join ASCOT, which was concerned with problems in Black Africa and Algeria.

Delouette made two trips to black Africa and two to Algeria. But ASCOT's financial situation began to worsen; thus Delouette, with a basic salary of 4,000 francs, was in financial straits once again.

He now badgered the SDECE, which put him in touch with Colonel Fournier, to whom he confided his grievances. Some days later the colonel remitted him 27,000 francs, representing the total of his loss of earnings since his departure from Cuba. But Delouette was still jobless. His difficulties were becoming increasingly pressing.

On 17 December 1970, Delouette was to meet a man at the café Le Paris on the Champs Elysées. He did not know him, but he knew that this man was to be sitting at a table with a *Paris-Match* in front of him.

The meeting was for six o'clock. The man looked about thirty and was smartly if soberly dressed. He proposed that Delouette should smuggle drugs into the United States. When Delouette gave his agreement, the man explained that the commodity was fifty kilos concealed in a car, a 'Volkswagen Camper'. His profit would be 6,000 francs a kilo, a total of 50,000 dollars.

On 7 January Delouette met the man again at Le King on rue François Premier. The car was to arrive in New York on a Saturday. He was given the delivery date of the brand new Volkswagen and its date of dispatch from Le Havre. The car would be taken out of the port of New York on the Monday.

The man then told Delouette that someone called Nicolas would contact him at the hotel. On 25 February Delouette went to Switzerland to deposit the money needed for the purchase of the car. He took possession of it on 3 March.

About 15 March, a Monday, the man telephoned him to give him instructions.

On Tuesday Delouette went to Pontchartrain. In a small lane, near the Chateau, he was to meet a man at the wheel of a green Simca Chrysler. It was one in the afternoon. He was to drive slowly by him. The unknown man would then gesture to him and ask him to stop and follow him.

The man at the wheel of the Simca took him into the forest of Rambouillet, beyond Monfort l'Amaury. Once well in the forest, he turned left, then right, and at last turned into a remote unmetalled road.

Both emerged from their cars. The strange man looked about forty. He was small but well built; badly dressed and taciturn.

Quickly he opened up the boot of the Simca and took out two cheap but new suitcases and a tool bag.

Skilfully he set to, dismantling certain panels of the Volkswagen, beginning at the front. He put the sachets from the suitcase in the panels and then discovered that all fifty kilos would not fit. He decided to keep eleven of them.

He took the two empty cases, and put them back in the Simca, together with the tool bag. They walked a few yards together. Then the stranger asked Delouette to set off in the opposite direction from the one he was going to take.

In Paris, Delouette telephoned the Pacific Intermountains Express to say that he would be in Le Havre the following day and would hand over the car to them to dispatch. He was told to arrive at sixteen hundred hours.

The next day, a Tuesday, Delouette arrived in Le Havre at fifteen hundred hours and went to the PIE office. He was told that the boat on which he had been intending to put the car had cancelled its sailing. There would thus be a week's delay.

The manager of the PIE asked him if he was going to leave the car in a locked garage or take it back to Paris.

Having no desire to drive back with a car crammed with drugs, Delouette decided to leave it in Le Havre. When he arrived in Paris he went to TWA to change the date of departure, and also reserved a room at the Park-Sheraton Hotel, which had been recommended to him by friends.

On Thursday the man telephoned him. Delouette informed him of the delay, which did not seem to concern him particularly; he confirmed his departure for 4 April.

On 4 April 1971, a Sunday, at fourteen hundred hours, Delouette was among the passengers emerging from the TWA Boeing 707, flight 803 from Paris.

Delouette proffered his passport to an immigration man: Christian names; Roger, Xavier, Léon, born in Paris, 10 May 1923; technical adviser in agronomy, height 1.82, address 30 rue Nungesser et Coli, Paris 16; American visa issued 30 March 1971. To the policeman who asked him how long he was staying in the United States. Delouette replied that he was intending to cross the States to go to Mexico with his car, which was coming from France by boat.

The customs man who was preparing to ask the ritual question found himself pipped to the post by Delouette, who promptly uttered 'Nothing to declare', while flipping open his tawny leather case. 'Okay, okay,' said the customs man.

The air was already spring-like, and there were a lot of passengers and not many buses at Kennedy Airport. After a good twenty minutes' wait, Delouette and two other passengers, both French, decided to share a taxi. Abroad, among compatriots, affinities began very soon to make themselves felt, if only because of a shared language. Delouette thus learned that one of his new acquaintances was a geologist, his ultimate destination being California, where he was to give a lecture. The other was a veterinary surgeon from Boulogne-Billancourt.

After dropping them at their respective hotels, Delouette arrived in front of his own, the Park-Sheraton. His room had been booked by TWA. The porter handed him an envelope from PIE transport, which was dealing with the dispatch of the car. This company asked him to go to its headquarters as soon as possible, at 17 Battery Park Place, New York, to collect the papers he would need to pick up his car . . .

That same Sunday, 4 April, Miss Lyn Pelletier, aged twenty-two, a pretty young red-headed inspector of customs, had received precise instruction from her bosses. They had drawn the attention of all inspectors to the increasingly widespread use of vans and minibuses to bring drugs, particularly hashish, into the United States.

Furthermore the Director of Customs, Myles Ambrose, had ordered a periodic search of every vehicle arriving in any US port. For twenty-four hours now the 'Volkswagen Camper' off the cargo boat *Atlantic Cognac*, coming from Le Havre, had been held in waiting on one of the wharves of Port Elizabeth, in New Jersey. This car was registered in the name of Roger Delouette, address in New York Park-Sheraton Hotel, 870 Seventh Avenue, Manhattan.

A few days earlier, Thursday 1 April, Claude Pastou, coming from Rio de Janeiro via Los Angeles, had booked in at the Edison, at 228 West 47th Street, in the name of German Schaffer. Pastou immediately made contact with his American buyer, and told him that he would telephone him as soon as he had seen the transporter of the goods.

On the agreed day, Sunday 4 April, he went to the Park-Sheraton. It was about six-thirty in the evening. But Pastou did not meet Delouette. The latter, after a brief spell in his room, just long enough to freshen up, had gone to breathe the air of Broadway which, despite the lingering daylight, was already aglitter with multicoloured neon. He went into a bar for a beer and about seven o'clock returned to the hotel, where he had a snack in the near-deserted restaurant.

At about eight o'clock, Pastou appeared again at the reception desk in the Park-Sheraton. He had trouble making himself understood. Suddenly he caught sight of a man waiting for a lift who corresponded to the description given.

'Are you M. Delouette?' he asked. The answer being in the affirmative, they decided to have a drink in the bar of the Taft, also on Seventh Avenue, indeed number 769, very near the Park-Sheraton. Delouette explained that he was to take delivery of his Volkswagen the following morning at Port Elizabeth in New York. They therefore agreed to meet at the Taft bar the following morning between midday and one, with a standby rendezvous between six and seven in the evening at the same place. As he was leaving Pastou, Delouette informed him that he had a ready-made system in case of trouble.

Delouette went to bed at midnight but had trouble getting to sleep, what with the time difference and the electric atmosphere of New York. However, after rising on the morning of 5 April, he went to 17 Battery Square. The offices were only just opening. A young man received him, glanced over the PIE letter and called a young employee who gave him a document with the number of the wharf in Port Elizabeth where he would find his car.

He left the office and hailed a taxi. One stopped, but on hearing the address, refused to take him there. A second and third did likewise. At last a fourth, going off duty in the direction of New Jersey, agreed to take him. There was more difficulty at the port, finding the office mentioned on the documents. However, when they at last arrived there, Delouette showed his papers to an employee who sent him to a customs inspector. There he had to fill in and sign two forms which were then stamped by the customs officer. 'Now,' he said, 'wait here a minute. Your car is being brought into the nearby garage for inspection.'

Customs Officer Larry Harris had chosen the young and attractive Miss Lyn Pelletier to examine the vehicle. He asked her to carry out a thorough search. 'I don't like this kind of car,' he said, 'You can put all sorts of things in it.'

Roger Delouette stood in front of Miss Pelletier. She saw a tall man, oval-faced and rather fleshy, with brown hair greying at the temples and dressed in a brown jersey wool suit with a Mao collar. Delouette had a certain English style. He could have been a playboy, he was still a charmer.

Miss Pelletier asked him for his licence. The address given on it was that of the French embassy in Cuba. This was enough to intrigue Miss Pelletier. Delouette explained that he was being sent to Cuba, for a French government agricultural body. She observed that his car was new. 'Indeed,' he said, 'I bought it in Paris on March 1. It's only done a thousand kilometres, accounted for by a trial run I did after running in, before putting it on the boat on 26 March.'

While chatting away, Miss Pelletier carried out a minute examination of the doors, armrests and seats. She might not yet have acquired the dexterity of an old hand at the job, but she had the heart-stopping, methodical slowness of the brilliant pupil of the customs training centre. The lessons of her masters were too fresh for her not to apply them scrupulously. At first her attention was attracted by an unusual phenomenon: a missing screw from a panel to the right of the dashboard. She slipped her hand behind this panel, felt something, pulled, and extracted a plastic bag containing some white powder. Faced with this discovery she asked for reinforcements, and a few minutes later one of her colleagues, Harry Dihmyre, was helping her pursue her researches. Forty-eight packets each weighing five hundred grams were discovered. After analysis, proving that they did indeed contain heroin, 92 per cent pure, Delouette was arrested, taken to 201 Varick Street, New York, under a heavy guard and there photographed, fingerprinted and thoroughly searched. He was found to be in possession of 150 dollars and 1,230 French francs in notes, 180 dollars in travellers' cheques, bought in Paris from the American Express on 29 March 1971, the addresses of two bank accounts, one on the Banque de Paris et des Pays Bas, Avenue George V branch, the other on the Credit Suisse ce Genève, numbered account 195.715, plus a letter from this bank telling Delouette that 14,000 Swiss francs had been received and paid out the following day for the purchase of the Volkswagen, as well as an invoice from the Michel-Ange garage where the car had been bought. This invoice for a total of 14,079 Swiss francs was paid by cheque on the Crédit Suisse account.

'Why,' a customs officer asked Delouette, 'does your licence say that you live in Cuba?'

'Because I've worked in Cuba and because all French Citizens living abroad have the right to a resident's identity card issued by their consulate. This card enabled me to buy the Volkswagen tax free, that is, paying twenty per cent less than the purchase price in France.'

The inspector then informed the accused man of his rights. In accordance with the ten points of the Fifth Amendment of the Constitution, he could refuse to make a statement. He could obtain the assistance of the lawyer of his choice, and legal advice would be granted him if he could not get a solicitor himself. He could renounce these rights and privileges and make any statement he liked, it being understood that he could invoke them again at any point. By pleading guilty he would incur a sentence of five to twenty years and a fine of 20,000 dollars maximum.

'You'll be in prison a long time, M. Delouette,' an inspector told him, 'and your bosses will be at liberty . . . unless you tell us all you know.' These were the last words the inspector said before the arrival of special agent Paul Boulad. Two other customs inspectors put handcuffs on Delouette. He had difficulty in understanding what he was being asked, and even more difficulty in making himself understood. His English was rudimentary and the customs men present spoke no French. Very soon special agent Paul Boulad arrived. He spoke French fluently. He was followed, a few moments later, by police officer Claude Chaminadas, of the New York French branch.

Paul Boulad asked the first questions in French. Delouette instantly adopted the pose of the complete innocent, incomprehending and completely ignorant of what was in the car. After all, it had been in a garage in Le Havre for ten days, hadn't it? He kept up this position until seven in the morning.

For his part Claude Pastou had twice gone to the agreed

rendezvous at the Taft bar, first at one o'clock and then at seven o'clock. He had been waiting for Delouette for more than half-an-hour. Certain that some 'accident' had occurred, Pastou left New York post-haste to go to Rio de Janeiro and meet Christian David. About seven-thirty Delouette was taken to a BNDD office in Manhattan and confronted with Inspector Hartung, who addressed Delouette in an almost brutal fashion, accusing him of lying all along the line. 'Your passport is false,' he said, 'your American visa faked, your card from the Consulate, worthless. What is your real identity?' All this in the presence of Paul Boulad, who decided to take Delouette back to his hotel, the Park-Sheraton. 'You'll be better off here,' he said smiling. 'Though you'll be moving to a bigger room, because naturally you won't be on your own . . .'

In fact he moved into one of the two communicating rooms. Delouette and Inspector Hartung slept in one of them, with two beds. A third bed was then brought in, and here, during the course of the night, various different policemen stretched out, including Chaminadas who was unlucky enough to have a bad dose of flu.

About seven in the morning, the telephone rang. The Inspector promptly answered it. It was a call from Paris for Delouette; it was his girl-friend, a young lady called Marie Jos Rt, who was surprised not to have heard from him yet.

Inspector Hartung answered that M. Delouette was not in his room, but at the intervention of an American policeman, he handed over the receiver to Delouette. He explained to his mistress that he had not been able to phone her because something incredible had happened, which he could not tell her about on the phone. Then he hung up. The American policemen then asked Delouette to ring her back. 'Tell her it's nothing serious, that she mustn't worry and that your trip to Mexico has just been postponed.'

Marie Jose Rt now knew how things stood. Her friend was up against it. It would have been easy for her to warn the rest of the gang.

'She knew nothing whatsoever about my affairs,' Delouette later stated.

Delouette advising himself to sleep on it, passed a virtually sleepless night. He spent most of the time reflecting. Should he shoulder the burden alone? He had not forgotten what an inspector had told him, at the initial questioning, and what Paul Boulad had reminded him of: if he co-operated, the sentence would be much lighter.

At nine in the morning, in the presence of Inspector Hartung, Delouette said to Paul Boulad: 'I'm renouncing my rights and privileges. I'll co-operate.'

We know now he did this. And his case would just have been an ordinary matter of traffickers and a courier, presumably an occasional one, if the SDECE and a colonel of this service had not been cunningly involved in it by him. In fact Delouette had been all the more skilful in that his story was an adroit amalgamation of truth and falsehood.

35

The Caprice des Temps *in Florida*

At dawn one day at the beginning of May 1971, a hired station-waggon drove through Nice and set off towards Grenoble. It had come from Villefranche and was driven by a bald, weatherbeaten man, of medium height and piratical appearance: Marcel Boucan.

The Caprice des Temps had been in the Voisin boatyard for several months awaiting various modifications. Bernard Voisin had received the sailor, whom he had known since 1947, almost as a friend. He had met him again when he had been involved in the smuggling of American cigarettes, then when he was in charge of the *Oiseau des Iles*, which was to be destroyed by fire in the Antilles. 'In 1969 he had asked me to find him a boat for lobster-fishing, then he telephoned me to cancel the search because he'd found what he wanted at Sables d'Olonne.'

Officially, again, Boucan was preparing himself for a lobster-fishing expedition. He intended to leave at the end of the month. The work carried out in the boatyard, in connection with the engine and a few bits of cabinet work, had been completed. Now the keel had to be cemented over and work on some concrete anchor buoys completed. After a winter of idleness, the team now worked at touching up the paintwork and did a bit of general spring cleaning in the living quarters.

Boucan arrived at the Nice wholesale market. He steered his station-waggon between the piles of crates and heaps of fruit as to the manner born, and approached a truck which two men were unloading. The vehicle had the trade name of a greengrocer from the Bouches-du-Rhône on its side. Boucan reversed, drove round the truck and let the back flap down.

Without exchanging a word, the two men emptied the truck,

took from it sacks identical to the others and put them in the station-waggon. Boucan closed up the back and got back into the car; one minute later he was driving away from the market and back towards Villefranche.

During the next few nights, he put plastic packets from the sacks in the hollow of the keel, inside watertight compartments. While the crew went to Cannes to see a film and have an evening off, Boucan made some cement and blocked up the opening with a trowel. Sawdust, a few shavings and the harbour dust disguised the evident newness of this piece of work.

There were still a number of packets which had not fitted into the keel, and they were destined for the anchor buoys, watertight metal containers in a cement shell. Again, a layer of cleverly applied cement could disguise the opening and a lead weight set within would bring them up to the weight of an ordinary anchor buoy.

During the days that followed, the crew loaded up the provisions and equipment necessary for the Atlantic crossing. There were to be several ports of call: Gibraltar, Ceuta, Casablanca and the Canaries. The destination was Pointe-à-Pitre; one final stage would take the *Caprice des Temps* to Miami where she would moor in the Jones boatyard – naturally, for further repairs: this time it was to be the propeller shaft which had gone – and to be unloaded safe from prying eyes.

Everything was ready for her. An associate of Orsatelli's, Ange Santoni, known as Louis, who spoke English fluently, had flown to the US at the beginning of April together with a young woman, Michele, divorced from an American husband. Santoni had been a policeman in Algeria, then a prison warder. His professional file included the following description: 'mediocre physical fitness, unemotional, cunning, not wholly reliable, unenterprising, depressed, not really fitted for the police force'.

The departure of the *Caprice* took place on 17 May, under Boucan's command. Lacascade was to take the helm at Pointe-à-Pitre. The crossing took only two weeks. Boucan was a first-class sailor.

* * *

The *Caprice* and its precious cargo arrived at Pointe-à-Pitre on 7 June, from the Canaries. Marcel Boucan had informed his numerous friends in the Antilles that he was off on a lobster-fishing expedition. Some tourists, whose movements often coincided with those of the *Caprice*, had made their appearance at the beginning of the month: Orsatelli, together with Mme Agvanian, and someone called Toussaint Astolfi.

Orsatelli went out in the boat several times, then flew to Miami where Santoni was waiting for him. Everything was ready for the *Caprice*. An obliging customs officer had been notified, as had the Jones boatyard. Officially the boat needed further modifications, which would be added to the hold covering built in Villefranche.

It was goodbye to the lobster-fishing expedition. On 25 June, the *Caprice* entered the harbour. She was promptly directed towards the boatyard where, before retiring to their hotel, the crew were visited by Orsatelli and Santoni. Somewhat unusual work then began: the anchor buoys were bludgeoned to bits, the concrete covering of the keel split up with a cold chisel.

The next day, two members of the crew were employed to transport sacks to the boot of a car they were never to see again.

A few days later, Santoni gave Boucan sixty thousand dollars in a Pan-Am bag. Once again delivery had been effected without incident. None the less the *Caprice* remained in dry dock until the end of July.

Orsatelli and Santoni set off again for Guadeloupe. Boucan had sent a cable to his wife asking her to reserve hotel rooms and to hire a car for the period of their stay. They flew back to France a few days later.

Towards the end of the month, the *Caprice* and her crew went to sea again, under command of Lacascade, with Boucan playing the part of the shipowner. As in the first return journey, the only freight consisted of five empty suitcases belonging to Orsatelli.

After putting in at the Bermudas, the pseudo-lobster-boat crossed the Atlantic and reached the Azores. It then went to Gibraltar where Marie-Françoise, his ex-wife, was to join Marcel and sail with him from there to Bastia.

36

A Series of Successful Deliveries

Richard Berdin had put off his trip to Marseilles where the twelve kilos of drugs bought for him by the syndicate with a part of his profits awaited him. His break with the association meant that he himself had to get the goods to his buyer. Through Dumerain, he learned that the Picpus crowd intended to smuggle several hundred kilos of heroin before the end of the year, to be hidden in cars. They asked Berdin to oversee delivery in New York. As for the twelve kilos, Dumerain agreed to include them in the first consignment he would be asked to take delivery of in New York for the Picpus group.

But first they had to be brought from Marseilles to Paris, and that was what exercised Berdin. The young Frenchman had been watched closely for over a month – more, perhaps – and did not want to be caught for a negligible parcel of twelve kilos after having handled such very large quantities.

Désiré D, whom he had met in Fresnes where he was doing time for currency fraud and for whom he had done certain favours, was eager to repay his debt. At the beginning of July, the two men set out for Marseilles, after having made sure they were not being followed.

A few hours later, Berdin deposited Désiré in the centre of town and drove towards the Vieux Port. He turned into the Belle de Mai district, in the direction of the café kept by Robert le Sourd. Salles had warned Robert to expect a visit.

'Come back in half an hour,' he said, taking a small beige canvas suitcase which Berdin handed to him. 'Le Noir will be here.'

Robert le Noir, another member of the local underworld, whose appearance was unnervingly piratical, was really Di Russo. One hour later he entered the café, his case considerably heavier. Berdin went up to him; they exchanged a few words and the Parisian went out again with his load. He put it in the car and drove towards the Canebière, where Désiré was waiting for him.

'Have you got the junk?' Désiré asked.

Berdin's affirmative reply was apparently the reverse of reassuring. Experienced by now, Berdin recognised in Désiré's reaction the anxiety he himself had felt over his first deal.

'Don't worry. I wasn't followed, I assure you.'

'What a scheme! Who'd go to Paris with this lot?'

A few minutes later, they entered the Gare St Charles. Désiré looked around him nervously. However, he took the suitcase and went towards the platform. Berdin watched him from afar. Then he went back to his car and drove off towards Paris. Two days later, Désiré brought the case to the studio that Dumerain had rented on rue Balzac, near the Champs Elysées. If the heroin reached the American buyer safely, the deal would net the young cat-burglar a hundred and fifty thousand dollars, almost eight hundred thousand francs, a first step on the road towards his stated ambition – retirement.

But Salles continued to badger him. If he, Berdin, would no longer work for him, he should have the decency to persuade Preiss to agree to replace him. Preiss listened to the proposal impassively.

'You suggest that I work for them, then you tell me you're leaving because they're always crooking you. Tell them I'll think about it.'

Berdin also met Signoli. His prompt release had made him the hero of the hour in the Paris underworld; his health was drunk in champagne at the Picpus and the Orphéon. The Marseilles crook was too pleased with himself to feel resentment about Berdin's defection. He simply thanked him for having suggested Preiss, who had a very good reputation as being reliable, cool, circumspect and not easily ruffled.

'But he hasn't accepted!'

'He will. There's too much money to be made in this game for an intelligent guy to be able to refuse. You would have stayed in yourself if you hadn't found another network. By the way, be careful, particularly with the Lyon group. They've sent two cars over this month. Lajoux and Grisoni were there, one at New York the other at Montreal. They had a car gone over by the Canadian police.'

Roger Preiss, who had joined the two men during their conversation, was later to state in his testimony in New York, 'My presence did not seem to embarrass them in any way. Berdin was telling Signoli that Labay was due for fifty million, because the kilos missing after the dismantling of the car delivered to New York had been found.

All Berdin had to do now was to await the end of the Picpus gang's St Tropez holidays and to keep up relations with the Lyon group. After their Canadian setback, they seemed to set great store by his collaboration. He sometimes met Preiss, who despite the poor report of his future associate, was increasingly inclined to reap his share in this apparently inexhaustible harvest.

A little before the end of the month, Nancy telephoned from New York. The police had been to question her about her French friend on several occasions, asking when he was proposing to come back to the United States; if she knew his address in France. They claimed that it was about some minor offences, but she was sure there was more to it.

'Do you promise me that your business is all above board? You never talk about it.'

He promised. He said he avoided the topic so as not to bore her.

It was the beginning of July. At about the same time, Anthony Pohl's report to the Senate Committee revealed, 'We were informed by the Paris Office for the Prevention of Drug Trafficking that the person who had taken delivery of the heroin in New York on behalf of the organisation was called Richard Berdin and that it was probable that he would be coming back to the States in the near future.'

Force of circumstances forced Berdin to remain in touch with

Salles and Signoli. Despite the fact that he was under surveillance, Signoli prepared to set off again for America. He asked Preiss to give him a definite answer, because he had to make arrangements. After a lot of hesitation, the young crook made up his mind.

'All right. But at the first backhander, I quit.'

Jo reassured him. There would be no funny business. He told him to get hold of two photos for the documents he would get him and to be ready to leave at the beginning of August.

Indeed, at the end of the following week, on the terrace of the Café de Flore on St Germain des Près, his new employer handed Preiss his passport, with a visa for the US, in the name of Patrick Lorentz.

'We're leaving this evening,' the Marseilles man informed him. 'I'll meet you at the Voile d'Or.'

Together they went to make a few purchases at Ted Lapidus: shirts, ties and sundry accessories. Jo offered his new associate a black crocodile belt. At nightfall, Vanverberghe drove them to the Gare de L'Est. They had a reserved compartment in a *wagon lit* on the express to Frankfurt, in the names of Yvon Tournier and Patrick Lorentz.

They crossed the frontier without difficulty, Signoli sighed with relief: 'They must have poster-sized copies of my photo.' He gave his companion two thousand five hundred dollars and two addresses, to be destroyed if anything went wrong – one in New York, the other in Miami, in case he, Signoli, got picked up.

'We mustn't go through the customs or immigration together when we arrive in the US. I'm as well known as Nixon. It's my last trip there. But I absolutely must contact the buyer before handing over to you.'

They bought their tickets at Frankfurt Airport the following morning and took off that afternoon on board a Lufthansa Boeing 707.

Roger Preiss left Signoli at Montreal and carried on to Miami, where Signoli was to join him after working out the details of a delivery of heroin concealed on board a Barracuda car.

But the changeover in Florida had been secured well before

he left France. The Syndicate was engaging in several operations at the same time. Towards the end of July, two somewhat atypical tourists had landed in Miami and been taken to the Deauville; the following morning they had rented a brand-new Cadillac.

One of them was called Herman. Sandy haired, stocky, of medium height, aged about thirty, he had been lent to the Syndicate, or rather, in this operation he was representing the interests of another group run by the Mafia. The other one, 'Meu' – his real name was Marius Lastroyani – was a friend of Signoli, another old acquaintance of the Marseilles police. With his two brothers and two other characters known as the 'Maltese', he had specialised in the form of procuring which consisted of forcing young women to become prostitutes by terror.

Before his departure, Signoli had given him a ring. Meu had to go to Tampa, in Florida, as soon as an Italian ship called there. On presentation of the ring, which would act as identification, a sailor was to hand over a considerable quantity of heroin.

On board the sumptuous hired Cadillac, Meu and Herman went to Tampa. But on entering the harbour, they had the feeling that they were entering a vast and very close-meshed net. Men in plain clothes, with grimly idle expressions, were sauntering along the quays and a positive battalion of customs men were swarming around the warehouses. The Cadillac left without its precious burden. The junk returned whence it came.

Preiss was unaware of Meu's presence. He knew him fairly well because he had had a disagreement with him in a Paris restaurant. Meu had threatened to 'make mincemeat of him'. As soon as he came off the plane, he went to the Newport Hotel, on Miami beach, and spent the rest of the day bathing, sunbathing and strolling around the town.

The next day, towards midday, he was at the airport waiting for the plane from Montreal; he took Signoli to the hotel, to the double room he occupied on the first floor overlooking the swimming pool. Signoli immediately telephoned this friend Meu to arrange a meeting. Then he had a long conversation in Italian with his buyer, Louis Cirillo.

'He asked me to go and see him alone,' he said to Preiss. 'I'll introduce you another time. Meanwhile, Meu has messed up the deal I put in his way. I'll try and sort it out.'

After lunch, the two men met Meu and Herman; the ensuing discussion was lively enough; but Signoli became really angry only when he saw the Cadillac they were using.

'Couldn't you find anything more eye-catching? Herman, take it straight back, as soon as Meu has hired a less striking one. Also leave the Deauville and go to the Castaway motel, two minutes from here. No point in wasting our time driving for miles.'

'During my stay in Miami,' Preiss was to state, 'I spent the time bathing and strolling. I also spent quite a lot of time in my room because of sunburn and also because I'd injured my forehead in a car accident and the wound had reopened in the water.'

Signoli left him to attend various rendezvous. One day he took Preiss to an apartment on the ground-floor of a two-story building. Louis Cirillo was expecting them, seated in an armchair. They sat down on a couch.

A half-open door gave on to an adjoining room. Intensive haggling about the price of heroin began. Louis suggested ten thousand dollars, Signoli asked for ten and a half, adducing the agreements made by Fiocconi. At last he made his point and promised a delivery to New York during the following week.

During this discussion, Preiss rose to stretch his legs. Whether intentionally or not was unclear, but he set off towards the open door, passing behind the seat occupied by Louis, who jumped. But already Signoli had leapt up and grabbed his companion by the arm.

'Don't be a fool,' Signoli murmured to him in French. 'There may be guys observing us who set store by their anonymity. They'll probably be quick off the draw. Don't ever do that sort of thing again.'

The incident put an end to the conversation.

The following morning, 18 August, Preiss and Signoli, pretending not to know one another, took their places on an Eastern Airlines plane bound for New York.

* * *

At New York they went to the Abbey Victoria, recommended to them by Jo Astuto. They met two days later in a snack bar on the corner of seventh Avenue and 57th Street, so as to arrange the final details of the delivery.

A further meeting was arranged for the following day, in the same place. 'We waited a good half hour,' Preiss was to say, 'and as I was beginning to lose patience, Signoli told me that that was quite normal, that we were probably being observed and our reactions registered.'

Astuto arrived at last together with Cirillo, then everyone went off again, the Frenchmen on foot and the Italo-Americans in Cirillo's green Continental. During the luncheon Signoli informed Preiss about the details of the delivery: it would take place the following morning at seven, at the corner of Seventh Avenue and 51st Street.

At the appointed time, Preiss met Signoli and Astuto, in Astuto's bronze Cutlass. One minute later, the car having set off, Signoli showed the empty Barracuda parked at the roadside to Astuto, who was driving. The Cutlass drove round the block. When it reappeared, the Barracuda drove out into the road in its wake, with a Marseilles member of the Syndicate at the wheel. One behind the other, the two vehicles set off towards Fort Lee, in New Jersey.

The Cutlass parked at the kerb, Astuto went to ring the door bell of the house. With a bunch of keys he was handed, he opened the doors of the garage and the Barracuda drove in. A few seconds later, the four men were plunged into a gloom which was promptly dispelled by a neon strip light. 'There were some tools,' Preiss recalled, 'and we began to dismantle the car. The Marseilles man from the Syndicate had a diagram of the chassis and coachwork. The places where the packets were hidden were marked on the plan.'

One hundred and sixty packets of white powder were successfully retrieved from the doors and the roof, from under the petrol tank, the floor and the chassis. Meanwhile, Jo Astuto put them together into bags which he took into the house. The garage was not well ventilated and the men were sweating heavily; they ended up stripped to the waist. Preiss, ever clumsy managed to tear a packet and heroin poured out. Astuto went into the house and came back with a spoon.

'Put it all back into the bag,' ordered Signoli. 'Try not to mix up any dust. And don't breathe, unless you want a fit of the vapours. And next time, try to be more careful.'

Having reconstituted the bag, Preiss sat down in a corner and watched his companions. Two other packets, in which the powder had turned to a dirty yellow, posed a problem. Astuto went off to the house for a consultation. He came back with the verdict. Those bags must stay with the others.

A little before the end of the unloading, the door to the house opened outwards and two hands holding a tray appeared. Astuto instantly leapt up, grabbed the tray and shut the door. He doled out cakes, coffee and soda in plastic cups. Once the unloading was over, the team washed their hands and faces in a basin at the top of the stairs leading to the cellar.

'Then,' stated Preiss, 'we all got into Jo Astuto's car, and he drove us to a cab rank. Then we went to Manhattan.'

During the afternoon Preiss went to the cinema and in the early evening met Signoli, Astuto and the man from Marseilles. During the meal they had together, Signoli announced that they would 'find some birds'.

'You'll see,' he said to his protégé, 'it's more than just work. After each delivery, Louis gives a party for everyone.'

Towards midnight, the Cutlass drew up in front of a smart building. A porter with a braided uniform came forward and ushered the group to the lifts at the back of the marble entrance hall. They went up to the seventh floor, following a corridor to a half open door from behind which floated chatter and music. They walked forward, sinking into the thick green carpet as if into turf, and discovered the welcome committee: Barbara, the mistress of the house, a friend of Jo Astuto, fair and slight, flanked by a small redhead and a luscious brunette.

'Beds and bedroom furniture were green like the carpet,'

Preiss recalled. 'A large bedside lamp was lit . . . I didn't take part in the general carry-on. I couldn't see any point in it. I was irritated rather than drunk.'

Cirillo joined his suppliers towards two in the morning. He got into an argument with Signoli about the delivery but finally agreed to pay for the two packets whose contents seemed to have deteriorated.

This problem solved, Signoli and Cirillo went to get the money to pay for the eighty kilos of heroin delivered and Preiss went back to the Abbey Victoria to bed. He was awoken the following day about midday by Signoli, who came in with a Samsonite case in his hand, and emptied its contents onto a locker: three hundred thousand dollars in wads of hundred-dollar bills, a roll of brown paper and a pot of glue. 'He poured a glass of boiling water into the case. After a moment, he pulled out the lining and put it to dry on the air-conditioning machine.'

'I'm leaving this evening,' stated Signoli, pursuing his work. 'You'll wait another two or three days. I'll give you my address and phone numbers in Paris and Marseilles. You can deal with the money later. Take two thousand for expenses.'

The deal concluded, they went to a jeweller's on 57th Street. Signoli bought a gold Piaget watch for fourteen hundred dollars. It was intended to strengthen the bond of business and friendship with Cirillo. A few hours later, the wealthy Syndicate boss flew off to Brussels in a Sabena 707 which carried a Samsonite case in its luggage compartment containing the equivalent of one million six hundred thousand francs in dollars.

Two days later, Preiss too flew off for Frankfurt, and then Rome, in a Lufthansa plane.

37

The First Real Setbacks

The plans of the Picpus and Lyon groups seemed to be taking shape. Almost every day, Berdin saw one or other of the members of the parallel syndicates who would advocate patience: it was sometimes his friend Jean Dumerain, or Riton le Juif, or André Lajoux, Pierre Simeoni, Antoine Grisoni, Jean-Claude Vela or Bakri.

At the end of the first week in September 1971, Roger Preiss, alias 'Eric', returned from Rome. He had stopped en route in Marseilles to meet Signoli, then he took the plane for Paris, where he met Berdin.

Eric's lack of enthusiasm for the Marseilles men and their syndicate suited Berdin. He needed a buyer. Why not Cirillo, approved of by Salles and Signoli? Preiss, who was in contact with the Italo-American, was thus particularly well placed to make the connection.

'Do you realise,' said Berdin, 'they are proposing sending a hundred kilos a week? At a thousand dollars a kilo for us, we'd make four hundred thousand dollars a month.'

The next day, the plan took shape. At the Bistingo, on rue St Benoit, Grisoni, Simeoni and Lajoux told Berdin that the first load was on its way, on board an Italian boat. It was concealed in a Ford Mustang belonging to a certain Giacomazzo, who was returning home to Astoria, in New York State, after a holiday in Italy.

The speciality of the Picpus plan was to utilise vehicles belonging to American citizens of Italian origin, who had been for a stay in the mother country.

A meeting was arranged for the following morning, so as to go to Lyon and work out final details. On 18 September in the morning, Berdin flew to Orly and found himself, one hour later, in a bar decorated with pictures of the Ile de Beauté – together with Grisoni and Lajoux. They were joined by a well-dressed man who sat down opposite Berdin and gave a clear, authoritative résumé of the plans put to him by his Picpus friends. Then he asked Berdin to go with him.

'I'm going to introduce you to the man who will contact you in New York and who will hand over the goods. He realises that he will have to abide by your decisions over there.'

A few minutes later, he parked his car at the kerb and entered a bar. He emerged again with a man of about thirty who took the wheel. Another rendezvous was arranged outside the Air France window on Fifth Avenue, between ten and eleven a.m. from 22 September onwards.

The young man grasped the wheel tightly. He stared at Berdin for some time, memorising his features. After having gone over all the procedures to be observed at the meeting, Michel – that was the name he had given – gave up his place to the elegant fifty-year-old who took his visitor back to his travelling companions. Everything had been arranged. 'I went back to Paris with Grisoni,' said Berdin. 'Lajoux spent the night in Lyon before leaving for Marseilles, where he was to take part in a trotting race.'

The next day, he met Preiss and informed him of the proposed deal.

'I'm leaving the day after tomorrow,' Berdin told him. 'I've got a passport in the name of Gilbert Koumoun. As soon as the car is in New York, I'll let you know.'

One hour later, Berdin was in Avenue Gabriel. Labay, back from Haiti, had informed him that he wanted to see him urgently. 'He explained to me that he had an excellent opportunity of smuggling quantities of heroin from a hundred to four hundred kilos from France to the US, thanks to the complicity of some American customs men in New York airport.'

'One piece of good news deserves another,' said Berdin. 'Salles has recovered the missing sixty-seven kilos. But you'll have trouble getting paid. They've had it in their possession for several months without saying anything and they're still making you work to make up for it.

Berdin then proposed that they should go into the customs men deal with the collaboration of the Picpus team. Until his departure, Preiss would serve as intermediary. The rest of the day was spent in rushing around obtaining the agreement of all concerned. Grisoni hesitated, then gave his agreement for a delivery of a hundred kilos at the end of the month, through the said network.

It was almost midnight when Berdin, who had gone to Brussels by road, presented himself at the Sabena ticket office. Just as he was getting his ticket for New York, he hesitated. Perhaps he was jumping into the lion's mouth? Then he said firmly, 'A return ticket to Montreal, please.'

On the morning of 22 September 1971, the Italian steamer *SS Raffaelo* entered New York. Among the passengers was an American citizen born in Sicily, Giuseppe Giacomazzo, aged thirty-four, living in Astoria, New York, accompanied by a woman called Corinne with whom he had spent several weeks in Italy.

They had left America with the Ford Galaxie which Giuseppe had bought the previous year. Some time beforehand his brother-in-law, Lorenzo d'Aloisio, who lived in the same town, had asked him if, for a payment of a thousand dollars, he would agree to bring back a considerable sum of money concealed in his car. Giuseppe had agreed. On 7 September, during his stay in Turin, he had handed over his car to some unknown men while his friend looked round the town. The Ford and its cargo were now in the ship's hold.

Three or four days earlier, the BNDD had been notified by a telex from the Office for the Prevention of Drug Trafficking in Paris, that Richard Berdin, travelling under an assumed name, was on his way to the US to supervise the delivery of loads of heroin contained in six successive cars.

The next day, the Canadian Mounted Police notified the Montreal Bureau of the arrival of Richard Berdin – whose description they had. He was immediately put under discreet surveillance. His departure for New York on board an Air Canada plane in the late morning of Tuesday 21 September, was reported, and the alert along the frontiers called off.

After the arrest of Edmond Taillet, which gave some idea of how widespread drug smuggling in cars was, and faced with the impossibility of searching all those arriving in American ports or crossing the Canadian or Mexican frontiers, the customs administration had decided to conduct a series of restricted operations: to search all cars on a boat chosen, not exactly at random, but as a result of apparently favourable pointers. The boat on which this technique was to be tried first would be decided upon at the last moment. Berdin's journey to New York, twenty-four hours before the arrival of the *Raffaello*, hastened the decision.

Giacomazzo and Corinne were going through immigration, when a team of customs men discovered the first packets of heroin inside a back door of the Ford Galaxie. They alerted their superiors and pursued their searches. From the back of the rear seat, they brought out a hundred and sixty-nine bags, or a total of eighty kilos of heroin.

Meanwhile, the owner of the car and his companion had been taken into a customs office. The young woman's innocence was obvious. She was immediately released after detailed questioning. Giacomazzo on the other hand was taken to the customs headquarters; for once, the customs authorities were in close collaboration with the BNDD. He learned the real nature of the goods he was transporting and came clean.

He agreed to collaborate with the authorities so as to enable them to arrest as many traffickers as possible. After a delay of ninety minutes, he left the harbour at the wheel of his Ford Galaxie and drove home. He parked his car at the kerb of Astoria Boulevard. Inside the vehicle, there was only half a kilo of heroin left. The remainder of the load had been replaced by bags of icing sugar.

Richard Berdin, who had arrived at Kennedy Airport the previous day, had gone through customs and immigration without any problems. He had taken the first taxi he saw – and whose driver was in fact a customs man – and driven to the Abbey Victoria. Despite his exhaustion, and his resolutions, he could not resist the temptation of contacting Nancy. He had telephoned her, she had come to meet him in a restaurant and they had spent the night together in the hotel.

The next day, after leaving her outside the hotel, Berdin went to his appointment with the unknown man from Lyon – known as Michel – in front of the Air France offices on Fifth Avenue. At a sign from Berdin, Michel followed him and went with him down a nearby street, still under the discreet surveillance of the BNDD and customs agents.

After reassuring his colleague – who had already come to the rendezvous the previous day – Berdin took the paper handed to him and read: '34th and Astoria Boulevard, 5T 289,' the location and number of the car.

'You can't imagine your job ends there,' he protested. 'What about proof that the guy hasn't had any problems and that the car isn't being watched? You'd better call him up so as to be quite certain.'

They went into a bar where Michel tried to reach Lorenzo d'Aloisio, his American contact, but unsuccessfully. Finally they decided to go and take a look round the spot themselves. They went out of the bar, hailed a taxi – whose driver was also a customs agent – and were driven to Astoria Boulevard. They continued their way along the boulevard on foot, went past the Ford Galaxie at 34th Street, went a few yards further on, then separated after having arranged to meet the following day.

The next morning, they met in front of the Abbey Victoria. Michel had already called Lorenzo's number several times, to no avail. Again they took a taxi to Astoria, cruised along the street and observed that the Ford Galaxie had disappeared. Who had moved it. – Lorenzo and his friends or the customs and BNDD?

Hoping to throw some light on the matter, Richard hired a car. For several hours he drove around Manhattan, then around the suburbs, then to Kennedy Airport, one eye permanently fixed on the rear mirror. No doubt about it. He was being followed. The car driving some distance behind his changed frequently, but one was always there.

He returned to his hotel, scrutinised the faces in the foyer, lift and corridors, and noted something odd about several of the 'guests', without coming to any very definite conclusion. As he went into his room, he turned round and saw a camera fixed above the door of the room opposite his and trained on him. He closed the door, went down the corridor, up the stairs and checked whether there was a similiar apparatus on the floor above. There was not.

'I had taken a risk coming back to the hotel. I thought that the American police, having identified me, were waiting for me to take possession of the drugs before questioning me. So I told myself that there was a chance that they would let me go back to France in the hope of arresting me with a quantity of drugs on me.'

Michel joined him again during the evening as arranged. He had finally managed to get through to Lorenzo. His friends had noticed suspicious goings on around the car, and had thought it would be better to wait twenty-four hours before moving.

'They'd do better to let it drop,' answered Berdin. 'If you have any way of getting them before tomorrow, tell them to drop it and lie low. It stinks.'

The helicopter blades whirled in the warm air of the Indian summer; the din of the engine drowned all other noises. The autumn sunlight softened the harsh outlines of the skyscrapers. In the streets of Manhattan, the slipways and expressways, the cars looked like serried ranks of multi-coloured ants. In whole regiments they stopped, started, accelerated and stopped again.

For the pilot and the customs agent with him, the problem, was to scan the distant swarm for a Ford Galaxie carrying seventy-nine kilos of heroin and to follow it to its destination. The helicopter was not alone in the sky. After taking off from the Floyd Bennett airfield on Long Island, to fly over the expressway, it had entered the mainstream of air traffic, the air space shared between Kennedy and La Guardia control towers; the authorities, notified of the operation under way, were allowing the forces of law and order priority over transcontinental Boeings.

The Galaxie was driving along, followed by a Buick and three cars from the customs, their outward ordinariness belied by the size of their radio aerials. From one of them, an operator called the helicopter pilot and directed him towards the Long Island expressway. The vehicle was spotted just as it was leaving the expressway to turn down a feeder road, followed by the Buick. The two cars stopped side by side, then went back to the expressway, having escaped the surveillance of their frustrated pursuers. The helicopter was being used for the first time in such an operation to cope with precisely such an eventuality. It described a large arc without the passenger losing the station-waggon from sight and resumed surveillance. The customs cars, now dispersed, followed the details of the chase on their radios. At last the Galaxie and then the Buick took refuge from the limelight in a secluded layby. The two vehicles were now screened from the drivers going along the expressway, but still visible from above.

The driver of the Buick, after having phoned from a public call-box, went up to the Ford Galaxie. It was immediately surrounded and its occupants arrested. The customs and BNDD men had not wanted to run the risk of losing it in the thick traffic.

One hour later, at the Abbey Victoria, the telephone rang in Berdin's room. He heard Michel's voice telling him that he could not come, had terrible toothache and was going straight home.

The young Parisian put down the receiver. This time he was on his own. He had already called his contacts in the trafficking world, but to no avail. He would have to wait several days, ask his Parisian friends for other meeting points, elude police surveillance by phoning from public call-boxes. It promised to be a hazardous business.

The only sign that all was not lost, was that he was still at liberty. He tried to convince himself that if he could not be caught red-handed, they would not catch him at all. To escape his loneliness he phoned Nancy, having resolved to put the whole matter out of his mind and make the most of her presence and affection.

The following evening, as they were going back to his room together, he shifted the lens of the camera trained on his door; it was a childish gesture of challenge. He was immediately surrounded by half a dozen police and customs men. Half an hour later, after putting his personal belongings hurriedly into his suitcase, he was taken to Varick Street, the first stage on the long journey which took the traffickers to the penitentiary through an endless succession of hearings, identifications, charges, repeated questionings and, above all, propositions that they collaborate with the law (which earned considerable remission for those who agreed, semi-freedom during the preliminary investigations and sometimes even immunity).

Berdin had decided to talk. During the days following his arrest, the BNDD officials presented him with the evidence of his guilt, carefully gathered over a year. The total sentence which could be passed on the young Frenchman as a result of these charges exceeded the average life-time.

He had no particular reason to remain loyal to his associates in any case: the Marseilles men had not stinted themselves when it came to carelessness, embezzlement, negligence and lies. He had never been more than a pawn in their game, never a full partner. On the other hand, his reward for co-operating with the police was freedom after a year.

But to earn such leniency, he had to do more than talk. Before embarking on a vast dragnet operation which would break up the Syndicate, the Federal Agents wanted to get their hands on the hundred and six kilos which Labay was soon to deliver, carefully concealed in expensive Vuitton suitcases. They were all the more eager because, according to what the businessman had told Berdin, a customs official was abetting him and was to help the goods through Kennedy Airport.

At the request of the French, who were not yet ready to cast their net, Berdin's arrest had not been revealed to the press. Only Giacomazzo, d'Aloisio and their American accomplices filled the front pages.

So Berdin was taken to a comfortable Manhattan hotel, where he enjoyed relative freedom. Several rooms around his were occupied by officials. He picked up the phone and asked for the Paris number of Lajoux's mistress, who lived in rue de Vaugirard. A few minutes later, the gentleman-driver was on the line.

'Michel tells us you're having problems.'

'Michel panicked needlessly. He was looking for an excuse to go home. The Italians have been hospitalised, but it's not likely to be catching. Our friends can come whenever they want. Still, I have changed my hotel. I'll give you my number so that you can let me know when you've made a decision.'

Two other calls during the days that followed reassured Roger Preiss and André Labay. Berdin hesitated before encouraging his two friends, to whom he bore no ill-will, to throw themselves into the lion's mouth. Of course, he had no choice, but he could have found ways of arousing their suspicions and bringing the operation to a standstill. But the customs men had one convincing argument: 'They'll be arrested whatever happens. The French police already have enough evidence against them. In Paris, they'll each get eighteen years. While here, if they are as co-operative as you have been, they will be free next year.'

The Picpus group therefore made contact with Labay and Preiss. It would take at least a week to buy the Vuitton suitcases and collect the junk from Marseilles where it had remained until the situation became clearer. 'Eric' was expected to leave at the beginning of October. The delivery of the drugs would be made at about the same time in Paris, at the Rond Point on the Champs Elysées, not far from Avenue Gabriel.

Labay was to leave as soon as his crossing could be timed to coincide with the duty hours of the accomplice at Kennedy. In his hotel in downtown Manhattan, Berdin received confirmation of the plan and the meeting-place between himself and Preiss was decided upon: the bar of the Waldorf Astoria, every day at eight, from 5 October. The conversation was registered on tape recorders installed in a neighbouring room.

Meanwhile, the French Office moved into action. Its inspectors, who were privy to Berdin's confession and the reports of the New York customs officials, had almost a hundred police on the watch. The Picpus suppliers were located. It was Lajoux, Grisoni and a man called Georges Burait who were in charge of the deal on this occasion. A fourth unidentified accomplice had bought four suitcases at Vuitton's for a thousand francs each. All these men were followed, their movements noted, their contacts scrutinised. Photos of them and everyone to whom they spoke were taken through telephoto lenses. Preiss and Labay were included in this series of checks.

It was then that Labay had one of his brilliant ideas. It very nearly succeeded. He sensed that the golden age of trafficking was drawing to an end. But he was so caught up in the machinery that he did not think it possible to extricate himself scot free.

He contacted former friends from the Special Services, for whom he had done a number of favours. Both French and Americans confirmed in guarded terms that the authorities were fully aware of his current activities.

Then the adventurer staked his life on a gamble. The French branch of the BNDD was housed in an annexe of the American Embassy, at 58 bis rue de la Boétie. On the morning of 5 October, Inspector Guy received a phone call. A Frenchman speaking almost perfect English was willing to inform on a whole network of drug traffickers, on certain conditions. Was he interested?

When Labay introduced himself a few minutes later, he was immediately ushered into an office where Guy and one of his colleagues were waiting for him, a bottle of bourbon and three glasses on the table.

'In two or three days,' the visitor said frankly, 'I'm supposed to deliver a consignment of more than a hundred kilos of heroin to the US, which should earn me a hundred thousand dollars which I urgently need for my business. Another delivery is to follow, this time of two hundred and fifty kilos.'

His plan was to reconcile the interests of the two parties. He would be allowed to deliver the first load, so that he could get his share of fifty million francs and in exchange for the immunity he would be granted, he would deliver the second consignment which would make it possible to lay a trap for all those involved in it. Furthermore, he would reveal everything he knew about the drug trade.

His listeners paid rapt attention. Then leaving him with the bottle of bourbon, they went to consult their superiors.

The arrest of Berdin, Giacomazzo and their accomplices was largely the result of co-operation between the American customs and the BNDD, although the glory redounded chiefly to the customs. Labay's proposition had an added advantage: it allowed the BNDD to arrest the receiver in New York and, with a little luck, to get their hands on the buyer who had eluded them for years.

When Guy and his colleague came back into the room where Labay was, they gave their agreement. The businessman did not realise that it was unthinkable that American policemen would deliberately allow a quantity of heroin which could cost the lives of thousands of young addicts from New York or elsewhere to enter the US. Thinking that he had won the round, Labay left the BNDD agents after announcing that the goods would be handed over to him the following day.

'I'd like to see it and taste it before you go,' suggested Guy, 'at least to reassure ourselves we haven't been had.'

Labay was to take delivery of the car and the cases filled with heroin the following morning. It was a Volkswagen which Burait had hired that same day. A meeting was arranged at the car-park of the Grandes Terres, at Marly-le Roi, near Labay's official residence.

At dawn on 8 October there was quite a crowd at the Rond Point in the Champs Elysées. Near one of the fountains three shady characters, deep in friendly conversation, kept their eyes glued to the Volkswagen, crammed with elegant luggage and parked near the Avenue Montaigne. The contents of the cases represented more than a million dollars on the retail market, enough to compensate for the loss represented by the load on the *Raffaello*: eight hundred thousand francs at cost. It was certainly worth the early morning surveillance.

There were other loiterers on the scene: a tourist was photographing the view; a delivery boy piled crates onto a truck; a street sweeper shuffled along the gutter; a managing director read the *Figaro* at the wheel of his car; other motorists stood chatting near their vehicles. All came from Place Bauveau, rue de la Boétie and the Fauborg St Honoré, the centres of the various police departments.

When Labay appeared crossing the avenue wearing a smart spring suit, an imperceptible ripple of excitement flowed through the assembled company. He approached the Volkswagen, took out his key-ring, opened the door, lifted a suitcase lid, closed it again, sat down at the wheel and drove off.

Already the motorists had returned, with studied calm, to their cars. Coolly, they turned on their engines and drove behind the Volkswagen up the Champs Elysées towards the Bois de Boulogne, the westbound motorway and Marly. Meanwhile, the other strollers, crooks and police had dispersed.

Guy had been waiting for some time in the Grandes Terres car-park, but showed no sign of impatience. He saw the Volkswagen arrive. Labay got out, opened the door and again lifted the lid of one of the cases. The two men leant over the rows of packets. With the hand of an expert, Guy nicked the plastic slightly, licked his finger and picked up a bit of the powder which trickled out.

'Excellent. Top quality.'

He made a gesture with his hand. As if by magic, a dozen men suddenly materialised in the middle of the car-park which had been empty a few seconds earlier. They came towards him. Labay understood: he did not protest. His world had just collapsed. He had lost everything on this last gamble. He glanced at Guy, who made a small gesture of apology. Labay held out his hands for the handcuffs which the nearest policeman had just produced from his pocket.

'My life is over,' he murmured.

* * *

The following evening, at about seven-thirty, Richard Berdin was driven for the third time to the bar of the Waldorf-Astoria where for a moment he would be able to savour a whisky and the illusion of freedom. He could imagine more congenial company, but his companions were not proving too disagreeable.

A little later Preiss, who had arrived during the night, crossed the foyer under the interested gaze of several women and a gentleman called Provencher, a BNDD agent. He made a sign to another loiterer, Agent Pavlick. They approached the traveller who was preparing to enter Harry's Bar, and showed their credentials. The Frenchman followed them unprotestingly. The Narcotics Bureau had just scored a point over the customs.

'He had on him a sheet of paper with a lot of scrawled numbers which didn't seem to make any sense,' Anthony Pohl stated before the Senate Committee. 'He admitted that these were coded telephone numbers of American buyers, Jo Signoli and others. After he had decoded them, the agents working on the affair discovered that they included that of Maria Schiotis, Louis Cirillo's mistress.'

Louis Cirillo's last conviction for drug offences dated back to 1945. Subsequently he had spent six years in prison for armed robbery. His police file was up to date and he was not hard to track down. The coded telephone numbers found on Preiss, and Berdin's revelations, supplied enough evidence to charge him.

On 8 December, the Miami section of the BNDD was notified of the probable arrival of the Italo-American in a new Buick station-waggon, together with one Anthony Rostaing: his destination was probably the Tahiti Motel, on Collins Avenue. And on the 9th he deposited Rostaing and continued on to the Oxford House apartments on Twenty-First Avenue. The same tailing led to the identification of a number of other individuals, mostly known to the police.

Surveillance was continued until 12 October, when the New York office informed Miami that an application for a warrant for arrest had been made. They suggested that Cirillo's arrest should be effected as soon as possible. At 17.30 the Buick, with Cirillo and

Rostaing aboard, drew up at a red light at the corner of West Park Road and Sheridan Boulevard, in Hollywood. It was immediately surrounded by BNDD agents and Cirillo was informed that he was under arrest for violating the law on narcotics. He was wearing red and white striped trousers, white shoes, a jersey wool shirt with vertical blue stripes, and sunglasses. He was immediately taken to the local office and informed of his constitutional rights. Among the personal objects seized was the Piaget watch which Signoli had given him.

The new Jersey garage, whose location had been given by Preiss, was thoroughly vacuumed. In the dust collected, chemists discovered indisputable traces of heroin. The investigation lasted several months and produced sufficient evidence for a number of convictions. 'The evidence and information obtained,' Anthony Pohl was to state to the Senate Committee, 'established that, during a period of seventeen months, from May 1970 to October 1971, Cirillo and his accomplices had introduced fifteen hundred kilos of heroin on to the American market; it had sold for ten and a half thousand dollars a kilo and was thus worth fifteen million, seven hundred and fifty thousand dollars.'

38

The Boarding of the Caprice des Temps

Since 24 August 1971, the *Caprice des Temps* had remained in the Voisin boatyard at Villefranche-sur-Mer. After her journey from Miami, after putting into port in the Azores, then at Gibraltar, where Mme Boucan met Marcel, the boat had sailed towards Corsica. She had arrived at Bastia about 15 August. Orsatelli, accompanied by his faithful 'courtesan', was waiting on the quayside. There were embraces and congratulations. In accordance with tradition, five empty suitcases were passed from the boat to the empty boot of the Corsican's DS 21.

Then everyone dined at the Mattei – with the exception of the sailors – at the *patron's* table. During the afternoon the *Caprice des Temps* had cast off her moorings and set sail for La Spezia, the last port of call before laying up for winter and more fitting out. 'The boat was a trawler with a forehold,' Voisin stated. 'She had a storeroom occupying her whole height. In this space, of about three metres sixty, a floor had been made with a panel in the middle and two bunks on either side.'

Meanwhile, the crew busied themselves with assorted tasks. The Boucan couple moved into the flat Boucan had conveniently acquired for his wife in the residential block Le Chantilly at Cagnes-sur-Mer. 'A most polite and charming man,' recalled the owner. 'He was always so punctilious.' They also made the best possible impression at the restaurant La Trinquette at Villefranche: 'M Boucan was always so courteous,' sighed the proprietress. 'He lived very simply. I never saw him with anyone at all suspicious.'

But despite their uneventful life, the couple had been the object of discreet but continuous surveillance. The police of the Côte d'Azur took over from the Guadeloupe police who, on the instructions of Divisional Inspector Guillaud, had been on the lookout since 22 June. They examined all the doings and movements of the Boucan family and the crew.

Tailing thus led the two inspectors from their hide-out in Cagnes to Marseilles, in the wake of the sailor, who had been lent a Peugeot 403 for the crew to drive around in. They then managed to observe the visit to the Voisin boatyard of two passengers in a Citroen-Maserati who had already mentioned in various reports: Orsatelli and Santoni.

It can easily be imagined what they had come to say to their courier: that the delivery of the large amount of heroin they intended to smuggle on this occasion was going to take time and that departure would not take place before 1972. Indeed, Lacascade and two members of the crew took the plane for the Antilles. Boucan returned the Renault 16 he had hired in Nice, then flew off again for Guadeloupe where the police resumed their watch. The year drew to a close. Lacascade gathered the members of the crew of the *Caprice* and flew them to Nice. In January 1972 the Boucans were once again living in Cagnes-sur-Mer on site, after a visit to Ile St Vincent.

Work at the Voisin boatyard was completed. The crew members bustled around over the finishing touches. Boucan went to Marseilles with his wife, whom he left in a hired car while he had a long converstion with Orsatelli.

After this visit, Ango Santoni and his friend Mme Le Gall took the plane for the US where the BNDD followed their movements as far as Miami. All this activity seemed to indicate that a consignment was about to be sent out.

In Nice Boucan hired a capacious station-waggon. On 23 February, he borrowed several tools and half a sack of cement from a mason in the shipyard. One morning, Mme Boucan came to fetch two other members of the crew. She needed their help for some removal, she said. They spent the day in her living-room, watching television.

In the middle of the night a greengrocer's truck, with its

crates of carefully packed vegetables, drove out of the gates of a suburban property in Nice and parked in the middle of the swarming activity of the wholesale market. Unloading began. Crates piled up. As in the previous year, Boucan appeared at the wheel of his station-waggon, reversed and lowered the tailboard. Behind the barrier of crates was a pile of jute sacks which were carefully placed on the floor of the car. Half an hour later, it was driving towards Villefranche.

The sacks were unloaded by Boucan in the empty shipyard, then stowed in the hold. It would take several hours of back-breaking labour for the adventurer to put the four hundred and thirty-eight kilos of heroin into the twenty-eight kit bags, eight card-board boxes and one basket, to pile them up in the depths of the keel and cover them with a thick layer of cement. The half bag of cement borrowed was intended to deflect attention from the scale of the work to be done; Boucan already had an adequate store of cement. When the crew came on board, everything was concluded.

Before setting sail, Boucan went to Marseilles to see Orsatelli one last time. On 29 February, the *Caprice* left Villefranche for another translantic crossing, destination Miami.

At 4.35 on 1 March, the decks were cleared for action on the *Sirocco*, the customs speedboat. Approached in the open sea, off the Ile du Levant, a boat had refused to stop; indeed it had increased its speed. After having unsuccessfully made the usual requests with the aid of signals, the customs men loaded the *mitrailleuse* and fired a burst into the air, then another. A man appeared on the deck of the pursued boat.

'I'll have to wake up the crew if you want me to stop,' he replied to the orders barked through a loudhailer.

A quarter of an hour later, the trawler finally stopped. Four customs men boarded the craft and ordered the captain to follow them to Marseilles.

'On 29 February,' Joseph Lanfranchi, the commander of the *Sirocco*, stated, 'the Marseilles police asked us to identify a boat of which they gave us a description, and to follow it on radar, seeing that it did not leave territorial waters. Level with the Ile de Porquerolles, it suddenly headed for the open sea. It was then that we decided to challenge it.'

Another customs coastguard vessel, the *Lissero,* had left Marseilles to give assistance to the *Sirocco.* Customs men boarded the deck of the *Caprice des Temps.*

In Boucan's cabin, they found a magazine whose cover bore the headline: 'How your children are being drugged'. An initial search produced nothing. Standing in a small bookshelf were works by Kafka, Camus, Kant and Balzac.

The *Caprice,* flanked by the two motorboats, re-entered Marseilles harbour.

About 11.30, it was moored near the Fort St Jean, which had become the customs post. A further search revealed nothing suspect. However, the customs men did seize some papers which Boucan had been trying to conceal: an address book, invoices for repairs to the boat, several thousand dollars and two 7·65 pistols.

At about 20.00 hours, an expert observed that the concrete covering of the boat's ballast extended surprisingly far forward. The search was put off until the next day.

On Thursday 2 March, at six in the morning, Boucan slipped noiselessly into the harbour waters. A hastily scribbled note left in his cabin exonerated his family and crew. Despite his fifty-eight years, he intended to attempt an escape by swimming across the arm of sea separating him from Fort St Nicolas. But the water was icy and his limbs become numb. He did however make it to a Thai junk where an American couple, Mr Ray Evans and his wife Barbara, were living with their children and a monkey, which gave the alarm with shrill cries.

With the help of his wife, Mr Evans pulled the swimmer aboard, rushed to Fort St Nicolas where he was given the brush-off by some jeering soldiers, rushed towards the harbour and was at last able to ask for help in a bar. Boucan, too feeble to attempt further escape, was taken in hand by the firemen. Dressed in trousers, a sweater and lumber jacket, he was carrying five thousand francs; people attempting suicide do not normally carry cash . . .

It was 8.30. On board the *Caprice* the customs men's searches were concentrated on the cement slab which extended the covering forward. A few blows with a crowbar were enough to uncover the eight hundred and seventy-six packets of carefully wrapped heroin. The 'Drug Syndicate' had been broken decisively.

When Louis Cirillo appeared in April 1972 before a jury that was three-quarters female, the network set up by Fiocconi and Kella and which had reached a peak of prosperity with Salles and Signoli (when it was divided into several extremely active subsidiary branches), was broken up completely.

Signoli, who had acquired the *café-brasserie* Le Consul, on the Avenue de Friedland in Paris in the interim, was arrested shortly after his American buyer, at the house of his friend Anne, in rue Etaix in Paris by Inspectors Fiori and Giordani, of the 'stups'.

They seized several papers, some coded telephone numbers that a schoolboy would have been able to decipher, and other documents which were promptly followed up. On 10 April Jean Dumerain, located in a bar on rue Feydeau, was arrested together with his mistress, Marie-Michele. His home on rue des Sablons at Neuilly was gone over with a fine tooth comb. Inspectors Perru and Rey just missed Salles at Boulogne, in front of the apartment Preiss had done up for his mistress. But he conveniently came back to be caught at the wheel of his Porsche together with his girl-friend Yaminé at the beginning of the afternoon.

That evening, the veteran Jo Orsini was sitting at home in front of his TV, watching the eight o'clock news. Suddenly he was confronted with some film showing the arrest of his two protégés. The shock was too much for his tired heart. It killed him, thus saving him from yet another period in prison.

On the 11th, it was Demeester's turn to be caught in his own house, in Avenue de Villiers; to be followed by Raymond Moulin at the Hotel Bergère. The next day, Inspector Perru visited a barber's shop in Pigalle and discovered the false passports factory'.

At the same time, police officer Andre Sarda set out to learn more about the four cars used in the trafficking which had been identified: the Lancia sold to Mireille, Moulin's friend, the Bentley 5764 TT 75 belonging to Labay and two vehicles in Demester's name, the Mercedes 300 and the Cadillac abandoned by Berdin in a grim New York suburb.

Two of these had been tracked down without difficulty by the American police. The Bentley was more problematical. Labay had sold it to a Yugoslavian dancer, a friend of Elizabeth F. He in turn had sold it to a Californian businessman, who had had the original radiator grille replaced by a Rolls-Royce one, for reasons of prestige.

When Customs Officer Bocchicio found it at last, it was in a shed together with other props belonging to a film company, the coachwork riddled with bullet holes; it had played a heroic part in a television serial about gang warfare, but it was still roadworthy, and indeed it was driven through Los Angeles, followed by a police car – just to be on the safe side – and hoisted onto an open truck, destined for New York, without arousing the slightest curiosity.

Anthony Pohl and his team went to Louis Cirillo's house in the Bronx. His wife and daughter had left. It was an unassuming place, with a small unkempt garden. Searches revealed nothing, although police had received information that his *mafioso*'s lost treasure was still hidden there. The BNDD agents proceeded with their search doggedly and spent a night with searchlights, reducing the building to rubble, which left the administration with a fairly hefty bill.

Wallpaper was stripped off, panelling torn down, various pipes dismantled. At last, in a sort of sports room equipped with a shower, a tin box was found in a niche behind the shower panelling. It contained a hundred thousand dollars.

This find encouraged the searchers to continue with their destructive activities. The whole garden was dug up, the paving battered with crowbars. Curious bystanders stood around the house, riveted, oblivious of time, indifferent to the first glimmers of dawn etching the buildings against the skyline.

At last, under a narrow strip of turf beneath a protruding window ledge, there appeared a row of half-rotten boards, hiding a black plastic bag. In this bag were five packets similiar to those containing the heroin and each holding two hundred thousand dollars. Altogether, the equivalent of six million, two hundred thousand francs.

On 25 May, Louis Cirillo was sentenced to twenty-five years in prison.

A few days earlier, Laurent Fiocconi and Jean-Claude Kella had finally gone for trial. The testimony of Berdin and the BNDD special agents, who had been hunting them for several years and had amassed a mountain of evidence against them, left no doubt of their guilt. They were sentenced to twenty-five years on each of three charges.

39

Second Arrest of the King of the Chemists

When Joseph Cesari came out of prison, having served his time for his part in the clandestine laboratories of the Clos St Antoine, he found himself free but penniless. He had lost his estates of 435 hectares and his four servants. The underworld had seen that his wife and children did not lack for anything, but once he was out, he would be obliged to get to work again if he did not want to die of hunger.

After the several months of rest which are always accorded to 'a friend who has been arrested and who hasn't talked', Cesari would have to make an effort to set up a laboratory again. It was the only work he could do which would enable him to earn enough money fast enough to reimburse his creditors and leave France for Peru, where a big cocaine deal was awaiting him.

Promptly approached by the traffickers – for it was impossible to find another chemist as good as he was, and because no one had dared to set up a laboratory since recent crippling setbacks – Cesari was to work to order.

But he needed premises, an organised team and the wherewithal to produce as much heroin as possible, as fast as possible.

It was at the bar Banon, where he was a regular, that Cesari was to meet his man, a twenty-eight-year-old taxi driver, Lucien Giraudo. The bar Banon, situated on the hill of Montolivet above Marseilles, belonged to a trafficker. The bar was registered in his brother-in-law's name. It was also a tobacconists and, adjoining the bar, there was an oyster stall.

Giraudo had no convictions; his form seemed to be good. He had always worked as a taxi driver. He suited Cesari's purpose ideally for buying tools, equipment and cars, without attracting unwelcome attention. Cesari, too well known to the 'stups', would have to keep a low profile.

The two men got on well and met almost every evening. At first Cesari asked him to see to various minor matters. Then he brought more, if subtle, pressure to bear and began to exert a positive spell over Giraudo, who was a simple man. He painted pictures of a readily accessible El Dorado. At last he asked him to rent a villa in Aubagne, through which the Huveaune ran; this was a small coastal river, the purity of whose water was well known. Pure water was essential for treating the raw morphine to obtain the best quality heroin.

The house, the Villa Suzanne, stood alone on an upland, set apart from the main town. Approach was difficult; it was situated near a small lane edged with coppices and fallow land. It was surrounded by pine trees and vines.

A low building with green shutters and roofed with red tiles, it had one story only, flanked by an outhouse with a chimney; ordinary tenants would probably have used this as a laundry. For Cesari and his accomplices, here were the ideal premises for their clandestine activities. The Villa Suzanne was the typical Provençal hide-out of which retired people dream. A couple called Georgiou were employed as caretakers. Lucien Giraudo was to be paid on output: five hundred francs per kilo of heroin produced.

But Inspector Morin, knowing that Cesari had been released from the prison at Poissy and had returned to the region, had had him watched.

Cesari was impatient to get his new laboratory into working order. He was to manage to produce four hundred kilos a month. One evening at the bar Banon he met an old friend from the Italian underworld. He had not seen this friend since the beginning of the sixties, when he had often been in Italy on business. Cesari introduced him to Jacquelin M, the owner of the Banon, and to another trafficker, Louis R.

The Italian gave them an order which the two men were to deliver to San Remo.

In January 1972, the two smugglers went to Italy, fell into the trap and were arrested. Cesari's friend had become an undercover agent for the BNDD.

Hearing the news, Cesari was very alarmed, fearing that he would be implicated. He decided to work only at night and to leave the laboratory before daybreak so as to be less easily located; he kept a revolver under his pillow. If the police arrested him, he intended to put up a fight or kill himself, anything rather than go back to prison.

The long period of surveillance carried out by Inspector Morin's men finally bore fruit. The Villa Suzanne was located.

'As soon as we approached the villa, we smelled the characteristic smell of the chemical products used. Once on the spot, we arrested Georgiou and his wife. One room was locked. Georgiou claimed that he hadn't got the keys. After forcing the door, we found a cupboard containing the fruit of a fortnight's intense activity: ten packets of heroin, with a total weight of a hundred kilos.'

Thanks to evidence found on the spot, the inspectors then went on to Cesari's home.

On Thursday 16 March 1972, at about 16.00 hours, an Aubagne taxi driver, François Cocco, parked his cab, a red Mercedes, at the taxi-rank. He had just returned from a trip to Marseilles. His engine was still running when a client whom he knew well approached him and asked him to drive him home, to a villa on the road to Gémenos. The man was pale and sweating, and seemed exhausted. As they arrived at the open gates, he asked the taxi driver to drive in.

Suddenly the car was surrounded by men in check caps and blue overalls.

'A hold-up,' thought the driver, his heart in his boots. Pistols were trained on him and his passenger.

'Cesari, you're caught, no funny stuff,' said one of the men. François Cocco was taken into the kitchen while Cesari, under heavy guard, was put in another room. His wife, Mme Renée

Cesari, was temporarily absent. When she returned, she was surprised to see François in her kitchen. 'What are you doing here?' she asked the taxi driver. But she soon understood. 'I'm so sorry you're caught up in all this.'

During the month preceding his second arrest, Cesari had been working furiously, about eighteen hours a day. 'He'd become a positive wreck, completely poisoned,' the police were to comment.

Facing investigation, he took refuge in the most adamant denial, saying merely: 'You came upon a fine business in Aubagne, but it's nothing to do with me.'

'They were quiet people,' recalled the neighbours who lived in a house on the other side of the road. 'They never spoke to us. I was amazed when I saw a whole fleet of cars driving up. At first I thought they were going to make a film.'

In Villa Suzanne the police also found 2,175 kilos of acetic anhydride (two kilos of which are needed to treat one kilo of raw morphine), 1,200 kilos of tartaric acid, 950 kilos of sodium carbonate, sixteen sacks of bone black, 200 litres of alcohol, 255 litres of acetone and 240 litres of hydrochloric acid. That stock would have enabled the 'king of chemists' to make 1,000 kilos of pure heroin.

Another team had gone to arrest Giraudo at his home, five kilometres from Aubagne. Once again Cesari had been prevented from exercising his lethal trade.

40

Death of Joseph Cesari

On 22 March 1972 an icy breeze blew down the Rhone valley and swept clear a pale blue sky.

At eight o'clock, the curfew plunged the Baumettes Prison in Marseilles into silence. Each of the sixteen hundred prisoners retired into solitude. A few assorted noises mingled into a vague murmur punctuated by the iron-tipped tread of the warders on night watch. In the central office, the others prepared for a long vigil.

A little after nine o'clock, a warder went into the first-floor corridor on a beat which would take him over the entire prison in an hour and a half. He stopped in front of each numbered door, pressed the switch lighting the cell and glanced through the peep-hole to check that the prisoner inside was indeed stretched out on his bed. It did not matter whether he was awake or asleep, provided he was obeying regulations. In the course of time the warder reached cell number 100; there, he paused. The accused occupying the long white-washed room was in solitary confinement. He was called Joseph Cesari. He had been arrested in the Espillières district, above Aubagne, in a villa he had turned into a laboratory for manufacturing heroin.

Chief Constable Morin and his men had seized a hundred and twenty kilos of remarkably pure heroin in the Villa Suzanne, as well as a large haul of chemicals. Cesari had been taken to the CID premises known as the 'Evêché' (once the Bishop's Palace). After attempting to deny the charges, he had retreated into total silence.

'He looked a complete wreck,' said one of the investigators. 'His face and hands were eaten away by the acid he had used to transform the raw morphine into heroin. His legs were covered with sores which opened up at the slightest impact, because of the anti-coagulant treatment he was forced to undergo all the time.' Despite his extreme frailness, this little man, with his high forehead and short, greying hair, had been working eighteen hours a day for the last few months in the poisonous atmosphere of his laboratory.

He had arrived at Les Baumettes on the Monday evening fifty hours earlier. Since then, he had not left his cell. He lay for hours on his narrow bed, his eyes fixed on the ceiling, lost in silent meditation.

Through the peephole, the warder inspected the room from right to left, glancing at the pail, the basin, the cupboard where the prisoner could put his clothes, his washing things and his blanket. His gaze stopped at the folding bedside table fixed to the wall and rapidly he made an inventory of its contents: a few sheets of white paper, envelopes, a pair of glasses, a ball-point, an orange, a book: *Le Jardin noir* by Christine Arnothy, a story of the daughter of a war criminal with a ravaged conscience.

In the bed, buried under the blankets, Cesari was lying still, apparently asleep. His breathing was regular. The warder pressed the light switch and walked on, leaving the room lit only by the dim glow of a nightlight. One detail escaped his conscientious inspection, but it was an anomaly he could not have noticed from outside: the prisoner's clothes were no longer in their place in the cupboard.

Hardly had he moved on, than Cesari threw back the covers and got up, dressed as he had been dressed the previous Thursday, the day of his arrest: blue trousers, black socks and shoes, white shirt and black leather windcheater. Calmly he sat down at his bedside table, put on his glasses, pulled the sheets of paper towards him and began to write, bending his head to make out the marks of the ink on the paper:

'To the examining magistrate, I would like to ask you to be good enough to remit my body to my family . . .' He wrote unhurriedly, his hand hardly trembling. His decision had been carefully considered. Whether recalling his past or trying to imagine the future, he could find no other way out. There were some obvious reasons for his decision; others, more subtle, proved equally imperative when he thought about them.

Only his love for Renée, his long-standing companion, could have held him back. He had married her five years earlier when he had been a prisoner at the Centrale in Poissy. When he thought of his children – Renée, already an adolescent, and Richard, still a young boy – he wondered whether it might not actually be better for them, for their future, that he should disappear once and for all.

In any case, he was unlikely to see them ever again, except in a prison visiting room. At worst he would receive a life sentence, at best, twenty years. In either case he would never know freedom again. He knew he did not have long to live. After his last arrest, in October 1964, he had undergone two surgical operations at Poissy and at Fresnes for serious cardio-vascular disorders. It was for health reasons that he obtained an early release at the beginning of December 1970.

Even if, by some miracle, he were to profit from extenuating circumstances or obtain a remission, his fate was sealed. His friends – suppliers or clients – would force him to set to work once again in the poisoned atmosphere of a clandestine laboratory.

They had seen to it that his family did not want for anything during his long detention. This was not a disinterested action; his debt to them had mounted over the months, the years. He now had little chance of realising the youthful dream in pursuit of which he had made all these mistakes: that of leading an easy life with his family on a large estate, where he could devote himself to stockbreeding.

After signing the few lines he had just written, Joseph Cesari calmly folded the sheet of paper and slipped it into an envelope, on which he wrote: 'M Saurel, Examining Magistrate.' He took another sheet of blank paper which he contemplated at greater length before writing, in a more hesitant hand: 'My darling, first let me tell you how much I love you. You have been the only love of my life, with the children. Excuse my handwriting. My fingers are stiff. Forgive me for all the harm I may have done you . . .'

He was not quite sure what he meant by that. All he had ever thought of was her happiness. But some images persisted in his mind: her slow ageing over the years against the background of prison visiting rooms; her increasingly resigned and despairing expression; the difficulty they had in resuming their past intimacy after his release. He also thought of his perfunctory embraces with the wife of one of his accomplices on a mattress in the Villa Suzanne, in the hope of fending off his anguish, and above all of the fleeting encounter with Renée, his wife, in a corridor of the Palais de Justice when she was leaving the judge's offices between two policemen. It was this last memory that had made him lose all desire to fight.

The harm he had done to others was something he thought about more and more often. Previously, the idea that each gram of heroin coming out of his laboratory meant the downfall or death of a human being had not crossed his mind. He belonged to the generation of the 'quiet men', often modest traffickers who supplied a traditional clientèle of night-birds, middle-class people and criminals. When, after his arrest in 1964, Judge Periès had painted a picture of the ravages caused by drugs, he had replied simply: 'All that matters to me is work well done.'

He had been quite sincere. He did not think it had been mere thoughtlessness or a refusal to face reality. He had always lived just outside the law, an inhabitant of the underworld. Sickly, scrawny, timid, silent and uneducated, he had decided that he would excel, and he had succeeded. He had pored laboriously over chemistry books; and he had improved the homespun methods at the time. He had claimed, 'You learn how to make heroin from chemistry books just as you learn how to make recipes from cookery books.'

He had realised his most ambitious dreams: buying a large estate, employing servants, living in a gentleman's sumptuous residence and even earning money from his pig farming. He was on the point of abandoning his clandestine activities when the police arrested him in October 1964.

At Les Baumettes, at Fresnes, at Poissy – where he had spent the previous six years – he had heard about the extraordinary expansion in heroin trafficking, the gold-mine it represented for a new generation of greedy and ambitious traffickers who had unloaded tonnes of white powder onto the American market. They would probably have offered fortunes to get their hands on the uniquely pure heroin that he alone was able to produce and that the *Cosa Nostra* buyers had positively fought over.

Towards the end of his sentence, he had felt something of the tide of hatred against the 'death merchants' and their suppliers sweeping over Europe and America. The peaceable clandestine trade of former times was front page news now. Heroin had become a symbol of revolt for the younger generation, ill at ease in the kind of world their elders had to offer. In inexperienced hands, it slowly destroyed the bodies and minds of its users – when, that is, it did not rapidly bring about their violent deaths.

It was then that Joseph Cesari, himself eaten away by the insidious ravages of his trade, had begun to examine his own conscience. But on his release he was caught up in the machinery. He was ruined, and after having paid his debt to society, he had to settle the other debts he had accumulated during his imprisonment.

'Ask forgiveness for me from my children and tell them how much I love them. The release I am seeking in death is necessary for all of us. For you, for the others, for myself. Goodbye my darling.'

Cesari folded the paper and put it into another envelope. He addressed it to 'Mme Renée Cesari, c/o Examining Magistrate Saurel.' He placed it next to the other letter, removed his white gold wedding ring and laid it on the first letter.

He had done everything; he had no time to lose. The warder doing the ten o'clock rounds would already be on his way. He had to finish everything before his step rang out in the stair well. Cesari opened the cupboard doors, took out a cloth which he twisted so as to make a rudimentary rope. He passed the end round the window hasp, six feet from the ground. Perhaps one last picture flashed through his brain: of a gaunt-faced, emaciated young addict to whom he had talked in the prison doctor's waiting room the previous evening; the chance meeting had upset him.

At eleven o'clock, the warder pressed the switch of cell 100, looked through the peephole and saw the prisoner's body hanging from the hasp, feet swinging forty centimetres from the ground. He ran to alert the warder in the central office, who had the keys. Together they returned to the cell, opened the door and cut down the body, still warm. While one tried to revive Cesari with mouth-to-mouth resuscitation, the other ran for the doctor. A few hours later, a welfare worker entered Renée's cell to tell her of her husband's death.

Cesari's death had occurred a few weeks after the boarding of the *Caprice des Temps*; Marcel Boucan had been about to deliver a cargo of four hundred and thirty-five kilos of heroin to Miami. It marked the twilight of an astonishing venture involving several dozen criminals. For eight years, they had sowed panic in the US and held out against the police of a dozen countries. Oddly enough, their enterprise had taken off just at the moment when Joseph Cesari had been arrested for the first time, in autumn 1964.

41

'We Must Get Ricord', Richard Nixon, 1971

The Latin American network had already brought more than five tonnes of drugs to the US and it was in Paraguay that Ricord had demonstrated his organisational talents to the full. He had managed to locate a number of helpful contacts in the entourage of the Paraguayan dictator, General Alfonso Stroessner, and it was General Patricio Coleman, in charge of repression of the *guerilleros*, who protected Ricord.

On the last trip of its journey, from Asuncion to Florida, the Marseilles heroin was transported by small private planes belonging to smuggler-pilots whom the American customs men had nicknamed the Mau-Mau.

Auguste Ricord had managed to obtain their co-operation and had set up relay points at Rio, São Paulo, Caracas and Panama. But the FBI was on the alert. In autumn 1971 the Miami police had received an anonymous letter informing them that a plane from 'Ricord's fleet' was to carry a load of heroin to an aerodrome in Florida.

On 18 October 1971 a Cessna, registered in Argentina, landed at Miami airport. Piloted by a Paraguayan named Cesar Bianchi, the plane pursued its route to North Perry, also in Florida.

Bianchi was blissfully unaware of the fact that, above him, an FBI plane was tailing him among the clouds. When the plane landed, the police found fifty kilos of heroin in the tail of the aircraft.

The pilot had already set off again for Miami where, once arrested, he agreed to co-operate and fell in with the plans of the BNDD agents.

Bianchi went to New York. In a hotel off Fifth Avenue, the St

Regis, he met two men, an American and a Frenchman. That evening the trio dined with a fourth man, an Argentinian, at La Brasserie, a restaurant on 53rd Street, between Park and Lexington Avenues.

The BNDD then decided to take action. Once arrested, the men pointed to Ricord. But the organiser of the drugs fleet showed every sign of being a law-abiding grandfather, a kind uncle; an elderly gentleman who loved children; at worst, perhaps, an over-zealous businessman; at all events not a 'death merchant'. Everyone in Paraguay knew he had made his money by buying and selling restaurants, bars and clubs all over Latin America.

'Since my arrival in Argentina,' he was fond of saying, 'I've had sixteen restautants. The Fètiche, the Lido Club, the Robinson, the Copacabana, El Sol which became L'Auberge Provençale and many more, including the Paris-Niza in Asuncion.'

Ricord certainly was a friend of General Coleman's, but simply because the general was a regular at his restaurant, which was frequented by the cream of Asuncion society. Furthermore his friend Papillon, the writer, had been his partner in Le Madrigal in Buenos Aires.

But, unfortunately for Ricord, Bianchi had talked. Small, stocky and obstinate-looking, Bianchi was a mercenary who owned three planes, including a DC3 and a twin-engined Cessna, which were used to transport heroin. He had made three trips to the US. In June 1970 he had delivered sixty kilos, in August thirty, and in October forty-two. That journey was his last.

Bianchi had explained to the BNDD agents that he had collected the drugs from the restaurant of El Viejo (Ricord), the Paris-Niza in the suburbs of Asuncion. He had waited outside the door and an intermediary had gone into the restaurant. Ricord had received him and had given him three suitcases, which Bianchi was to carry.

As a reward for his co-operation with the American authorities, Bianchi was allowed to 'escape' from Miami prison and merge into the background.

On 25 March 1971, the American Government categorically

demanded Ricord's extradition on the basis of an agreement made between the United States and Paraguay in 1913.

'We are considering trying him for conspiracy against the United States,' said John Mitchell, the Attorney-General. The American request fell upon the Paraguayan Government like a bolt from the blue. It would be awkward for them to leave the owner of the Paris-Niza at liberty. Several policemen were sent to arrest him. But Ricord had been tipped off.

That morning at nine, a fat man with jet-black hair and a burnished complexion, Police Officer Salvador Ibarola, presented himself at the Paris-Niza. He asked to see the establishment's police licence, went out into the garden and ordered an al fresco cup of coffee. Another policeman accompanying him asked to speak to M Ricord.

Just at that moment an unknown man with a shock of hair and dark glasses emerged from the restaurant, leapt into a red Torino and drove rapidly towards the Argentinian frontier, which was less than a kilometre away. On the other side of the river lay Argentina, of which he was a citizen. The man was 'El Viejo'.

Unfortunately for him, that day the Paraguayan police, who had previously been willing to turn a blind eye, had been given their instructions, and a boat. They pursued the runaway and when they caught up with him Ibarola's first move was to seize Ricord's wig.

Then an incredible process of blackmail began.

'We can't possibly hand Ricord over to you,' said the Paraguayan Government to the Americans. 'Our liberal traditions would not allow it.'

'If you persist in keeping him,' the Americans replied, 'we shall take reprisals. First of all we shall stop buying your sugar at advantageous prices. If you co-operate, we can increase our economic aid.'

In December President Stroessner was on the point of giving in. The Attorney-General of Asuncion broadcast a communiqué hinting that he might be favourable to Ricord's extradition.

But in January 1972 hopes faded. A Paraguayan court decided

that Ricord could not be handed over to the US: 'He is not a US citizen and has never set foot there.' The Asuncion judges decided, therefore, that the extradition treaty did not apply to him.

'Ricord is more powerful than we are,' they said in Washington.

Nixon was furious: 'We must get Ricord,' he said to Attorney-General John Mitchell.

Ricord, meanwhile, had organised a comfortable life for himself in prison in Asuncion. He had furnished his cell in the English style and had had a TV installed. Twice a day the head waiter from his restaurant Paris-Niza brought him his meals. He played cards with the warders and received journalists whom he plied with champagne. His nieces came to see him twice a week.

'I'm just a prosperous restaurateur,' said Ricord in his defence statement. 'My specialities are meat balls and *coquelets à la creme* with mushrooms.'

He had spent fourteen months in prison before the judges reached their decision.

42

The End of the Grupo Frances

The denunciation which led to the arrest of Ricord caused panic among those criminals still in South America.

The most important of them, Lucien Sarti, was then living at Ibasema in the residential suburbs of Rio under the name Roberto Sconamiglio. He had just met a superb brunette, Helena Ferreira, and had set her up in a flat. The couple's affair was predictably turbulent and a complaint of disturbance of the peace was lodged against Sarti and his volcanic friend. At the same time Sarti, having learnt of Ricord's arrest, felt it politic to flee to Peru with Helena.

At Lima airport the customs men were in for a surprise. Searching through the couple's eleven suitcases, they discovered a fortune in dollars. The young woman was arrested. Sarti was allowed to carry on to Mexico. His legitimate wife joined him in Mexico City. On 8 March, the couple moved into a handsome apartment in the residential district. They went out and entertained. Sarti never suspected that the police had been on his trail ever since his late entry into the country. The Guatemalan authorities were after him for an armed attack on a bank, he was wanted by the Bolivian police. Interpol had issued descriptions of him everywhere.

On the evening of 17 April, about nine o'clock, Sarti and Liliane, his wife, decided to go to the cinema. They went out into the street and were about to get into their car. At this moment four policemen appeared. Sarti turned round sharply. He was not armed, but the police fired and hit him. His wife was arrested.

The next day the Mexican Minister of Justice announced that an international drug trafficker had been killed during a confrontation with the police.

* * *

On 2 September 1972 François Chiappe (Rubber-lips) and his girl friend Margarita Nadal were at the shooting lodge he had just purchased at Serenade la Falda, near Cordoba in Argentina.

Suddenly the police burst in, arrested them and discovered forty-six kilos of heroin destined for the American market.

Less than a year later, François Chiappe managed to break out of prison in a most improbable fashion. When the new President of the Republic took office, the Argentinian Government decided to mark the event by granting the country's political prisoners a general amnesty. At the Villa Devoto Penitentiary the warders had simply opened the cell doors and the hundred and eighty-six prisoners walked out, as intended. What had not been envisaged, however, was that assorted gangsters and some common law prisoners should follow in their wake, with François Rubber-lips well to the fore . . .

Coincidentally, this same 2 September, the day of Chiappe's arrest in Argentina, the Asuncion Attorney-General telegraphed Washington: 'You may take Auguste Ricord.' A few days earlier, he was still under the impression that he had a friend in the Republic of Paraguay, General Stroessner. He had told journalists, 'I have nothing to fear, and if I have nothing to fear, it is because I have done nothing. Let the Americans come and get me if they can. As far as I'm concerned, everything is open and above board. I will gladly face US justice if necessary. But it will not be necessary. To charge me, they need evidence, and that is what they have not got.'

But on 3 September, Auguste-Joseph Ricord, alias El Viejo, alias Cori, alias Senor Andres, landed, handcuffed at Kennedy Airport, with an impressive escort: ten policemen, two nurses and a doctor (he suffered from diabetes and had a weak heart). He was driven off in a Cadillac. The bail for this small, grey-faced, wrinkled, bony little man was set at a million and a half dollars.

It may have been Ricord's arrest which precipitated the fall of his right-hand man, Christian David, 'beau Serge'. When his boss had been arrested in 1971, he had drawn ahead, leaving Paraguay suddenly for Brazil. It was the BNDD agents who tracked him down and notified their Brazilian colleagues.

David was living with a woman in a hotel in Feira de Santana, in Bahia. The Brazilian police had been tailing his mistress for some days. On 21 October they decided to take action. David was always armed and knew he was being followed. The police were prepared for a struggle.

At dawn the hotel was surrounded. Caught just as he was getting out of bed, he did not have the time to escape; determined to stake his all, he opened fire, but the police rushed forward, threw themselves upon him, disarmed him and took him to the prison in São Paulo. Here he tried to commit suicide on two occasions, but failed, thanks to the vigilance of the warders. Transferred to the US, he was to be sentenced to twenty years for drug trafficking. At the end of November 1972 the members of what the Rio underworld called the *grupo frances* were all dead or in priosn.

With the help of their South American colleagues, the BNDD agents had achieved the impossible: they had broken up the network used by the Marseilles Mafia to unload seventy per cent of all heroin trafficking.

43

The Mysterious Trunk

At the beginning of 1972, the Central Office for the Suppression of Drug Trafficking identified the man whom the American Narcotics Bureau was still calling Mario Deniz, believed to be in Uruguay. He was in fact André Condemine, a Frenchman.

During all the years he had acted as a link between the South American traffickers and the French suppliers, Condemine had managed to conceal his activities behind the identity of Mario Deniz. He had tested this cover to the full, as he had remarried Gilberte G under this false name when he had already married her under the name Condemine.

At the beginning of 1972, the couple lived in Brussels, where Gilberte had a decorating business. She also owned a light grey BMW which her husband often used.

In the spring, the BNDD learned that some American traffickers had called the telephone number 25 77 20 in Brussels, from New York; it was Condemine's number.

Condemine was in the process of organising a sixty-kilo consignment to the United States via Spain and the Argentine. He had enlisted the services of a man called Pedro Caballero-Linares.

At the end of September, Caballero-Linares was arrested in Buenos Aires. Obviously, he must have helped the authorities because sixty kilos of pure heroin were then seized, concealed in a consignment of kid skins on a cargo boat, the *Normacoltair*, when it called in at Rio on its way to New York.

After the seizure, Condemine left his Belgian address: he was tracked down a few weeks later in Paris, where he was arranging for another consignment of sixty kilos, using the Mexican General Mariles as courier.

On 10 November the 'stups' learned that Condemine might be living in a studio on a quiet street in the sixteenth *arrondissement*.

On the 14th, he was located. The studio was on rue des Patures. At this address, a man calling himself Alphonse Mostin had been living in a studio overlooking the courtyard on the third floor, since 1 November. The concierge was shown Condemine's photo and recognised 'that nice M Mostin'; she added that he drove around in a light-coloured BMW with a Belgian registration plate.

The concierge also stated that M Mostin had told her that he would be away for a few days around 14 and 15 November.

From 17 November surveillance was organised at the rue des Patures, but to no avail. Condemine seemed to have disappeared. As the organiser of such an important deal he would have had to be on the spot.

Investigations were made in hospitals and prisons, since he could have been hospitalised under his false name of Mario Deniz. The police made enquiries in a small village in Haute Saone, where the parents of his wife Gilberte lived.

'He would never have crossed my threshold,' said Gilberte's father, 'if I'd known what he really was. When he presented himself hoping to marry my daughter, he told us he was the owner of an automatic car-washing outfit in Brussels. He was handsome, gentlemanly, well dressed and charming; I would have given him my wallet if he'd asked for it. Now he's simply never mentioned in the family . . .'

The old man, a former employee of the Ponts et Chaussées, had had fifteen children. Gilberte was the youngest.

'He never stayed more than two days, he said he couldn't leave his business. He liked to play *boules*. He used to have endless games with the neighbours on the pavement in front of our house. Sometimes he would go for a bike ride or have a drink in the bistro. He didn't seem at all like a hunted man. He didn't try to lie low . . .'

On 28 July 1973, at St Cloud, on the banks of the Seine, a fisherman noticed a trunk sailing downstream. He informed the police, who called the firemen. They seized the trunk and pulled it out of the water. When they opened it, they found the body of a young man. After lengthy investigations, the police discovered, to their amazement, that this was undoubtedly André Condemine, alias Mario Deniz. His wife Gilberte recognised several accompanying objects unhesitatingly. 'That gold chain with the medallion. It's identical to the one I gave him. The cuff-links are identical to the pair my husband wore. He told me he'd had them made in Buenos Aires. I recognise the fastening system.'

The biggest trafficker between the old and new worlds was thus well and truly dead, presumably the victim of his accomplices. His friends in the underworld, whether out of jealousy, or because they knew he was done for, had felt the need to silence him once and for all. Suddenly suspicious and seized with panic as a result of the severe blows the police had already dealt them, the underworld purged itself of its own accord.

This did not necessarily mean the death of the 'Marseilles network'. It had certainly been hard hit, and the Marseilles underworld has not yet managed to find any alternative activity which would be equally profitable.

If the Marseilles heroin problem was to recur it would not be likely to recur in the form of another 'French connection'. In the past, Marseilles enjoyed a virtual monopoly of the drug. Today, if production were resumed in Marseilles, the Chinese traffickers from Hong Kong would not give up their privileged positions without a fight. Amsterdam is their bridgehead in Europe.

Furthermore, Turkish nationals, arrested in West Germany, have been found to be carriers of perfectly refined white heroin. This seems to indicate that the Turks are no longer mere suppliers of opium or raw morphine, but also have their own laboratories. Despite Ankara's assurances that the poppy harvest would be rigorously controlled, the American authorities have sounded the alarm and are now more vigilant than ever.

Index